W9-BQZ-662

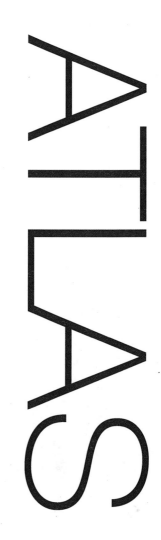

ATLAS

OF GLOBAL DEVELOPMENT

Fourth Edition

Contents

Acknowledgments

The text and data for the fourth edition of the *Atlas of Global Development* were prepared by the Development Economics Data Group of the World Bank under the management of Shaida Badiee. The team consisted of Liu Cui, Mahyar Eshragh-Tabary, Neil Fantom, Juan Feng, Shota Hatakeyama, Masako Hiraga, Wendy Huang, Bala Bhaskar Naidu Kalimili, Buyant Erdene Khaltarkhuu, Soong Sup Lee, Hiroko Maeda, Johan Mistiaen, Esther G. Naikal, Beatriz Prieto-Oramas, William Prince, Evis Rucaj, Sun Hwa Song, Emi Suzuki, Jos Verbeek, Olga Victorovna Vybornaia, and Sergiy Zorya. Eric Swanson was the general editor. Aziz Gökdemir, Stephen McGroarty, Santiago Pombo, Stuart Tucker, and Shana Wagger from the World Bank's Office of the Publisher managed the development and dissemination of the book and its online companion. Jeff Lecksell, in the Bank's Cartography Group, provided guidance on maps.

The Publishing, Design, Editorial, Creative Services, and Database teams at Collins Bartholomew, HarperCollins Publishers, provided overall design direction, editorial control, mapping, and typesetting.

Picture credits

Front cover, top to bottom Simone D. McCourtie/World Bank; Curt Carnemark/World Bank; Curt Carnemark/World Bank; Stanislas Fradelizi/World Bank; **Back cover, top to bottom** Julio Pantoja/World Bank; Aziz Gökdemir; Yosef Hadar/World Bank; Curt Carnemark/World Bank; **16** Ami Vitale/World Bank; **20, 34, 106, 117 (top)** Michael Foley/World Bank; **28** John Isaac/World Bank; **30** David A. Cieslikowski/World Bank; **36, 53, 94, 102, 109, 110, 114, 118, 126** Curt Carnemark/World Bank; **39, 68, 105** Scott Wallace/World Bank; **40** Tran Thi Hoa/World Bank; **43** Trevor Samson/World Bank; **44** Armine Grigoryan/World Bank; **48** Bill Lyons/World Bank; **50** Steve Harris/World Bank; **54, 78** Eric Miller/World Bank; **56** Yosef Hadar/World Bank; **60, 75, 113** Arne Hoel/World Bank; **64** Masaru Goto/World Bank; **67 (top)** William Taufic/Corbis; **67 (bottom)** Ray Witlin/World Bank; **71** Gennadiy Ratushenko/World Bank; **72** Lars Plougmann/Creative Commons license, creativecommons.org/licenses/by-sa/2.0; **76** Yuri Mechitov/World Bank; **80** Yang Aijun/World Bank; **86** Guiseppe Franchini/World Bank; **88** Cory Doctorow/Creative Commons license, creativecommons.org/licenses/by-sa/2.0; **92** Shannon Stapleton/Reuters/Corbis; **98** UNHCR/T. Irwin; **117 (bottom)** UNEP; **120** Julio Pantoja/World Bank; **123, 124** Dominic Sansoni/World Bank.

ECO-AUDIT

The World Bank is committed to preserving natural resources. This atlas is printed on recycled paper with 100 percent postconsumer waste in accordance with Green Press Initiative standards. See www.greenpressinitiative.org for details.

Saved:

- 46 trees
- 21 million Btu of total energy
- 3,985 pounds of net greenhouse gases
- 21,612 gallons of waste water
- 1,446 pounds of solid waste

Foreword

We are very pleased to bring you the fourth edition of the *Atlas of Global Development* and the fortieth atlas produced by the World Bank documenting development trends over the past 50 years. The atlases represent the longest continuing publication of the World Bank. Data presented in an atlas help us to understand the geographic relationships among countries and their economic and social development. In designing the atlas, we have illustrated these relationships with maps, charts, tables, and photos.

Geography is not destiny, but geography strongly influences the ways economies can and do develop. Geography encourages exchange and human interaction. It also creates barriers and nourishes disputes and conflicts. Neighboring economies may share common resources and interests, but economies at great distance may also be linked by historical ties of settlement and migration that still influence political alliances and economic exchange. Landlocked economies have a harder time bringing their goods to markets and have generally been slower to develop, but Botswana and Switzerland are two examples of landlocked economies that have flourished. Small island economies, because of their isolation and limited internal markets, face similar challenges, but Mauritius has overcome those obstacles and prospered. And because climate and geography are closely linked, economies in the same region face similar risks from climate change and from natural hazards such as storms, flooding, and earthquakes. All of these are important reasons for taking a comprehensive view of the geography of global development.

Understanding the development process, formulating policies, and evaluating outcomes require reliable data.

The *Atlas of Global Development* draws on the World Development Indicators database, which has been compiled from the work of the World Bank, other international organizations, and the national statistical offices of member countries. To improve the quality of international statistics, the World Bank in collaboration with national and international partners supports programs for the development of statistics in developing countries.

While new technologies have not eliminated geographic barriers to the movement of goods and peoples, they have made it possible for information to move far more quickly and to reach a larger audience. Online databases and electronic publications can be accessed from anywhere in the world. Nevertheless, barriers to information remain. In some places economic and social statistics are treated as privileged information, restricted in their use or priced so as to limit access. Such policies deny citizens the use of data collected with public funding and prevent the development of innovative new applications of benefit to all.

As part of the World Bank's Open Data Initiative, the World Bank has adopted a policy of providing open, free, and unrestricted access to its databases, which are available on the Web at data.worldbank.org. You can also access the *Atlas* online at data.worldbank.org/atlas-global. Throughout the *Atlas* you will find links to other public sources of data. We encourage you to explore these databases, to employ the data in your own work, to disseminate them to others, and to send us feedback on how we could improve our ways to make data more accessible and usable.

Shaida Badiee
Director, Development Data Group
The World Bank

Guide to the online atlas

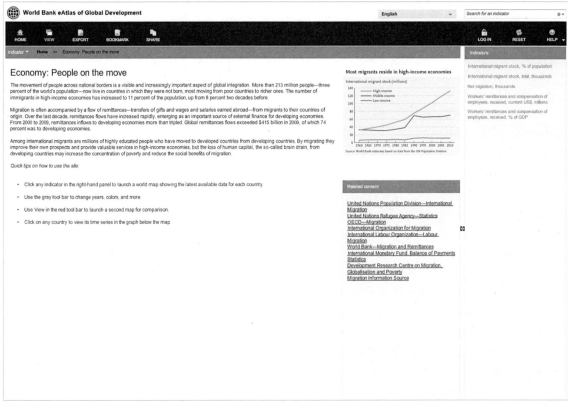

Figure 1

USER'S GUIDE TO THE WORLD BANK eATLAS OF GLOBAL DEVELOPMENT

Easy navigation from the home page (accessible via data.worldbank.org/atlas-global)

- Use the **right-hand panel** to select a main topic and see related indicators for mapping. (When you make a selection, a description appears, and the panel refreshes with the indicators [figure 1])
- Use the **search box** (top right) to search for any word in an indicator title or description (e.g., "malnutrition").
- Use **indicator** (top left, gray toolbar) to drill quickly from topic to indicator.
- However you start, selecting a specific indicator launches a world map that shows the latest available data per country, with many other visualizations and options.

Mapping basics (figure 2)

Once you have selected your indicator, the mapping application launches.

- The **world map** shows your indicator with the latest available data for each country. Mouse over the map to see country names, details, and indicator data.
- The **indicator name** (above the map, gray toolbar) is linked to the definition and source information.

- The **ranking table** (bottom right-hand panel), which shows indicator data, toggles from table to chart.
- A **time series chart** (across the bottom) is created; clicking on any country adds data to the chart.
- **View** (top left, red toolbar) lets you launch a second map alongside the first, providing a *Comparative View*.

Changing and viewing countries (figure 2)

- View and zoom to countries:
  - Click any country on the map or in the **ranking table** to zoom, or
  - Use **countries** (above the map, gray toolbar) to select a country, or
  - Use **locations** (above the map, gray toolbar) to select a country.
- Restore the full view by clicking the map area or by using the inset map at the top.
- Each time you zoom to a country, it is
  - Added to the **time series chart** (bottom).
  - Given more context (top right-hand panel)
  - Highlighted in the **ranking table** (bottom right-hand panel)

data.worldbank.org/atlas-global

6

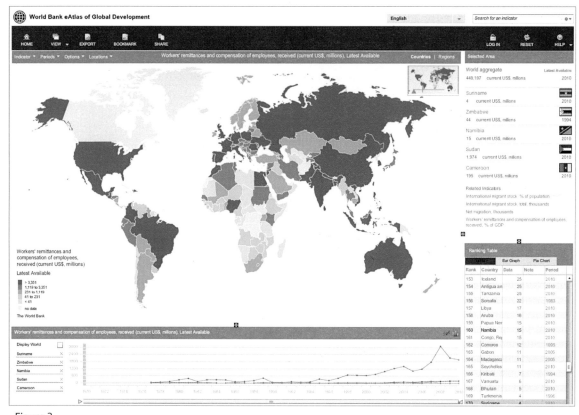

Figure 2

Changing years, colors, intervals, and more (figure 2)

- Use **periods** (above the map, gray toolbar) to select different years and "latest available" data.
- Use **options** (above the map, gray toolbar) to change colors, intervals, and analysis methods.
- Use **locations** (above the map, gray toolbar) to select a country.

Comparing maps and data

- Use **view** (top left, red toolbar) to select *Comparative View* and see two maps.
- Use **indicators, periods, options,** and **locations** (above each map, gray toolbar) to select what you want to compare, including any combination of indicators and years.
- Select the tabs below each map to see the **ranking table**, the **time series chart**, and more.
- Use **view** (top left, red toolbar) to select *Standard View* and return to one map with all the features.

Using the time series chart (figure 2)

- When you select a country (up to five), related time series data appear on the **chart** (bottom); country name and data are shown when you mouse over.

- Use the **play** button below the chart to dynamically map the time series for your indicator. As the map changes for each year, the **ranking table** and other information refresh.

NEW FOR THIS EDITION

The *Atlas of Global Development* is also available as part of the Atlas by Collins app. It is available for both iPhone and iPad.

For further information and technical advice go to www.atlasbycollins.com

7

CLASSIFICATION OF ECONOMIES

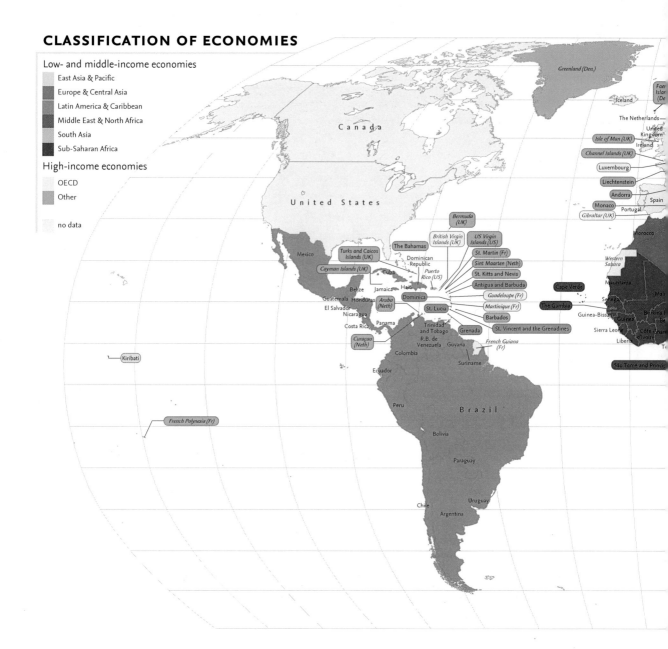

Low- and middle-income economies
- East Asia & Pacific
- Europe & Central Asia
- Latin America & Caribbean
- Middle East & North Africa
- South Asia
- Sub-Saharan Africa

High-income economies
- OECD
- Other

- no data

The World Bank classifies economies as low-income, middle-income (subdivided into lower-middle and upper-middle), or high-income based on gross national income (GNI) per capita. Low- and middle-income economies are sometimes referred to as *developing economies*. This is not intended to imply that all economies in the group are experiencing similar development or that other economies have reached a preferred or final stage of development.

The regions used in this atlas are based on the regions defined by the World Bank for analytical and operational purposes.

8

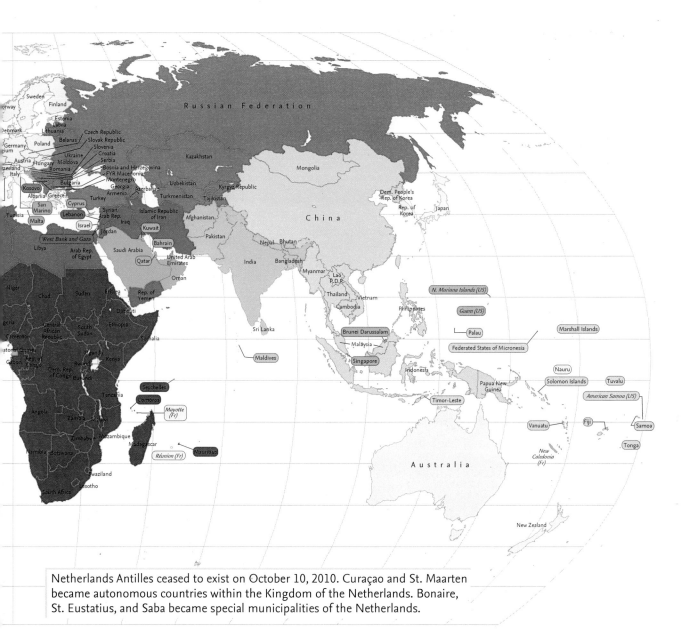

Netherlands Antilles ceased to exist on October 10, 2010. Curaçao and St. Maarten became autonomous countries within the Kingdom of the Netherlands. Bonaire, St. Eustatius, and Saba became special municipalities of the Netherlands.

These regions may differ from common geographic usage or from the regions defined by other organizations. Regional groupings and the aggregate measures for regions include only low- and middle-income economies.

Data are shown for economies as they were constituted in 2011. Additional information about the data is provided in *World Development Indicators 2012* or on the World Bank website (data.worldbank.org).

The Millennium Development Goals

The Millennium Declaration, ratified in 2000 by the 189 member states of the United Nations, committed rich and developing countries to work in partnership to achieve a set of critical development outcomes. Those commitments are embodied in the eight Millennium Development Goals (MDGs) for 2015, supported by 18 quantified targets and 60 indicators measuring progress since 1990. Progress has been uneven and many countries will not reach the targets set for 2015, but others have met or exceeded the targets, improving the lives of hundreds of millions of people.

Goal 1: Eradicate extreme poverty and hunger
Defined as average daily consumption of $1.25 or less, extreme poverty means living on the edge of subsistence. In 1990, more than 1.9 billion people lived on less than $1.25 a day. Since then, the poverty rate in developing countries has fallen from 43 percent to 22 percent in 2008, reducing the number of people in extreme poverty to less than 1.3 billion. Between 2005 and 2008, poverty rates fell in all six developing regions, the first time that has happened. By 2015, the global rate of extreme poverty is expected to be 16 percent and the number of people living in poverty will fall to around 1 billion. At the global level, the goal of halving the poverty rate has been reached, and all regions except Sub-Saharan Africa are expected to reach the target by 2015.

Goal 2: Achieve universal primary education
More than 20 years ago, the world community committed itself to providing at least a primary school education to every child. Providing all children with a good quality education is the foundation

All regions but Sub-Saharan Africa are on track to reach the poverty reduction target

East Asia & Pacific   Middle East & North Africa
Europe & Central Asia   South Asia
Latin America & Caribbean   Sub-Saharan Africa

People living on less than $1.25 a day (%)

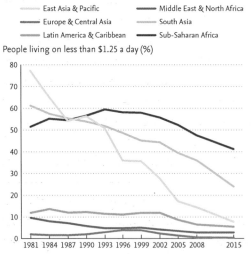

Source: PovcalNet, an online poverty analysis tool developed by the World Bank (iresearch.worldbank.org/PovcalNet/index.htm), and *Global Monitoring Report 2012*

To reach the goal of universal primary education, children must remain in school

East Asia & Pacific   Middle East & North Africa
Europe & Central Asia   South Asia
Latin America & Caribbean   Sub-Saharan Africa

Primary school completion rate (%)

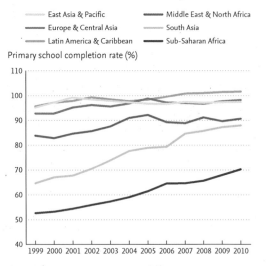

Source: UNESCO Institute of Statistics

Gender parity in enrollment has improved, but gender gaps remain large in some regions

Ratio of girls to boys in primary and secondary enrollment

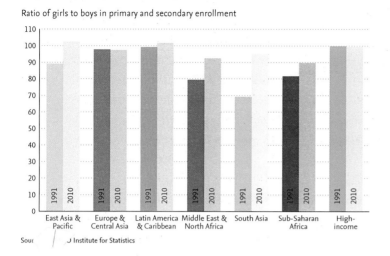

Source: UNESCO Institute for Statistics

Measles is the leading cause of vaccine-preventable deaths in children

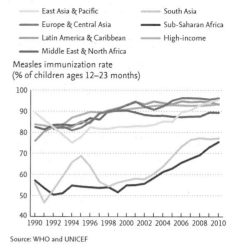

Source: WHO and UNICEF

of sustainable development and poverty alleviation. In 2010, the primary school completion rate reached 89 percent for developing countries: 94 percent for middle-income countries but just 68 percent for low-income ones. But 67 million children worldwide were out of school in 2009—and about half of them will receive no formal education.

Goal 3: Promote gender equality and empowering women

Promoting gender equality and empowering women are important in their own right and because they foster progress toward other MDG targets, such as those for reducing poverty, hunger, and disease and improving access to education. When women make decisions, household resources tend to be shared more equitably. And educated women are better able to care for children and more likely to send their children to school.

Education opportunities for girls have expanded since 1990. Enrollment patterns in upper-middle-income countries now resemble those in high-income countries, and those in lower-middle-income countries are nearing equity. But gender gaps remain large in low-income countries, especially at the primary and secondary levels.

Goal 4: Reduce child mortality

Deaths of children under age 5 have been declining since 1990. By 1999, for the first time, the number of children who died before their 5th birthday fell below 10 million. Child

mortality rates in developing countries dropped nearly 35 percent between 1990 and 2010, from 98 to 64 per 1,000 live births. Though this progress is impressive, it is insufficient to meet the fourth MDG of reducing under-5 child mortality by two-thirds.

Success in reducing infant and child mortality is a general indicator of progress toward the human development outcomes under the MDGs, reflecting falling poverty rates, improved nutrition, increasing female literacy, disease prevention, access to medicine and health facilities, and safe water and sanitation. Immunizations for measles—a leading cause of vaccine-preventable deaths among children—continue to expand worldwide. Coverage in all regions now exceeds 70 percent, markedly improving child survival rates.

For more information about the Millennium Development Goals, see the World Bank eAtlas of the MDGs: data.worldbank.org/mdg-atlas

Goal 5: Improve maternal health

Every year, hundreds of thousands of women die from complications related to pregnancy or childbirth. Some 99 percent of these deaths occur in developing countries. And for every woman who dies, about 20 suffer from injury, infection, or disease. In developing countries, pregnancy-related complications are among the leading causes of death and disability for women between 15 and 49.

Prenatal care and the presence of skilled health workers at delivery is critical to reducing maternal mortality. In developing countries, the share of births attended by skilled health staff rose from 58 percent in 1990 to 65 percent in 2010, and the proportion of pregnant women receiving prenatal care is rising. Countries in Europe and Central Asia have made the most progress in ensuring safe deliveries. Most have achieved universal coverage, and the rest are on track to achieve it by 2015.

Goal 6: Combat HIV/AIDS, malaria, and other diseases

For many reasons—including poverty, climate, bad policies, and inadequate services—people in developing countries are highly susceptible to life-threatening diseases. Some of these, such as malaria and tuberculosis, have been eliminated or largely contained in high-income countries, yet continue to kill millions a year in developing countries, and HIV/AIDS remains a global pandemic.

Worldwide, more than 30 million people have died from AIDS, and more than 16 million children have been orphaned since AIDS was first reported more than three decades ago. In 2010, 33 million people were living with HIV, but less than half of them were believed to be aware of their infection. With better treatment, death rates are declining and more people are living with AIDS. There were 1.8 million AIDS-related deaths in 2010, down from 2.2 million deaths in 2005. But there were over 7,000 new HIV infections every day, mostly among people in low- and middle-income countries. Sub-Saharan Africa contains just over one-tenth of the world's population but is home to two-thirds of the people living with HIV/AIDS, with women far more likely to be infected than men.

The World Health Organization estimates that in 2010, there were 216 million cases of malaria, leading to 655,000 deaths. Though malaria is endemic in many tropical and subtropical regions, most deaths occur among children living in Africa, where a child dies every minute from malaria.

The number of new tuberculosis cases peaked globally in 2004 and is leveling off, but prevalence is still high in Sub-Saharan

Better care during childbirth improves mothers' chances of survival

Births attended by skilled health staff (%)

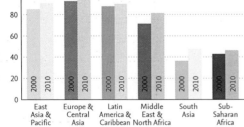

Source: UNICEF, *State of the World's Children*; Childinfo; and Demographic and Health Surveys by Macro International

Prevalence rates have risen as more people are living with HIV/AIDS

Prevalence of HIV among population ages 15–49 (%)

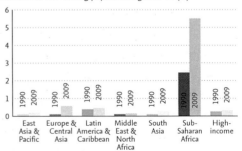

Source: UNAIDS and WHO

Most regions will achieve the 2015 target for access to an improved water source

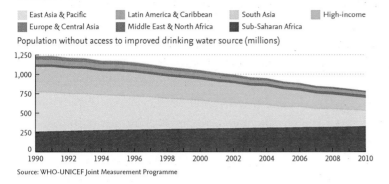

East Asia & Pacific Latin America & Caribbean South Asia High-income
Europe & Central Asia Middle East & North Africa Sub-Saharan Africa

Population without access to improved drinking water source (millions)

Source: WHO-UNICEF Joint Measurement Programme

Aid efforts by DAC donors have increased since 2000, but most still fall short of their commitments

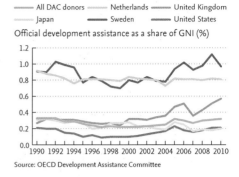

All DAC donors Netherlands United Kingdom
Japan Sweden United States

Official development assistance as a share of GNI (%)

Source: OECD Development Assistance Committee

Africa, and some South Asian countries appear to have returned to 1990 levels. In 2010 there were 8.8 million cases of tuberculosis globally—down from 14 million in 2007.

Goal 7: Ensure environmental sustainability

The 1992 Earth Summit adopted comprehensive global, national, and local responses for every area where humans affect the environment. This agenda was incorporated into the Millennium Declaration along with commitments to reduce greenhouse gas emissions, protect biodiversity, and prevent desertification.

Also included among the MDGs' targets are commitments to reduce the number of people lacking access to improved water and sanitation facilities. An improved water source meets basic standards for access to a protected water supply, but water from improved sources—such as public taps or hand pumps—may not meet standards set by the World Health Organization and may require considerable fetching and carrying. In 1990, more than 1 billion people in developing countries lacked access to such a minimal convenience. In 2010, 786 million people—42 percent of whom live in Sub-Saharan Africa—still lack access to improved sources for drinking water, but most regions made progress.

Around the world, 2.6 billion people lack access to toilets, latrines, and other forms of improved sanitation, and more than 40 percent of these people practice open defecation. In developing countries, the share of people with access to improved sanitation rose from 37 percent in 1990 to 56 percent in 2010. To halve the proportion of people without basic sanitation by 2015, more than 1.3 billion people would have to gain access to an improved facility—so the global target will be missed.

Goal 8: Develop a global partnership for development

Prospects for sustaining the current economic recovery will be enhanced if advanced and developing countries continue to cooperate in implementing policies aimed at increasing growth, protecting the poor and vulnerable, maintaining infrastructure investment, and sustaining private sector growth.

Private investment and remittances from migrants have become increasingly important sources of financing for developing countries. However, official development assistance—grants and loans made at low interest rates—remains an important source of support for development programs in the poorest countries. In 2005, the leaders of the richest industrial countries made specific commitments to increase aid to Africa. Aid received by all developing countries has increased substantially in real terms—from $79 billion in 2000 to $130 billion in 2010, measured in constant 2010 U.S. dollars. Aid to Africa increased to $45 billion in 2010, but remains far short of the commitments made in 2005.

Measuring income

Standards of living vary substantially across the globe. Comparing income or consumption or poverty levels among countries requires a common unit of measurement. Exchange rates reflect the relative value of currencies as traded in the market. Purchasing power parities take into account differences in price levels. Both have important roles in measuring the size of economies.

What is a developing country? Because development encompasses many factors—economic, environmental, cultural, educational, and institutional—no single measure gives a complete picture. However, the total earnings of the residents of an economy, measured by its gross national income (GNI), is a good measure of its capacity to provide for the wellbeing of its people. The World Bank classifies countries according to their average income, or GNI per capita, converted to U.S. dollars using three-year average market exchange rates (commonly called the World Bank Atlas method). Countries with average incomes of less than $12,476 in 2011 are classified as low- and middle-income (often referred to as developing economies). Countries with average incomes of $12,476 or more in 2011 are classified as high-income or developed economies. In 2011, the 1.1 billion people in high-income economies had an average income of $39,783 per person; the 5 billion residents in middle-income economies had average incomes of $4,121; and the 800 million people in low-income economies earned only $567, with some as low as $190.

Comparing incomes: The share of developing economies is higher when measured using purchasing power parity

GNI, PPP (current international $), 2011

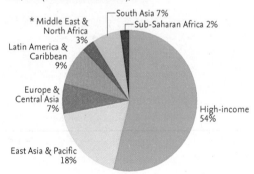

GNI, Atlas method (current US$), 2011

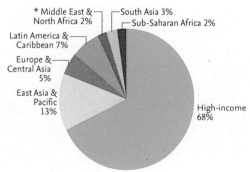

* Middle East & North Africa data are 2009, latest available

Source: World Bank, World Development Indicators database

Even measured using purchasing power parity, large differences remain

GDP per capita measured at PPP (constant 2005 international $)

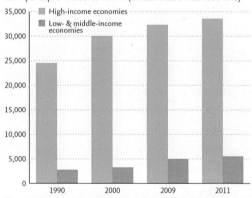

Note: GDP in constant prices measures the total volume of goods and services produced in the global economy

Source: World Bank, World Development Indicators database

To measure differences in welfare, comparisons of income among economies should take into account differences in domestic price levels. This is done using purchasing power parities (PPPs). Using PPPs instead of market exchange rates, the standard of living among countries can be compared in real terms, as if the people purchased goods and services at the same prices using a common currency. Measured using PPPs, developing economies receive 46 percent of world income. But when measured using the World Bank Atlas method, they receive only 32 percent. The difference is due to the lower cost of services and nontraded goods in developing economies, a fact that travelers frequently observe.

As the most comprehensive measure of living standards, GNI per capita is closely related to other, nonmonetary measures of the quality of life, such as life expectancy at birth, the mortality rate of children, and enrollment rates in school. Low incomes are both a cause and effect of low levels of health, education, and other human development outcomes. Poor people have a hard time obtaining good health care and education, while poor health and poor education leave them less able to improve their incomes.

Countries with higher GNI per capita often have higher life expectancy at birth ....

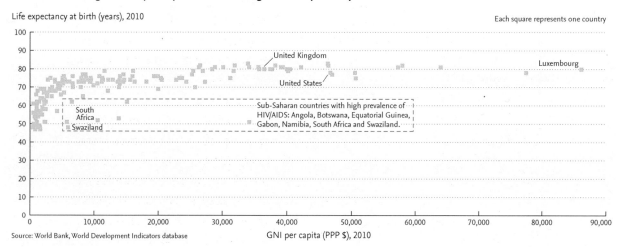

Life expectancy at birth (years), 2010

Each square represents one country

Source: World Bank, World Development Indicators database

GNI per capita (PPP $), 2010

.... and higher net school enrollment rates in secondary education

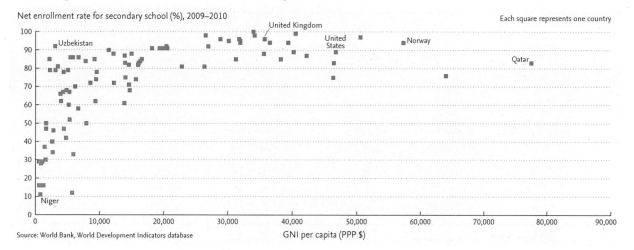

Net enrollment rate for secondary school (%), 2009–2010

Each square represents one country

Source: World Bank, World Development Indicators database

GNI per capita (PPP $)

INCOME

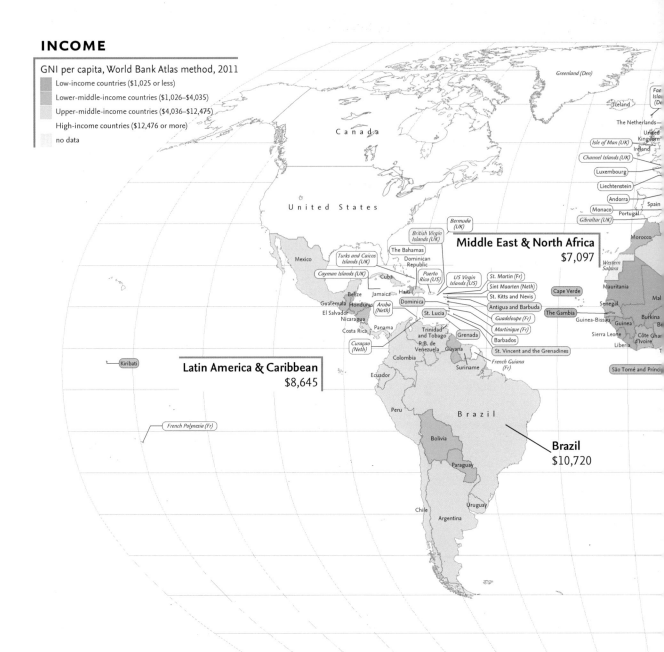

GNI per capita, World Bank Atlas method, 2011

- Low-income countries ($1,025 or less)
- Lower-middle-income countries ($1,026–$4,035)
- Upper-middle-income countries ($4,036–$12,475)
- High-income countries ($12,476 or more)
- no data

Middle East & North Africa
$7,097

Latin America & Caribbean
$8,645

Brazil
$10,720

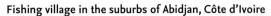

Fishing village in the suburbs of Abidjan, Côte d'Ivoire

Largest economies, 2011

Rank	Country	Gross national income PPP current international $ (billions)
1	United States	15,232
2	China	11,325
3	Japan	4,539
4	India	4,488
5	Germany	3,283
6	Russian Federation	2,845
7	France	2,346
8	United Kingdom	2,316
9	Brazil	2,261
10	Italy	1,966

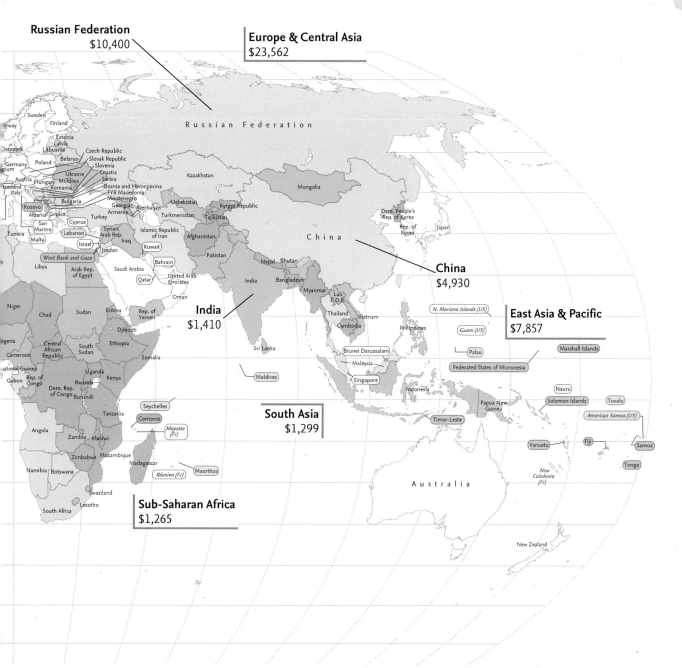

Russian Federation
$10,400

Europe & Central Asia
$23,562

China
$4,930

India
$1,410

East Asia & Pacific
$7,857

South Asia
$1,299

Sub-Saharan Africa
$1,265

Facts

► Of the 36 economies classified as low-income in 2011, 27 are in Sub-Saharan Africa, eight are in Asia, and one is in Latin America and the Caribbean.

► Most economies in Latin America and the Caribbean, Middle East and North Africa, and Europe and Central Asia are middle-income economies.

► Variations of income within each region can be large. For example, in 2011, Botswana's GNI per capita surpassed $7,480, while GNI per capita in neighboring Mozambique was only $470.

► Average GNI per capita in the low- and middle-income countries was $3,628 in 2011, while in high-income economies it was $39,783.

► Since 1989, 26 economies had moved from developing to high-income status, two of them in the last three years.

Internet links

► World Development Indicators	**data.worldbank.org**
► Organisation for Economic Co-operation and Development—Statistics	**www.oecd.org/statistics**
► International Monetary Fund Dissemination Standards Bulletin Board	**dsbb.imf.org**
► United Nations— Statistics Division	**unstats.un.org/unsd/snaama**
► International Comparison Project	**www.worldbank.org/data/icp**

Growth and opportunity

Economic growth reduces poverty. As a result, fast-growing developing countries are closing the income gap with high-income economies. But growth must be sustained over the long term and the gains from economic growth must be shared to make lasting improvements in the wellbeing of all people. The recent financial crisis has interrupted that process and recovery has been uneven.

Sustained growth is essential to reducing poverty, but few developing countries—especially low-income countries—have seen strong and steady growth in the past. Fewer than one-third of low-income countries have increased per capita income by 3.0 percent a year or more since 1980. For many countries in Sub-Saharan Africa, the 1990s were a lost decade, with little or no growth. But growth accelerated in the following decade. Since 2000, more than half of all developing countries achieved an average growth of per capita income of 3.2 percent a year or more. In Sub-Saharan Africa, three-quarters of the countries grew faster than 3.2 percent a year, despite formidable development challenges such as conflict and epidemic disease.

The financial crisis, which began in 2007 and spread from high-income to low- and middle-income economies in 2008, became in 2009 the most severe global recession in 50 years. Gross domestic product (GDP) fell by 3.7 percent in high-income economies and grew by only 2.7 percent in developing economies. The crisis was transmitted from high-income countries to developing countries as exports, private capital flows, commodity prices, and workers' remittances all declined. Many developing countries

Global recession in 2007–2009 reversed years of record economic growth

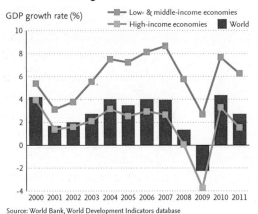

Source: World Bank, World Development Indicators database

Recovery from the financial crisis has been slow and uneven

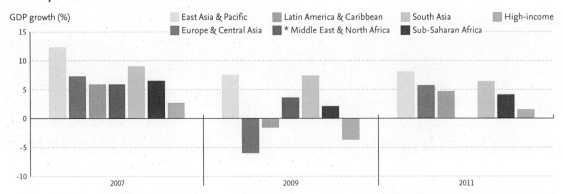

Source: World Bank, World Development Indicators database

* 2011 data not available for Middle East & North Africa

Income inequality has fallen in roughly half of the developing countries from the late 1990s to late 2000s

Annual change in Gini coefficient in 74 developing countries, late 1990s to late 2000s
Percentage points per year

Source: World Bank, World Development Indicators database
'The late 1990s' is the most recent year between 1995 and 1999, or 2000. 'The late 2000s' is the most recent year between 2005 and 2011

entered the crisis in better shape than in previous recessions, but for countries with large portions of their populations clustered around the poverty line, even brief periods of economic slowdown can have severe effects. In the poorest developing countries, health and education outcomes move with the economic cycle; they deteriorate during economic crises and take a long time to recover.

Since 2009, the global economy has shown signs of recovery, expanding by 4.3 percent in 2010. However, the pace of recovery has been uneven. High-income countries grew only 3.3 percent while developing countries grew 7.6 percent. East Asia and the Pacific was the fastest-growing region with 9.7 percent followed by South Asia and Latin America and the Caribbean, which grew 8.7 and 6.2 percent, respectively. The recovery has proved to be fragile; it suffered a setback in 2011, with global growth slowing to 2.7 percent. High-income countries grew only 1.5 percent while developing countries showed more resilience posting 6.2 percent growth. Weak recovery will likely resume in 2012 in the major advanced economies, and activity could remain relatively solid in most emerging and developing economies. However, since commodity prices are unlikely to continue the recent fast pace of growth, these economies may have to adapt their policies to promote economic growth in the post-crisis environment.

Economic growth reduces poverty. But in some countries, high growth has been accompanied by rising inequality of incomes, impeding the pace of poverty reduction. Moreover, a country with high initial inequality will need to grow faster than a country with more equal income distribution to achieve the same poverty reduction. Rising income inequality may also lead to social tensions, undermining the social impacts of economic growth and poverty reduction. Therefore, policies will need to simultaneously stem rising inequality of income and accelerate economic development and poverty reduction. Since the late 1990s, income inequality, measured by the Gini coefficient, has increased in roughly half of the developing countries with available data, and decreased in the other half.

In addition to inequality of incomes, inequality of opportunities is a challenge facing most developing countries. Personal circumstances at birth, such as gender, race, ethnicity, location, wealth, and parents' education, are associated with the level of access to those services needed for a productive life, such as safe drinking water, sanitation, electricity, basic education, and nutrition. Achieving universal access to these services is critical to the poverty reduction and development agenda.

ECONOMIC GROWTH

average annual growth of GDP per capita, 2000–2011

- less than 0.0%
- 0.0–1.9%
- 2.0–3.9%
- 4.0–5.9%
- 6.0% or more
- no data

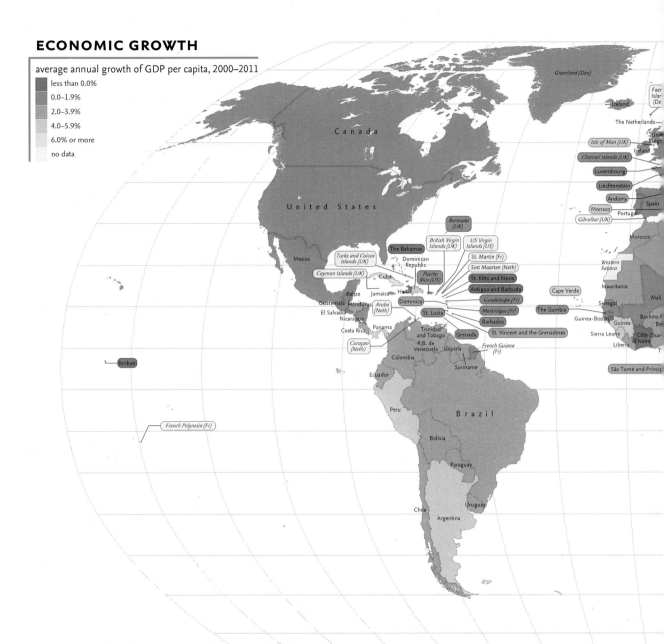

Small businesses, such as the one run by this dressmaker, contribute to economic growth

Recent growth of GDP per capita

Rank	Country	Average annual growth rate (%), 2000–2009
1	Azerbaijan	16.7
2	Vanuatu	14.3
3	Equatorial Guinea	13.6
4	Turkmenistan	12.3
5	Armenia	10.5
6	Angola	9.9
7	China	9.7
8	Belarus	8.7
9	Kazakhstan	7.9
10	Cambodia	7.3

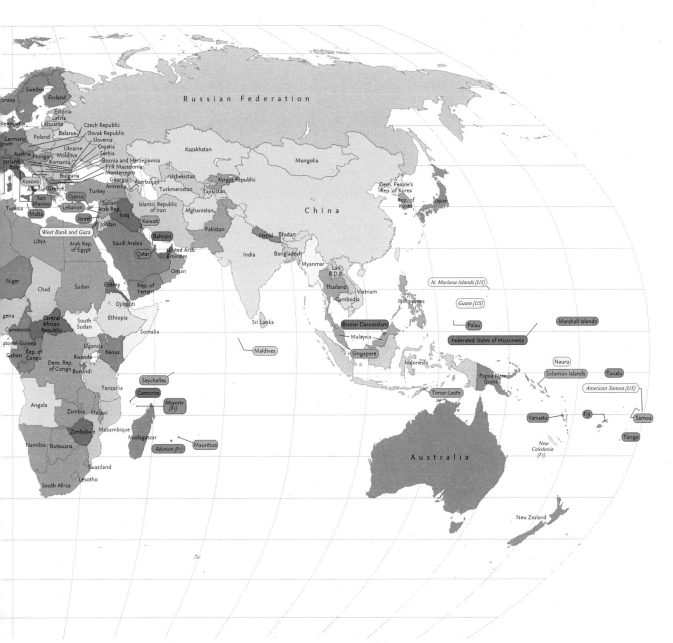

Facts

▶ In contrast to record economic growth from 2000 to 2007, the global economy fell by 2.2 percent in 2009 as a result of the 2008 financial crisis.

▶ GDP fell by 3.7 percent in high-income economies and grew by only 2.7 percent in developing countries in 2009.

▶ While the global economy is showing signs of recovery, low-income countries continue to suffer the consequences of the global recession.

▶ Between 1990 and 2011, GDP per capita grew 4.7 times in East Asia and the Pacific, but still ranked fourth among regions, behind Latin America and the Caribbean, Middle East and North Africa, and Europe and Central Asia.

▶ Among 10 developing countries with the highest GDP per capita growth in 2000–2011, two are from low-income economies, and two are from Sub-Saharan Africa.

Internet links

▶ World Development Indicators	**data.worldbank.org**
▶ World Bank—Global Economic Prospects	**www.worldbank.org/prospects**
▶ IMF World Economic Outlook	**www.imf.org/weo**
▶ OECD statistics	**www.oecd.org/statistics**
▶ The Commission on Growth and Development	**www.growthcommission.org/**

INEQUALITY

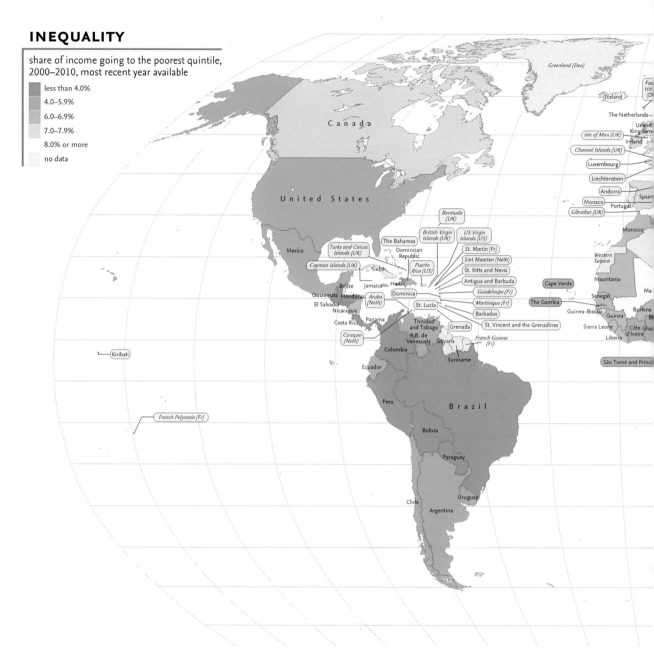

share of income going to the poorest quintile,
2000–2010, most recent year available

- less than 4.0%
- 4.0–5.9%
- 6.0–6.9%
- 7.0–7.9%
- 8.0% or more
- no data

One commonly used measure of income inequality is the inequality ratio, calculated as the ratio of income or consumption shares of the richest 20 percent to the poorest 20 percent of the population. A ratio of 10 means that the top 20 percent of the population earns (or spends) 10 times as much as the bottom 20 percent of the population.
Generally the higher this ratio, the more unequal the income distribution. Countries with high inequality ratios are mostly in Latin America and Africa. The highest inequality ratio among Asian countries is 12.

Countries with highest inequality ratios

Rank	Country with population over 1 million	Year	Inequality ratio
1	Honduras	2009	30
2	Bolivia	2008	28
3	South Africa	2009	25
4	Brazil	2009	21
5	Colombia	2010	20
6	Guatemala	2006	20
7	Central African Republic	2008	18
8	Paraguay	2010	17
9	Panama	2010	17
10	Zambia	2006	17

Facts

▶ Latin America and the Caribbean has persistently been the region with highest average inequality within countries, but inequality has been falling noticeably in the region since around 2000.

▶ East Asia started out as the region with lowest inequality within countries in early 1980s, but has seen a steady rise in inequality (side by side with a downward trend in inequality between countries).

▶ Between one-quarter and one-half of income inequality observed among adults in Latin America and the Caribbean is due to personal circumstances endured during childhood that fell outside their control or responsibility, such as race, gender, birthplace, parents' educational level, and father's occupation.

▶ In South Africa, circumstances at birth are important drivers for the unequal opportunities in childhood and later reemerge to contribute to unequal access to jobs.

Internet links

▶ World Bank— *World Development Report 2006*	www.worldbank.org/wdr2006
▶ United Nations Development Programme— *Human Development Report*	www.hdr.undp.org
▶ Inequality in Focus	go.worldbank.org/CCKE912HN0
▶ World Bank—Poverty Reduction and Equity	www.worldbank.org/poverty
▶ Poverty and Equity Data	povertydata.worldbank.org/ poverty/home/
▶ Human Opportunity Index, Latin America and the Caribbean	go.worldbank.org/A9Z0NUV620

Where is the wealth of nations?

Development can be seen as a process of building and managing a diversified portfolio of assets that contribute to economic wellbeing. For wellbeing to be sustainable, the total value of assets must be maintained at a constant level or increased. Adjusted net saving is a measure of the net change in a country's assets and thus a powerful indicator of sustainability.

A country's wealth includes not only physical capital such as buildings and machinery, but also natural capital, such as oil deposits, forests and crop land, and human and social capital. The capacity of a country to sustain and increase wellbeing depends on how well these assets are managed. Adjusted net saving (ANS) provides a measure of net change in wealth. It is defined as gross saving plus investment in human capital (education expenditures), minus depreciation of produced capital, depletion of natural capital (energy, mineral, and forest assets), and damage from global and local pollution. If ANS is negative, it means that the country is exhausting its resources at the cost of future generations; hence it is on a path of unsustainable development.

Adjusted net saving for a resource-rich country can be negative despite high gross saving

Adjusted net saving in Kazakhstan (% of GNI), 2010

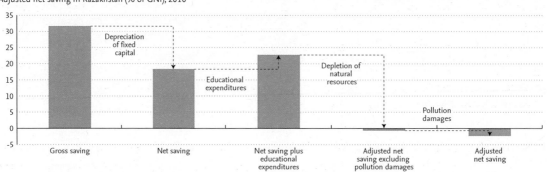

Source: World Bank, *Little Green Data Book 2012*

Adjusted net saving is often low in countries with high exhaustible resource rents

Adjusted net saving (% of GNI), 2010

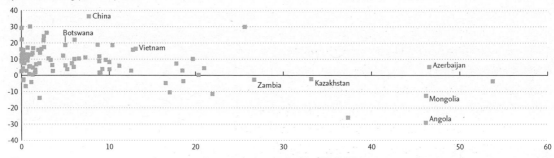

Energy and mineral rents (% of GDP), 2010

Source: World Bank estimates

Asia has sustained positive adjusted net saving rates over the past three decades

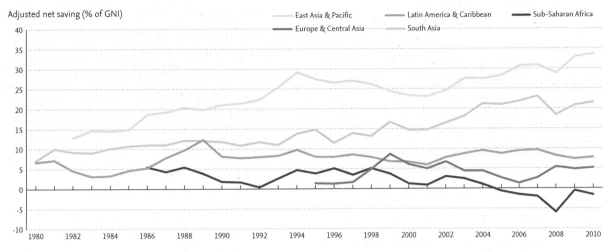

Source: World Bank estimates

Countries rich in natural resources have an advantage over others in financing development. Natural resource rents can be effectively deployed for this purpose, but it is important to reinvest such rents in other types of capital, notably human capital and institutions. The data show that natural resource abundance often leads to low or negative ANS. This is true for many resource-rich countries in the developing world. Adjusted net saving as a percentage of gross national income (GNI) often has a negative relationship with the share of energy and mineral resource rents of gross domestic product (GDP). Countries such as Angola, Mongolia, Kazakhstan, and Zambia, with resource rents greater than a quarter of GDP, have negative ANS rates as low as −30 percent of GNI. With relatively fewer natural resource endowments, China has achieved a high ANS rate by investing in produced and human capital. But natural resource abundance need not be a curse. At the other end of the spectrum are countries such as Botswana and Vietnam, rich in mineral wealth and energy resources but with positive ANS rates. Those countries are good examples of how reinvesting resource rents can boost social and institutional capital with positive results on growth. Vietnam's GDP grew by 7.5 percent over the past 10 years, and Botswana, one of the fastest-growing economies in Sub-Saharan Africa, grew by 4.1 percent.

Adjusted net saving trends across regions have varied widely over time. Sub-Saharan Africa generally has a declining trend in ANS, suggesting that this region is on an unsustainable development path. But if one looks more closely, distinct stories emerge. In Sub-Saharan Africa, a relatively small handful of countries have dragged down performance for the entire region, relative to the rest of the world. But nearly two-thirds of African countries have had positive saving rates over the decade. This group was led by the largest African economy, South Africa, and includes others such as Botswana, Ethiopia, Kenya, Mauritius, Namibia, and Uganda. The South Asia and East Asia regions stand out as achieving almost steadily increasing ANS rates generated mostly via their high gross saving rates in recent years. Other regions do not show a clear trend.

WEALTH OF NATIONS

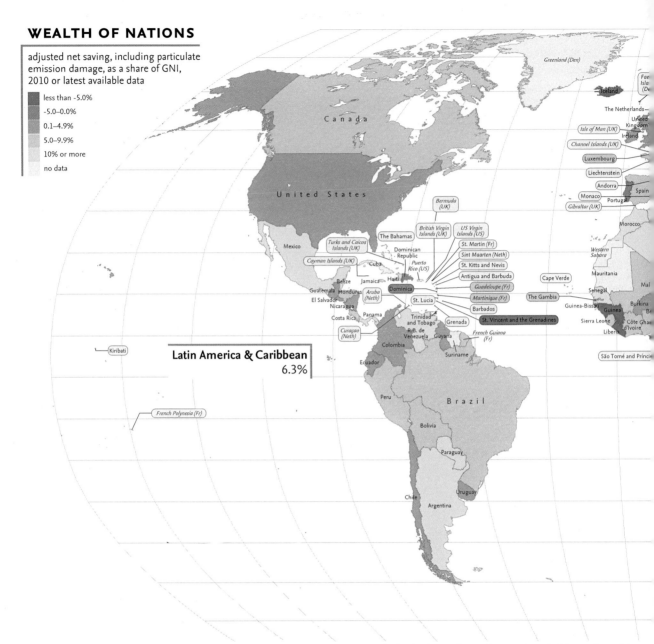

adjusted net saving, including particulate emission damage, as a share of GNI, 2010 or latest available data

- less than -5.0%
- -5.0–0.0%
- 0.1–4.9%
- 5.0–9.9%
- 10% or more
- no data

Latin America & Caribbean
6.3%

Natural capital as a share of comprehensive wealth is most important in low- and lower-middle-income countries. But countries differ substantially in terms of adjusted net saving.

Countries with the highest share of natural capital in total wealth

Rank	Country, population over 30 million	Natural capital as a share of wealth (%), 2005	Adjusted net saving (% of GNI), 2010
1	Congo, Dem. Rep.	69	..
2	Sudan	56	-3.6
3	Nigeria	55	..
4	Iran, Islamic Rep.	53	..
5	Algeria	52	29.8*
6	Russian Federation	43	4.5
7	Vietnam	39	15.8
8	Tanzania	35	12.1
9	Ethiopia	32	7.5
10	Pakistan	28	9.4

* 2009

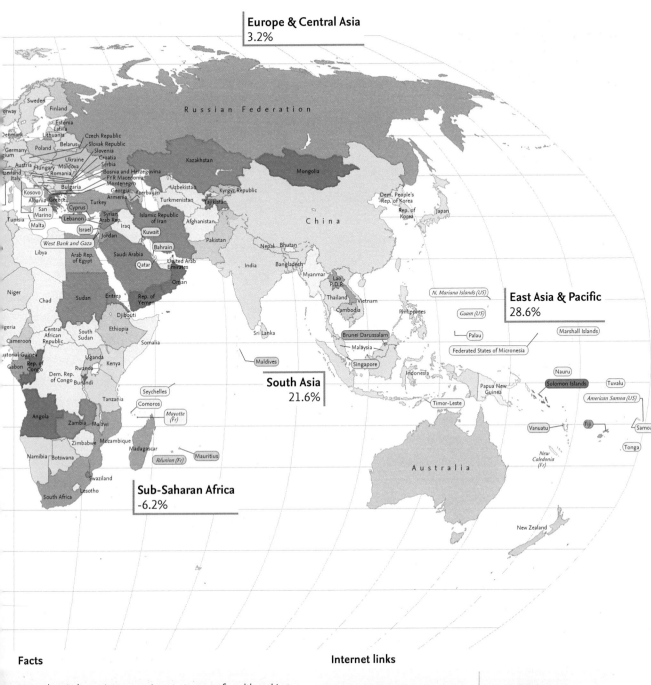

Europe & Central Asia
3.2%

East Asia & Pacific
28.6%

South Asia
21.6%

Sub-Saharan Africa
-6.2%

Facts

▶ Natural capital constitutes a major component of wealth and is a principal source of income in developing countries.

▶ If Trinidad and Tobago had reinvested all resource rents from oil and gas into manufactured capital, it would have accumulated more than three times as much manufactured capital between 1980 and 2005.

▶ In 2010, the ANS rate was 10.4 percent of GNI for the world as a whole, 18 percent for low- and middle-income countries, and 7.1 percent for high-income countries.

Internet links

▶ *Where Is the Wealth of Nations?*	**go.worldbank.org/ 2QTH26ULQ0**
▶ *The Changing Wealth of Nations*	**go.worldbank.org/ TF3U5N1AO0**
▶ *Report of the Commission on the Measurement of Economic and Social Progress*	**www.stiglitz-sen-fitoussi.fr**
▶ Environmental Economics at the World Bank	**www.worldbank.org/ environmentaleconomics**

How poor is poor?

Poverty and hunger remain, but fewer people live in extreme poverty. Between 1981 and 2008, the proportion of people in the developing world living on less than $1.25 a day fell from 52 to 22 percent, and nearly 650 million people were lifted out of poverty. Despite the 2008 financial crisis and food and fuel price increases, global poverty has continued to fall, but progress has been uneven and more than a billion people remain in dire need.

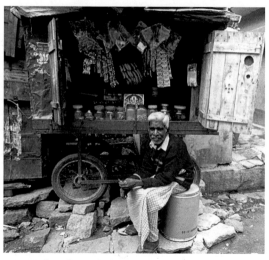

Man selling household goods out of a cart in the slum district of Bangalore, India

Poverty is found everywhere that poor health and lack of education deprive people of productive employment; where environmental resources have been depleted or spoiled; and where corruption, conflict, and bad governance waste public resources and discourage private investment. Poverty needs to be tackled on many fronts: by creating more and better jobs, delivering quality public services and infrastructure, and by protecting vulnerable people such as women, children, and the elderly. There is no single solution; the best strategies will depend on the circumstances in each country.

Definitions of poverty vary from country to country. A poverty line set at $1.25 a day in 2005 purchasing power is used by the World Bank as the working definition of extreme poverty. It represents the level of consumption of the poorest people in the poorest countries of the world. Since

While the number of people living on less than $1.25 a day has fallen, the number living on between $1.25 and $2.00 a day has increased

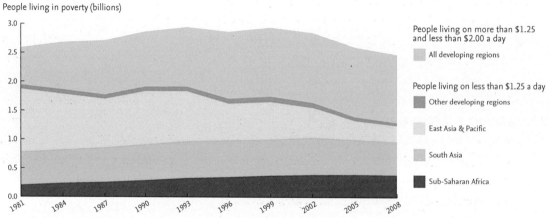

People living in poverty (billions)

People living on more than $1.25 and less than $2.00 a day

All developing regions

People living on less than $1.25 a day

Other developing regions

East Asia & Pacific

South Asia

Sub-Saharan Africa

Source: World Bank, PovcalNet – an online poverty analysis tool, iresearch.worldbank.org/PovcalNet/index

Purchasing power parity (PPP) and the international poverty line

To measure poverty in the world as a whole, a common standard is required. Because market exchange rates tend to understate the real incomes of developing countries and overstate the extent of poverty, PPPs are used to compare income and consumption levels between countries. PPPs are calculated to compensate for differences in the price of goods and services between countries. The result is a conversion factor that can be used like an exchange rate to convert values in one currency into those of a reference currency (such as the U.S. dollar). In 2008, new PPP estimates for 2005 became available from the International Comparison Program. The World Bank's original '$1 a day' international poverty line was based on the poverty lines in the world's poorest countries. By focusing on the standards of the poorest countries, the $1 a day line gave the global poverty measure a salience in focusing on the world's poorest. Using the new 2005 PPP rates, the international poverty line was revised to $1.25 a day, which is the average poverty line of the 10 to 20 poorest countries in the world.

1981, the proportion of people living in extreme poverty in the developing world has fallen from 52 percent to 22 percent (as of 2008). In absolute terms, the number of people living in extreme poverty fell from nearly 2 billion in 1981 to less than 1.3 billion in 2008.

But global success in reducing extreme poverty over the past three decades has disguised uneven progress across regions. The greatest drop occurred in East Asia and the Pacific, where the poverty rate fell from 84 percent in 1981 to 13 percent in 2008 and the number of people living on less than $1.25 a day fell by 662 million. In South Asia, the poverty rate fell from 61 percent to 36 percent over the same period. However, due to rapid population growth, the number of extremely poor people in the region increased and only returned to the 1981 level by 2008. In Sub-Saharan Africa, the poverty rate rose from 52 percent in 1981 to 58 percent in 1999, as many countries suffered a long period of civil discord and slow growth. By 2005, the number of people living in extreme poverty had almost doubled. But the poverty rate fell to 48 percent in 2008, and the number of people living in extreme poverty fell to 386 million. Africa's success was echoed everywhere: between 2005 and 2008, both the poverty rate and the number of poor people fell in all six developing regions for the first time since the World Bank began monitoring global poverty.

Rising incomes have brought more countries into middle-income status, so that nearly three-quarters of the world's poor people now live in middle-income countries. In many of these countries, a poverty line of $2 a day or higher is more representative of the extent of serious poverty. There are almost 2.5 billion people living on $2 a day or less, and

Children from poor households are more likely to die before reaching age 5

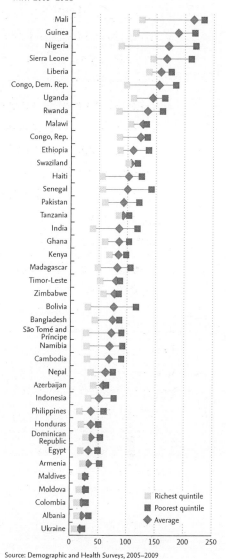

Under-5 mortality rate (10 year rate, per 1,000 live births), MRY 2005–2011

Legend:
- Richest quintile
- Poorest quintile
- Average

Source: Demographic and Health Surveys, 2005–2009

progress in reducing their numbers has been slow. The number of people living on between $1.25 and $2 a day is expected to remain constant at about 1.2 billion for the next decade. These are still very poor people whose prospects will improve only through continued growth.

POVERTY

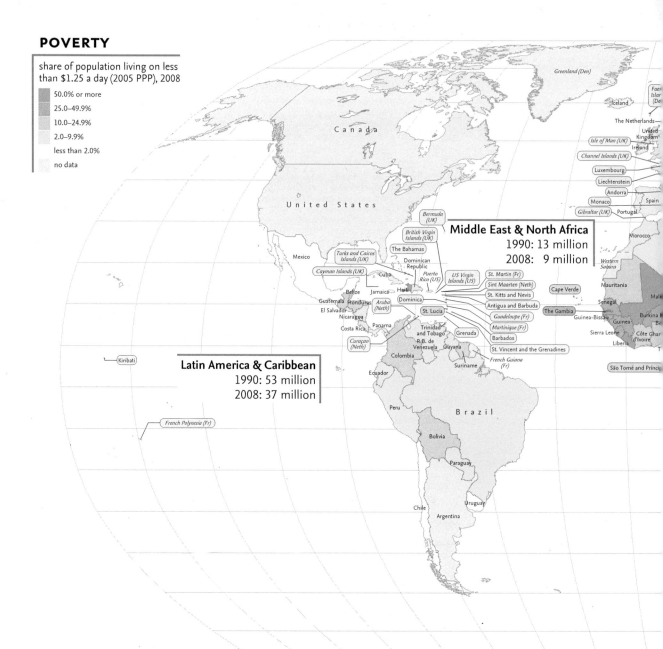

share of population living on less than $1.25 a day (2005 PPP), 2008

- 50.0% or more
- 25.0–49.9%
- 10.0–24.9%
- 2.0–9.9%
- less than 2.0%
- no data

Middle East & North Africa
1990: 13 million
2008: 9 million

Latin America & Caribbean
1990: 53 million
2008: 37 million

Public services are lacking in slum areas

People living on less than $1.25 a day

Developing country	Number of people (millions, most recent data 2005–2010)
India	568
China	276
Nigeria	108
Bangladesh	64
Indonesia	64
Congo, Dem. Rep.	51
Pakistan	35
Ethiopia	29
Tanzania	28
Philippines	17

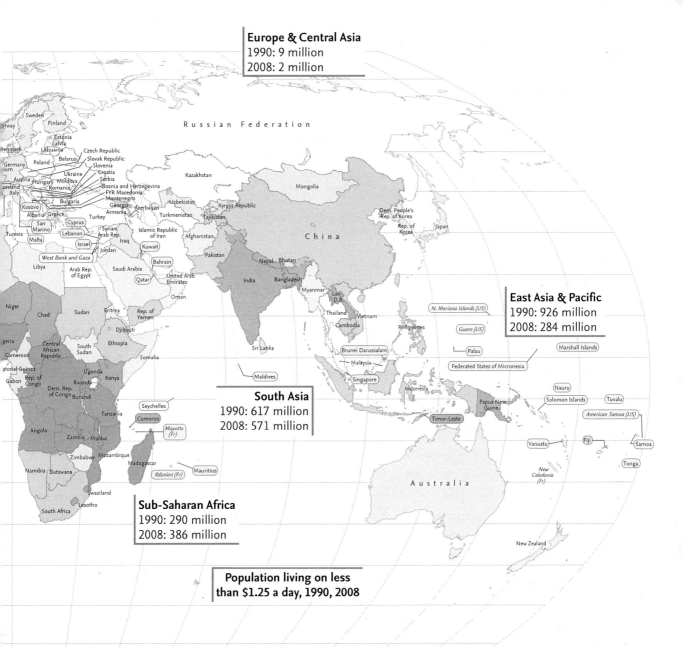

Europe & Central Asia
1990: 9 million
2008: 2 million

East Asia & Pacific
1990: 926 million
2008: 284 million

South Asia
1990: 617 million
2008: 571 million

Sub-Saharan Africa
1990: 290 million
2008: 386 million

Population living on less than $1.25 a day, 1990, 2008

Facts

▶ Two-thirds of the world's poor people live in the world's three most populous middle-income countries: China, India, and Indonesia.

▶ While Sub-Saharan Africa has the highest poverty rate, South Asia has the most people living in extreme poverty.

▶ China reduced its extreme poverty rate from 84 percent in 1981 to 13 percent in 2008 and lifted 662 million people out of poverty.

▶ Although extreme poverty occurs mostly in rural areas, urban slums also have high poverty rates.

▶ Preliminary survey-based estimates indicate that the Millennium Development Goal of halving poverty from its 1990 level by 2015 has been achieved at the global level in 2010.

Internet links

▶ World Bank—PovcalNet Online Poverty Analysis Tool	**iresearch.worldbank.org/ PovcalNet**
▶ World Bank Poverty & Equity Data Website	**povertydata.worldbank.org/ poverty/home**
▶ World Bank—Country Poverty Assessment	**www-wds.worldbank.org** (go to 'By Doc Type' in the left-hand bar and select 'Poverty Assessment' from 'Economic and Sector Work')
▶ United Nations Millennium Project	**www.unmillenniumproject.org**

Population growth and transition

The world is undergoing rapid demographic change, resulting from changes in the key determinants of population growth and structure: fertility, mortality, and migration. By 2050, there will be 9 billion people, most living in today's developing countries. More people will live in cities and the average age will increase, bringing new opportunities and challenges.

The world's population grew at an extraordinary rate in the 20th century—from 1.6 billion in 1900 to 6.1 billion in 2000, reaching 6.9 billion in 2010. Eighty-four percent of the world's people live in developing countries. East and South Asia, with half the world's population in 1960, added 2 billion people over 50 years. Sub-Saharan Africa, whose population more than tripled in the same time period, from 230 million to 850 million, grew fastest.

In developing countries, life expectancy at birth increased steadily, from 47 years in 1960 to 68 years in 2010. Fertility rates declined, but at 2.6 births per woman, they remain well above those of high-income countries, fueling population growth as births exceed deaths. Fertility rates are particularly high in Sub-Saharan Africa, averaging five births per woman in 2010.

In high-income countries, life expectancy has reached 80 years, 11 years longer than in 1960. The increase in life expectancy has coincided with income growth. With a fertility rate of 1.8 births per woman—well below replacement level—the average age of the population will rise, and population size may fall in the absence of immigration. A majority of international migrants are from developing countries, and these migrants make up a significant part of population growth in industrial countries. However, the number of migrants leaving most developing countries is too small to have much impact on the countries' population growth.

The world's population is expected to grow to 7.2 billion in 2015 and 7.9 billion in 2025, with more than 90 percent of the growth occurring in developing countries.

East and South Asia hold half the world's population, but population growth has been fastest in Sub-Saharan Africa

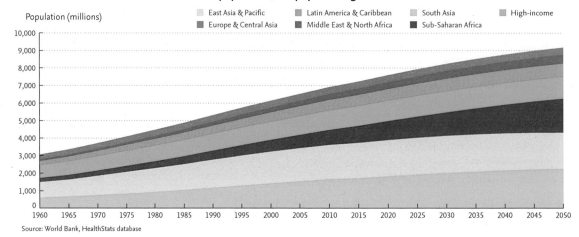

Source: World Bank, HealthStats database

Fertility rates are falling, but they remain highest in Sub-Saharan Africa

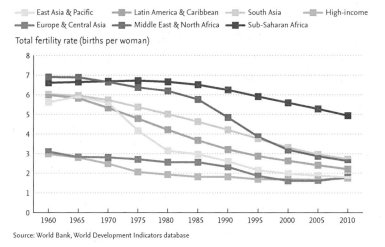

Total fertility rate (births per woman)

Legend:
- East Asia & Pacific
- Europe & Central Asia
- Latin America & Caribbean
- Middle East & North Africa
- South Asia
- Sub-Saharan Africa
- High-income

Source: World Bank, World Development Indicators database

More than 90 percent of population growth will occur in developing countries, particularly in South Asia and Sub-Saharan Africa

Share of population increase by region, 2010–2030

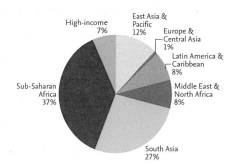

- High-income 7%
- East Asia & Pacific 12%
- Europe & Central Asia 1%
- Latin America & Caribbean 8%
- Middle East & North Africa 8%
- South Asia 27%
- Sub-Saharan Africa 37%

Source: World Bank, HealthStats database

Urbanization will intensify. About 90 percent of the additional population will be in urban areas. A third of people in urban areas will live in slums that lack basic social services such as clean water and sanitation and decent housing. In Sub-Saharan Africa, about 60 percent of urban dwellers will live in slums.

The average age of the population will increase as fertility slows and people live longer. About 20 percent of the population will be 65 years and older in high-income countries in 2025. The population will age at a higher rate in developing countries, although the share of elderly will remain lower than in high-income countries. In 2025, 9 percent of the population in developing countries will be 65 or older, a 42 percent increase since 2010.

Future population growth, mainly concentrated in urban areas, poses challenges for many countries. Those that cannot meet the needs of their current populations will be hard pressed to provide more schools, health care, employment opportunities, and infrastructure for growing populations. Although cities offer more favorable settings to deliver services because of their advantages of scale and proximity, the challenge is how to take advantage of their possibilities. Aging populations bring their own burden of chronic and noncommunicable diseases such as heart disease and stroke, cancer, and diabetes. Such diseases currently account for 60 percent of all deaths, and they are rapidly increasing in developing countries, putting additional pressure on health budgets.

The population is aging in both developing and high-income countries

Legend:
- Population ages 65 and older
- Population ages 15–64
- Population ages 0–14

Age structure (% of total population)

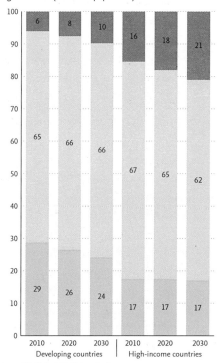

	Developing countries			High-income countries		
	2010	2020	2030	2010	2020	2030
65 and older	6	8	10	16	18	21
15–64	65	66	66	67	65	62
0–14	29	26	24	17	17	17

Source: World Bank, HealthStats database

POPULATION GROWTH

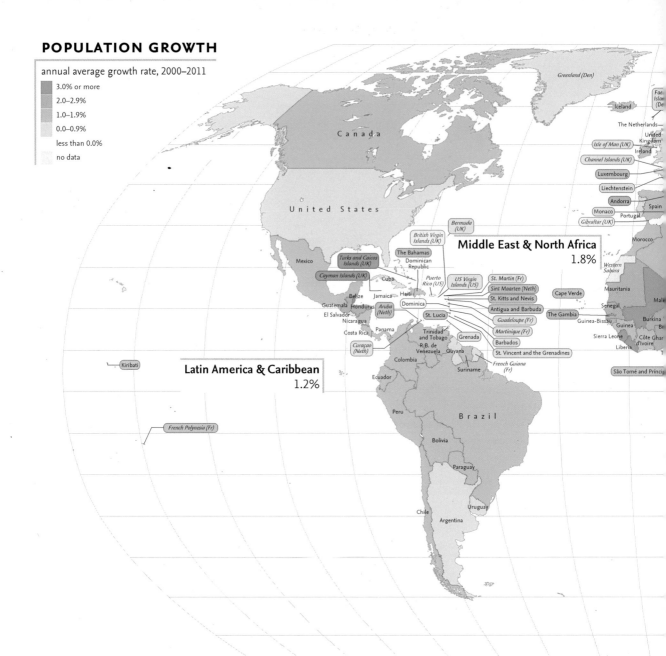

annual average growth rate, 2000–2011

- 3.0% or more
- 2.0–2.9%
- 1.0–1.9%
- 0.0–0.9%
- less than 0.0%
- no data

Greenland (Den)

Iceland

Faer Islan (De

The Netherlands

United Kingdom

Isle of Man (UK)

Ireland

Channel Islands (UK)

Luxembourg

Liechtenstein

Andorra

Spain

Monaco

Portugal

Gibraltar (UK)

Canada

United States

Morocco

Western Sahara

Middle East & North Africa
1.8%

Mexico

Bermuda (UK)

British Virgin Islands (UK)

Turks and Caicos Islands (UK)

The Bahamas

Dominican Republic

Cayman Islands (UK)

Cuba

Puerto Rico (US)

US Virgin Islands (US)

St. Martin (Fr)

Sint Maarten (Neth)

Cape Verde

Mauritania

Male

Belize

Jamaica

Haiti

St. Kitts and Nevis

Senegal

Guatemala

Honduras

Aruba (Neth)

Dominica

Antigua and Barbuda

The Gambia

Guinea-Bissau

Guinea

Burkina

Be

El Salvador

Nicaragua

St. Lucia

Guadeloupe (Fr)

Sierra Leone

Côte Ghar d'Ivoire

Costa Rica

Panama

Martinique (Fr)

Liberia

Curaçao (Neth)

Trinidad and Tobago

Grenada

Barbados

R.B. de Venezuela

Guyana

St. Vincent and the Grenadines

São Tomé and Princi

Kiribati

Colombia

French Guiana (Fr)

Latin America & Caribbean
1.2%

Ecuador

Suriname

Peru

Brazil

French Polynesia (Fr)

Bolivia

Paraguay

Chile

Uruguay

Argentina

Father and son in Bhutan

Countries with the largest population in 2020

Rank	Country	Projected population (millions)
1	India	1,385
2	China	1,382
3	United States	335
4	Indonesia	262
5	Brazil	210
6	Pakistan	205
7	Nigeria	204
8	Bangladesh	167
9	Russian Federation	139
10	Mexico	126

Europe & Central Asia
0.2%

East Asia & Pacific
0.8%

South Asia
1.5%

Sub-Saharan Africa
2.5%

Facts

▶ It took human history up to the early 1800s to reach 1 billion people; today the world gains 1 billion people every 12 to 14 years.

▶ The world's population is expected to reach 9 billion by 2050, with virtually all population growth occurring in developing countries.

▶ Sub-Saharan Africa will experience the largest proportional increase in population, from 12 percent of the world's population today to 21 percent by 2050, while East Asia and the Pacific's share, which stands at 29 percent today, is expected to fall to 23 percent by 2050.

▶ Almost all population growth between 2008 and 2030 will occur in urban areas, the vast majority of them in developing countries.

Internet links

▶ UN Population Information Network	**www.un.org/popin**
▶ UN Population Fund	**www.unfpa.org**
▶ Demographic and Health Surveys	**www.measuredhs.com**
▶ World Bank—HealthStats	**datatopics.worldbank.org/hnp**
▶ Population Reference Bureau	**www.prb.org**
▶ U.S. Census Bureau	**www.census.gov**

LIFE EXPECTANCY

life expectancy at birth, 2010

- less than 50 years
- 50–59 years
- 60–69 years
- 70–74 years
- 75 years or more
- no data

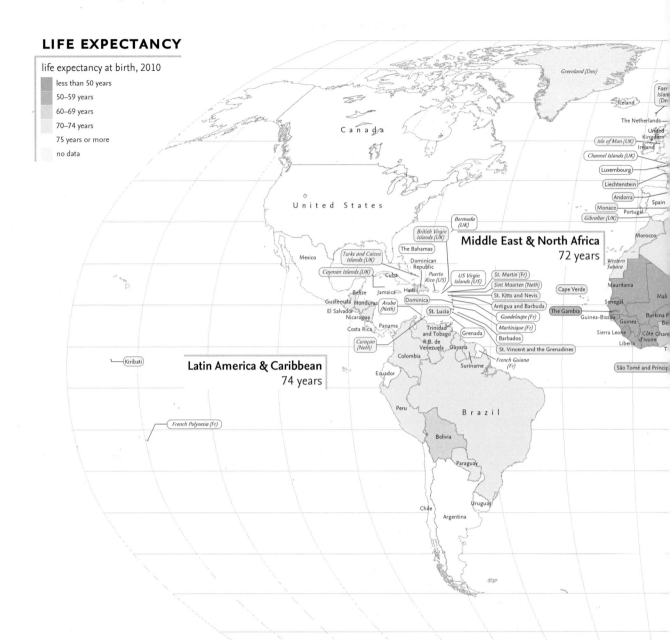

Greenland (Den)

Iceland

The Netherlands

Canada

United States

Bermuda (UK)

British Virgin Islands (UK)

The Bahamas

Turks and Caicos Islands (UK)

Dominican Republic

Cayman Islands (UK)

Puerto Rico (US)

Cuba

Mexico

US Virgin Islands (US)

St. Martin (Fr)

Sint Maarten (Neth)

Middle East & North Africa
72 years

Belize

Guatemala Honduras

El Salvador Nicaragua

Jamaica

Haiti

Dominica

Aruba (Neth)

St. Lucia

St. Kitts and Nevis

Antigua and Barbuda

Guadeloupe (Fr)

Martinique (Fr)

Cape Verde

Mauritania

Mali

Senegal

The Gambia

Guinea-Bissau

Guinea

Sierra Leone

Liberia

Burkina F

Côte Ghana d'Ivoire

Western Sahara

Morocco

Costa Rica

Panama

Curaçao (Neth)

Trinidad and Tobago

R.B. de Venezuela

Grenada

Guyana

Barbados

St. Vincent and the Grenadines

Colombia

Suriname

French Guiana (Fr)

São Tomé and Príncip

Kiribati

Latin America & Caribbean
74 years

Ecuador

Peru

B r a z i l

Bolivia

French Polynesia (Fr)

Paraguay

Chile

Uruguay

Argentina

Faer Islan (De

United Kingdom

Ireland

Isle of Man (UK)

Channel Islands (UK)

Luxembourg

Liechtenstein

Andorra

Monaco

Gibraltar (UK)

Spain

Portugal

A child in Sub-Saharan Africa can only expect to reach, on average, the age of 54

Economies with the longest and shortest life expectancies, 2010

Longest	Years
San Marino	83
Japan	83
Hong Kong SAR, China	83
Switzerland	82
Italy	82
Shortest	
Congo, Dem. Rep.	48
Guinea-Bissau	48
Central African Republic	48
Sierra Leone	47
Lesotho	47

Europe & Central Asia
71 years

East Asia & Pacific
72 years

South Asia
65 years

Sub-Saharan Africa
54 years

Sweden
Finland
Norway
Estonia
Latvia
Lithuania
Denmark
Germany
Belgium
Austria
Switzerland
Italy
Czech Republic
Slovak Republic
Slovenia
Croatia
Serbia
Bosnia and Herzegovina
FYR Macedonia
Montenegro
Bulgaria
Kosovo
Albania Greece
San Marino
Cyprus
Malta
Tunisia
Libya

Poland
Belarus
Ukraine
Moldova
Hungary
Romania
Georgia
Armenia
Azerbaijan
Turkey
Syrian Arab Rep.
Lebanon
Israel
Jordan
West Bank and Gaza
Arab Rep. of Egypt
Saudi Arabia
Qatar
Bahrain
United Arab Emirates
Oman
Rep. of Yemen

Russian Federation
Kazakhstan
Uzbekistan
Kyrgyz Republic
Turkmenistan
Tajikistan
Islamic Republic of Iran
Afghanistan
Iraq
Kuwait
Pakistan
Nepal Bhutan
India Bangladesh
Myanmar
Lao P.D.R.

Mongolia
China
Dem. People's Rep. of Korea
Rep. of Korea
Japan

Niger
Chad
Nigeria
Cameroon
Central African Republic
Sudan
South Sudan
Eritrea
Djibouti
Ethiopia
Somalia
Equatorial Guinea
Rep. of Congo
Gabon
Dem. Rep. of Congo
Uganda
Rwanda
Burundi
Kenya
Tanzania
Seychelles
Comoros
Mayotte (Fr)
Angola
Zambia Malawi
Mozambique
Zimbabwe
Madagascar
Réunion (Fr) Mauritius
Namibia Botswana
South Africa
Swaziland
Lesotho

Thailand Vietnam
Cambodia
Sri Lanka
Maldives
Philippines
Brunei Darussalam
Malaysia
Singapore
Indonesia
Timor-Leste
Papua New Guinea

N. Mariana Islands (US)
Guam (US)
Palau
Federated States of Micronesia
Marshall Islands
Nauru
Solomon Islands
Tuvalu
American Samoa (US)
Vanuatu
Fiji
Samoa
Tonga
New Caledonia (Fr)

Australia
New Zealand

Facts

▶ Life expectancy at birth has reached 80 years in high-income countries, 11 years longer than in 1960.

▶ In 1960, life expectancy in South Asia and Sub-Saharan Africa was 43 years and 41 years, respectively, but today there is a 11-year gap between South Asia (65 years) and Sub-Saharan Africa (54 years).

▶ Life expectancy for Zimbabwe and Swaziland is over 10 years shorter today than in 1990, the result of the HIV/AIDS epidemic.

▶ Male life expectancy in Europe and Central Asia fell from 64 years to 61 years between 1988 and 1994. Life expectancy started to recover and was back to 66 years in 2010.

▶ In four countries, all of them in Europe and Central Asia, female life expectancy is longer than male life expectancy by more than 10 years.

Internet links

▶ UN Population Information Network	**www.un.org/popin**
▶ UN Population Fund	**www.unfpa.org**
▶ Demographic and Health Surveys	**www.measuredhs.com**
▶ World Bank—HealthStats	**datatopics.worldbank.org/hnp**
▶ Population Reference Bureau	**www.prb.org**
▶ U.S. Census Bureau	**www.census.gov**

Children at work

There are 215 million child laborers across the developing world. Some perform simple tasks within the family; others endure long hours in harsh and damaging conditions. Children's work interferes with their education and can impede physical and mental development, reducing their prospects for leading healthy and productive lives.

The number of working children ages 5–17 fell by 30 million between 2000 and 2008. The progress was significant among the younger child laborers ages 5–14, but the population of the older working children ages 15–17 still grew. Sixty percent of child laborers are found in agriculture, and 68 percent work for their own families without pay.

Fewer children are working in hazardous occupations. The ratio of children in hazardous occupations to all child laborers improved to 54 percent in 2008 from 70 percent in 2000. Boys are more likely to be engaged in hazardous work. Asia and the Pacific had the largest population of children in hazardous occupations while Sub-Saharan Africa recorded the highest incidence in 2008. Exposure to workplace hazards at an early age has consequences for children's immediate safety and long-term health.

A substantial proportion of working children manage to attend school, at least some of the time, but children cannot benefit from their time in the classroom if they are tired or stressed by work or made ill by hazardous working conditions. And many drop out early to devote more time

Fewer young children are available to enter the labor force

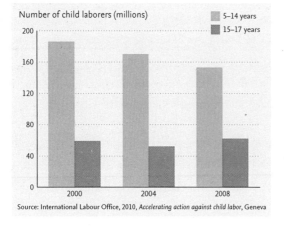

Source: International Labour Office, 2010, *Accelerating action against child labor*, Geneva

As age increases, children are more involved in economic activity

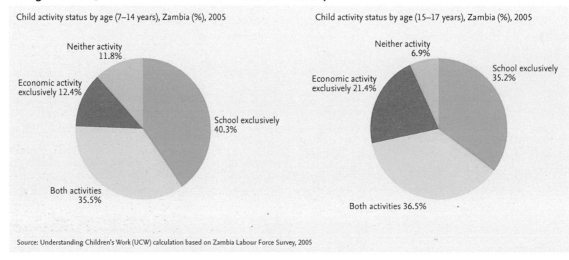

Source: Understanding Children's Work (UCW) calculation based on Zambia Labour Force Survey, 2005

Sub-Saharan Africa has a large share of children doing hazardous work

Children in hazardous occupations by region (5–17 age group, % of total children), 2008

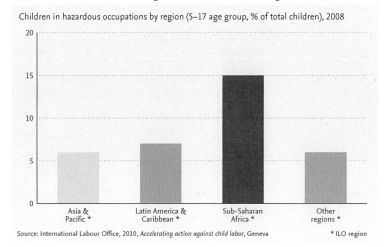

Source: International Labour Office, 2010, *Accelerating action against child labor*, Geneva

* ILO region

The number of working children increased during an economic downturn (2002–2003)

Children ages 10–14 years in R.B. Venezuela, by activity status (%)

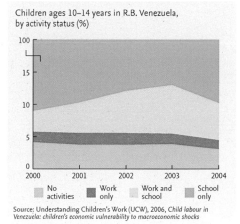

No activities   Work only   Work and school   School only

Source: Understanding Children's Work (UCW), 2006, *Child labour in Venezuela: children's economic vulnerability to macroeconomic shocks*

to work. Especially during financial crises, increased rates of child labor and school dropout can be observed. In the little time available to them, children balancing school and work are deprived of leisure and rest. Girls are particularly disadvantaged, as they often undertake household chores after work. However, their situation may be improving, evidenced by the 15 percent decrease in the number of girl child laborers.

The effects of child labor extend into adulthood. Lacking adequate education, young people are likely to wind up in low-paid, insecure work, or to be unemployed. They are more likely to be self-employed or in unpaid family work rather than paid employment. They also suffer from lower productivity, social stigma, and lower job aspirations.

Child labor, for too long seen as an isolated issue, not only is a serious violation of the rights of children, it also has broader consequences for national development. Because child labor cuts across many development issues including schooling, health care, labor market conditions, labor standards and legislation, and social protection, it requires action by governments, employers, labor organizations, and schools as well as by families themselves.

Long hours of work affect children's health

Reported work-related ill health, children ages 5–17 years (%), by hours worked, 2001–2003

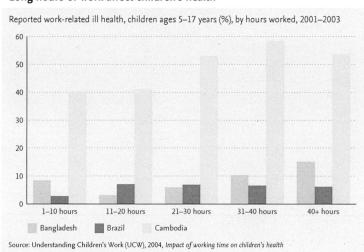

Bangladesh   Brazil   Cambodia

Source: Understanding Children's Work (UCW), 2004, *Impact of working time on children's health*

Boy tending field of potatoes with his family in Brazil

CHILDREN AT WORK

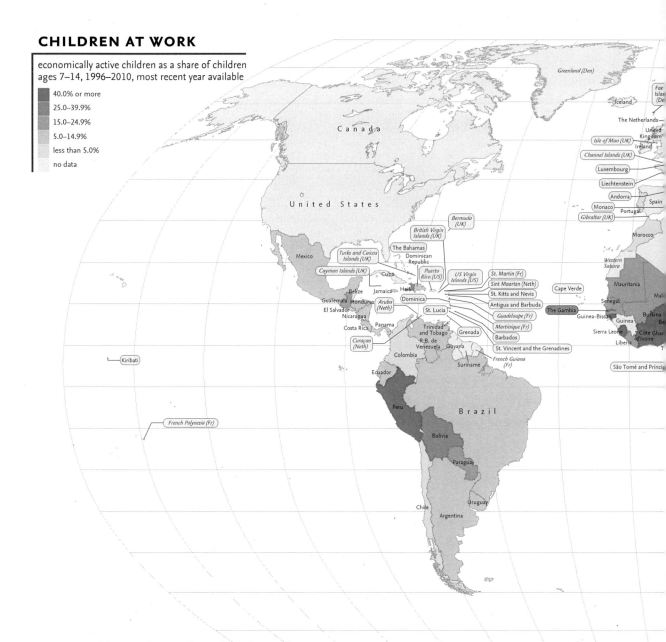

economically active children as a share of children
ages 7–14, 1996–2010, most recent year available

- 40.0% or more
- 25.0–39.9%
- 15.0–24.9%
- 5.0–14.9%
- less than 5.0%
- no data

**Children on their way home from farmwork, Son La province,
northern Vietnam**

Highest proportion of working children

Rank	Country	Children at work (% of children ages 7–14, most recent year 2006–2010)
1	Benin	74.4
2	Sierra Leone	53.7
3	Guinea-Bissau	50.5
4	Ghana	48.9
5	Niger	47.1
6	Côte d'Ivoire	45.7
7	South Sudan	45.6
8	Somalia	43.5
9	Cameroon	43.4
10	Peru	42.2

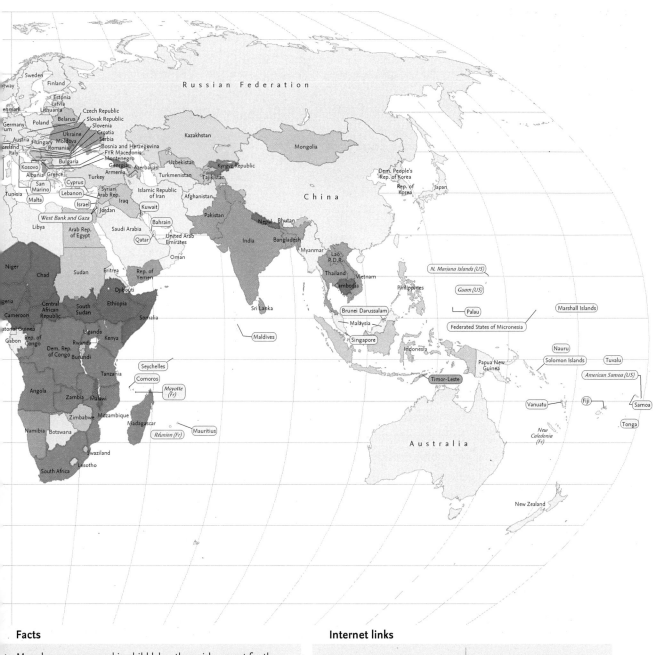

Facts

▶ More boys are engaged in child labor than girls, except for the Democratic Republic of Congo, Lao P.D.R., and Nepal. But there are wide variations among countries. In Bangladesh and Nicaragua, the gender difference is more than 10 percentage points.

▶ More than 75 percent of child laborers in Morocco, Pakistan, and South Sudan do not attend school, while almost all working children in Belarus, Bosnia and Herzegovina, and Ukraine attend school.

▶ In the Kyrgyz Republic, Romania, and Timor-Leste, over 97 percent of working children are engaged in the agricultural sector. In Chile, the Dominican Republic, and Uruguay, 60 to 70 percent of child laborers work in the service sector and fewer than 30 percent in agriculture.

Internet links

▶ Understanding Children's Work Project	www.ucw-project.org
▶ UNICEF Childinfo— Child Labor	www.childinfo.org/ labour.html
▶ International Labour Organization— Child Labor	www.ilo.org/global/topics/ child-labour/lang--en/ index.htm

Education opens doors

The promise of full primary education for everyone by 2015 has been around since 1990. Enrollment rates are rising, but many children still do not start, attend, or complete primary school. A good quality education is key to sustainable development and poverty alleviation and accelerates improvement in other areas.

Progress has been made toward universal primary education since 1990. In 2010, 89 percent of the world's school-age children were enrolled in primary schools. Primary completion rates—the proportion of children completing the last year of primary school—measure progress toward this goal. In East Asia and the Pacific, Europe and Central Asia, and Latin America and the Caribbean, most children enroll in and complete primary school. But South Asia and Sub-Saharan Africa, with primary completion rates of just 88 and 70 percent, respectively, lag far behind. Worldwide, some 60 million primary school-age children remained out of school in 2010. About 75 percent of those were in South Asia and Sub-Saharan Africa. There are many reasons children drop out or never attend school. Schools may be inaccessible or inadequate; teachers may be absent or indifferent, especially in rural areas; parents may not be able to afford school-related costs; or there may be demands for children's labor and their income. Children in poor families and those living in rural areas are less likely to enroll and attend school and more likely to drop out earlier.

Enrollment and completion rates are important measures of education, but they

Primary completion rates have improved, but regional differences remain

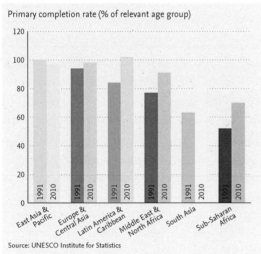

Primary completion rate (% of relevant age group)

Source: UNESCO Institute for Statistics

Children from poor families and those living in rural areas are less likely to complete schooling

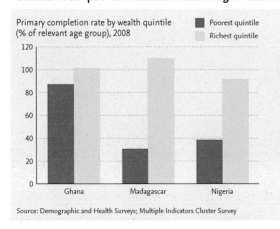

Primary completion rate by wealth quintile (% of relevant age group), 2008

Poorest quintile
Richest quintile

Source: Demographic and Health Surveys; Multiple Indicators Cluster Survey

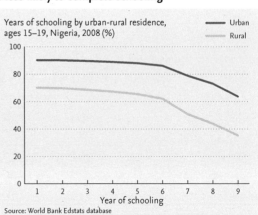

Years of schooling by urban-rural residence, ages 15–19, Nigeria, 2008 (%)

Urban
Rural

Year of schooling

Source: World Bank Edstats database

Rural children walking to school near Ulundi in Kwa-Zulu Natal, South Africa

do not always indicate successful education. Some students complete primary school without acquiring adequate literacy and numeracy skills. Hence there is an increased focus on measuring and monitoring education quality and learning achievement. Many countries conduct national assessments to monitor progress in learning outcome, but differences persist. Results from international assessments, such as the Progress for International Student Achievement (PISA) and Southern and Eastern Africa Consortium for Monitoring Educational Quality (SACMEQ), reveal large achievement gaps among countries, especially between developing and developed countries.

Beyond primary schooling

To compete in today's knowledge-driven economy and shifting global markets, countries need a flexible, skilled work force, able to create and apply knowledge. This is usually achieved through strong secondary and tertiary education systems. While all regions have made progress in expanding secondary and tertiary enrollments between 1991 and 2010, disparities remain between regions, and by gender, household wealth, and rural/urban location. Europe and Central Asia and Latin America and the Caribbean have enrollment rates of about 90 percent in secondary education, but only Europe and Central Asia has tertiary enrollment reaching 50 percent. In Sub-Saharan Africa, where primary enrollment is lower than all other regions, the secondary enrollment ratio is even lower, about 40 percent, and a huge gender gap persists: the ratio of female to male secondary enrollment is only 82 percent. Achieving widespread and equitable access to education will remain a development goal for many years to come.

Standardized tests reveal achievement gaps

Average mathematics score on the SACMEQ exam, 2007

Female
Male

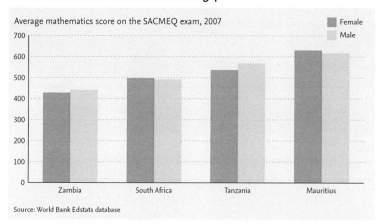

Source: World Bank Edstats database

Achievements in secondary and tertiary enrollment vary among regions

Gross enrollment ratio (% of relevant age group), 2010

Secondary
Tertiary

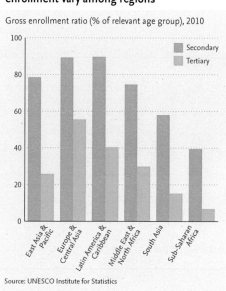

Source: UNESCO Institute for Statistics

EDUCATION FOR ALL

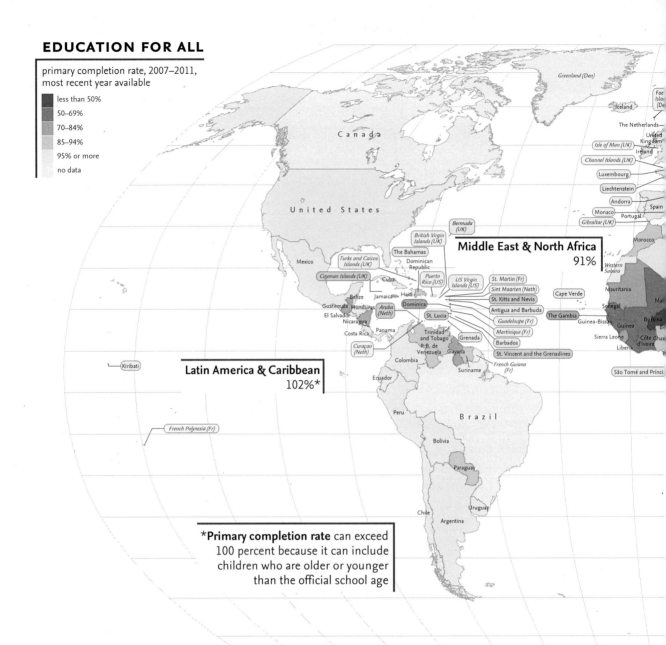

primary completion rate, 2007–2011, most recent year available

- less than 50%
- 50–69%
- 70–84%
- 85–94%
- 95% or more
- no data

Middle East & North Africa
91%

Latin America & Caribbean
102%*

*Primary completion rate can exceed 100 percent because it can include children who are older or younger than the official school age

Map labels: Greenland (Den), Iceland, Faeroe Islands (Den), The Netherlands, United Kingdom, Ireland, Isle of Man (UK), Channel Islands (UK), Luxembourg, Liechtenstein, Andorra, Spain, Monaco, Portugal, Gibraltar (UK), Morocco, Western Sahara, Mauritania, Mali, Cape Verde, Senegal, The Gambia, Guinea-Bissau, Guinea, Burkina Faso, Sierra Leone, Côte d'Ivoire, Liberia, São Tomé and Príncipe

Canada, United States, Mexico, Bermuda (UK), British Virgin Islands (UK), The Bahamas, Dominican Republic, Turks and Caicos Islands (UK), Cayman Islands (UK), Cuba, Puerto Rico (US), US Virgin Islands (US), St. Martin (Fr), Sint Maarten (Neth), St. Kitts and Nevis, Antigua and Barbuda, Guadeloupe (Fr), Martinique (Fr), Barbados, St. Vincent and the Grenadines, Belize, Jamaica, Haiti, Dominica, Guatemala, Honduras, Aruba (Neth), El Salvador, Nicaragua, St. Lucia, Panama, Costa Rica, Trinidad and Tobago, Grenada, Curaçao (Neth), R.B. de Venezuela, Guyana, Colombia, French Guiana (Fr), Suriname, Ecuador, Peru, Brazil, Bolivia, Paraguay, Chile, Uruguay, Argentina, Kiribati, French Polynesia (Fr)

Preschool micro-project in Armenia

Lowest primary completion rates, 2007–2011

Rank	Country	Completion rate (%, MRY 2007–2011)
1	Chad	35
2	Djibouti	36
3	Eritrea	40
4	Central African Republic	43
5	Burkina Faso	45
6	Niger	46
7	Angola	47
8	Equatorial Guinea	52
9	Mali	55
10	Burundi	56

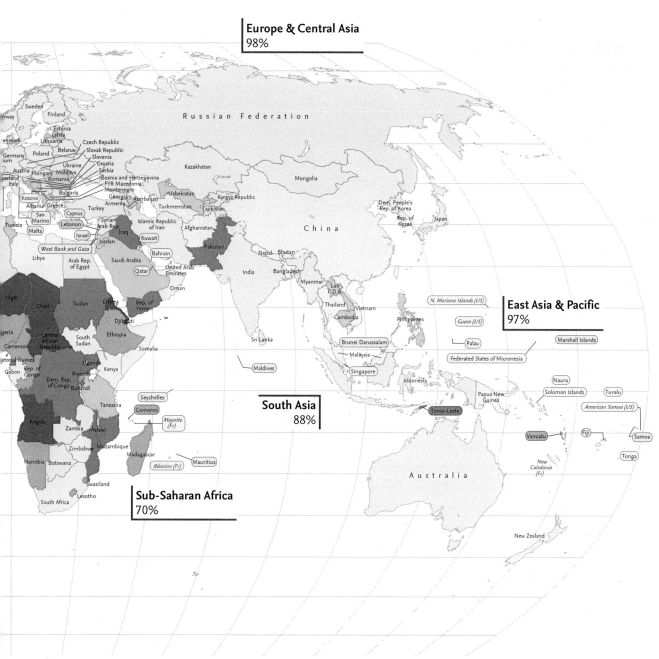

Europe & Central Asia
98%

East Asia & Pacific
97%

South Asia
88%

Sub-Saharan Africa
70%

Facts

▶ There are 60 million children of primary school age who are out of school. About 50 percent of them are in Sub-Saharan Africa.

▶ Latin America and the Caribbean has one of the highest primary net enrollment rates at 95 percent, but also one of the highest percentage of repeaters at 8 percent—the same level as that of Sub-Saharan Africa, which has the lowest net enrollment ratio.

▶ In Sub-Saharan Africa, the adult literacy gap between men and women is more than 20 percentage points. The gap is much smaller among young people ages 15–24, reflecting the recent improvement in education participation.

Internet links

▶ UNESCO—Education	www.unesco.org/new/en/education/
▶ UNESCO Institute for Statistics	www.uis.unesco.org
▶ World Bank Edstats	data.worldbank.org/data-catalog/ed-stats
▶ Demographic and Health Surveys	www.measuredhs.com
▶ UNICEF Childinfo—Education	www.childinfo.org/education.html
▶ UN MDG Indicators	unstats.un.org/unsd/mdg

Gender equality and development

Women around the world have made unprecedented progress in education, health, and access to some labor market opportunities in the past quarter century. However, gender inequality still has a significant effect on many aspects of women's lives. Established institutions may be unfavorable to women, while societal and cultural norms often limit their economic opportunities, which in turn constrain their social and political influence.

The last quarter century has witnessed an unprecedented narrowing of gender gaps in education, health, and access to some labor market opportunities. Gender gaps in primary schooling have been closed, and in one-third of the developing countries, female students now outnumber male students in secondary and tertiary education. Women make up 40 percent of the global labor force and 43 percent of the world's farmers. Moreover, as women have gained better access to health services, their health outcomes have improved dramatically in the last two decades. More women than ever now have access to antenatal care and birth assistance provided by trained health professionals. Women also live longer than men in every region of the world.

Yet progress has not come evenly to all countries or to all women or along all dimensions of gender equality. Women and girls still face discrimination and constraints in different areas of their lives. Gender gaps in secondary and tertiary education remain persistent in regions like South Asia, the Middle East and North Africa, and Sub-Saharan Africa. In almost all countries, societal norms and expectations have strong influences on the choice of subjects of studies in higher education by men and women. Social and cultural stereotyping also biases the roles and remuneration of women in the labor market. Despite a high female labor force participation rate, the types of

Secondary and tertiary enrollment rates of girls are much lower than those of boys in Sub-Saharan Africa, South Asia, and the Middle East and North Africa

Female-male ratio of gross enrollment ratios (%), 2010

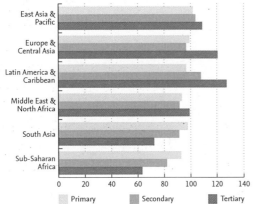

Source: UNESCO Institute for Statistics

Despite narrowing gender gaps in education, women are more likely than men to work as unpaid family workers

Contributing family workers as a percentage of employed males and females (%), 2010

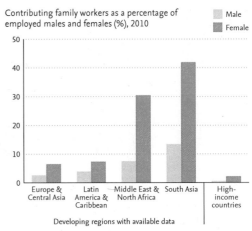

Developing regions with available data

Source: International Labour Organization, Key Indicators of the Labor Market database

Women in wealthier households are more likely to have their babies delivered by skilled health professionals than those from poorer households

Percentage of births assisted by skilled health personnel (%)

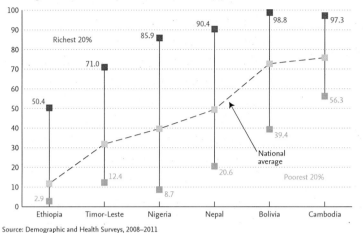

Source: Demographic and Health Surveys, 2008–2011

In many countries, a noticeably higher percentage of men than women have an account at a formal financial institution

Percentage of females and males (age 15+) who have an account at a formal financial institution (%)

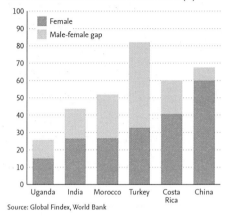

Source: Global Findex, World Bank

employment and the levels of earnings of women are generally inferior to those of men. Women, especially poor women, also bear a disproportionate share of domestic and care-giving responsibilities, leaving them very little time for market activities. In addition, women among disadvantaged groups still lack access to services such as transportation, education, and health care. Inadequate delivery of health services in the rural areas and among the poorest individuals places women at a higher risk of death during infancy, childhood, and reproductive years. Women also have less access than men to productive assets and services, such as land, capital, financial services, and information communication technologies (ICTs).

There has been progress in the past decade, but women still hold less than a quarter of parliamentary seats

Percentage of seats held by women in lower or single house (%)

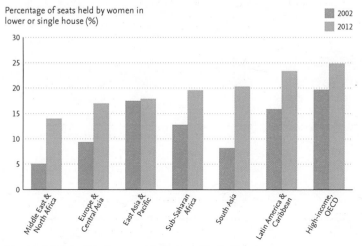

Source: Inter Parliamentary Union (data represent the situation as of May 31 of the year)

The many biases and constraints women face in different stages of their lives leave a vast number of them isolated and without bargaining and decision-making power, whether within the household, in the marketplace, in civil society, or in politics.

Evidence has shown that growth and economic development alone do not lead to gender equality in all its dimensions. Public action plays an important role. Promoting gender equality has received heightened attention and commitment of the international development community in recent years. Ongoing public efforts need to be intensified in four priority areas: reducing excess female mortality and closing the remaining gender gaps in education, improving access to economic opportunities for women, increasing women's voice and agency in the household and in society, and limiting the reproduction of gender inequality across generations.

GENDER EQUITY IN EDUCATION

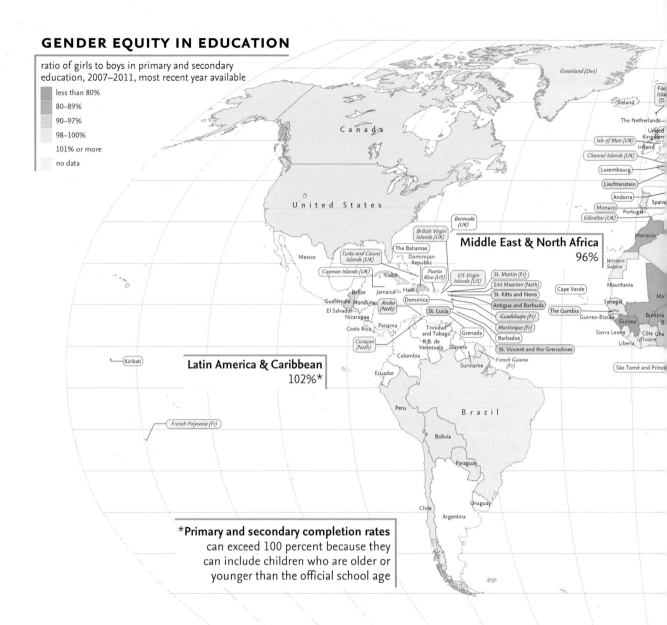

ratio of girls to boys in primary and secondary
education, 2007–2011, most recent year available

- less than 80%
- 80–89%
- 90–97%
- 98–100%
- 101% or more
- no data

Middle East & North Africa
96%

Latin America & Caribbean
102%*

*****Primary and secondary completion rates**
can exceed 100 percent because they
can include children who are older or
younger than the official school age

Students taking year-end exams at Martyr Kardi School in
Sana'a, Yemen

Countries with lowest ratio of girls to boys
gross enrollment rates in primary and
secondary education, MRY 2007–2011

Rank	Developing country	Ratio (%)
1	Somalia	53
2	Afghanistan	64
3	Chad	66
4	Central African Republic	69
5	Yemen, Rep.	75
6	Togo	75
7	Guinea	77
8	Niger	78
9	Congo, Dem. Rep.	79
10	Angola	79

Europe & Central Asia
97%

East Asia & Pacific
102%*

South Asia
91%

Sub-Saharan Africa
88%

Facts

▶ In 2010, 64 percent of the 800 million illiterate adults (ages 15 and above) in the world were women—a share that has remained unchanged since 1990.

▶ The gross enrollment ratio of girls in secondary and tertiary education in the Middle East and North Africa, South Asia, and Sub-Saharan Africa is still considerably lower than that of boys.

▶ Gender stereotyping in education largely reflects societal norms and expectations and has implications for gender gaps in job placement and earnings. In many countries, females constitute 70 to 90 percent of the total university graduates in education and health, but only 10 to 30 percent in law, engineering, manufacturing and construction.

▶ Some countries have experienced reverse gender gaps in school enrollment, especially at the secondary and tertiary levels. Male disadvantage in education needs to be closely monitored.

Internet links

▶ World Bank Gender Data Portal	**data.worldbank.org/gender**
▶ *World Development Report 2012: Gender Equality and Development*	**www.worldbank.org/wdr2012**
▶ *The Little Data Book on Gender 2011*	**data.worldbank.org/products/data-books/little-data-book-on-gender**
▶ UNESCO Institute for Statistics	**www.uis.org**
▶ UNICEF Childinfo—Education	**www.childinfo.org/education.html**

GENDER EQUITY IN THE LABOR MARKET

ratio of female to male labor
participation, 2010

- less than 55%
- 55–69%
- 70–79%
- 80–85%
- 86% or more
- no data

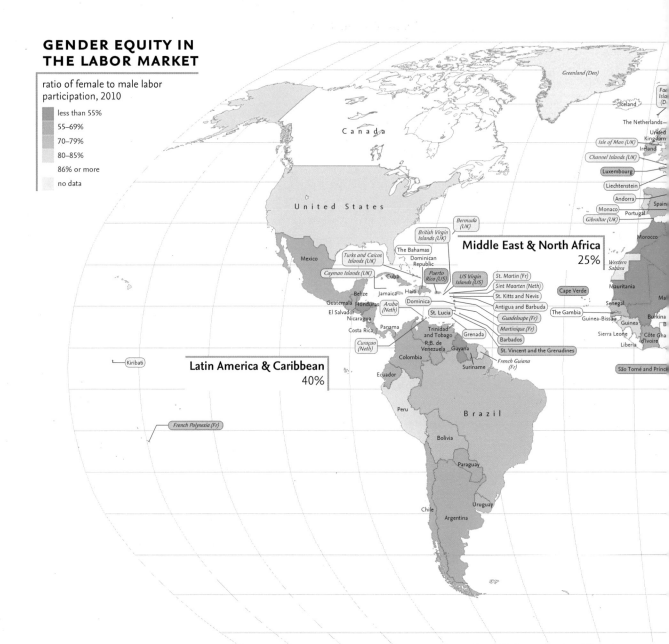

Middle East & North Africa
25%

Latin America & Caribbean
40%

Woman at work in the fields near Nongma village, southwest China

Countries with lowest ratio of female to male
labor participation rates, 2010

Rank	Developing country	Ratio (%)
1	Syrian Arab Republic	18
2	Afghanistan	19
3	Algeria	21
4	Iraq	21
5	West Bank and Gaza	22
6	Iran, Islamic Rep.	22
7	Jordan	23
8	Pakistan	27
9	Egypt, Arab Rep.	32
10	Lebanon	32

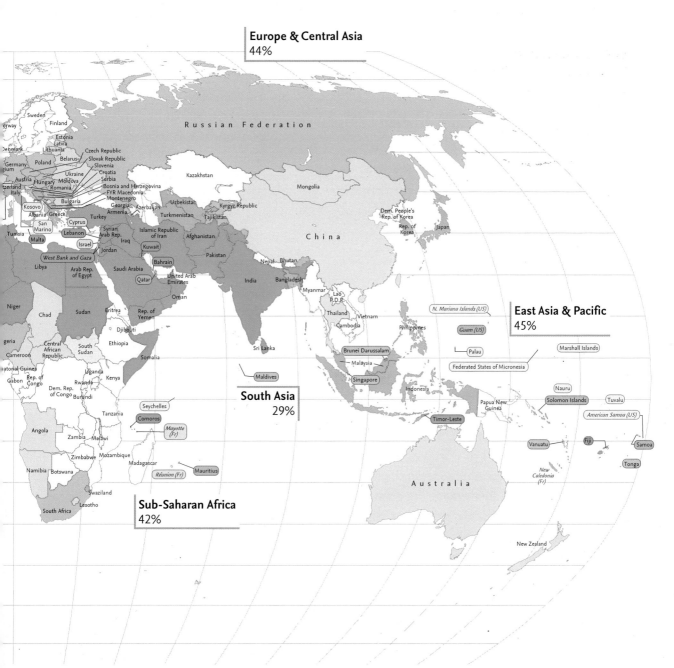

Europe & Central Asia
44%

East Asia & Pacific
45%

South Asia
29%

Sub-Saharan Africa
42%

Facts

▶ Women are more likely than men to be vulnerable workers—that is, less likely to have social protection and safety nets to guard against economic shocks. In developing countries, 65 percent of women were in vulnerable jobs in 2010 compared with 57 percent for men.

▶ In almost all countries, including high-income countries, women are more likely than men to engage in low-productivity activities, and they are more likely to be employed in informal sectors. As a result, women earn only 10 to 80 percent of what men earn.

▶ Women shoulder a much larger burden in household chores than men do. For example, the time women spend on fetching water each day can be two to four times the time men spend.

▶ Women's political participation remains low in both developed and developing countries. Only 20 percent of the parliamentary seats were occupied by women globally by mid-2012.

Internet links

▶ World Bank Gender Data Portal	**data.worldbank.org/gender**
▶ *World Development Report 2012: Gender Equality and Development*	**www.worldbank.org/wdr2012**
▶ International Labour Organization, Key Indicators of the Labour Market	**www.ilo.org/empelm/what/ WCMS_114240/lang--en/ index.htm**
▶ The Global Financial Inclusion (Global Findex) Database	**go.worldbank.org/ VMW3ST4CQ0**
▶ Women in National Parliaments, Inter-Parliamentary Union	**www.ipu.org/wmn-e/ world.htm**

Children under 5—struggling to survive

Seven million children died before their fifth birthday in 2011, the vast majority from causes that are preventable through a combination of good care, nutrition, and simple medical treatment. Child mortality is closely linked to poverty, and poor children are twice as likely to die before their fifth birthday compared with children from rich families.

Child mortality has improved in every region since 1970, when one in six children died before the age of 5. By 2011, this rate had fallen to 1 in 18 children. Latin America and the Caribbean and the Middle East and North Africa made the greatest progress: in 2011, child mortality there was less than one-sixth the level of 1970. Much of the improvement in these regions occurred among the poorest segments of the population. Better health care and public health measures such as immunization, use of insecticide-treated bednets for malaria

prevention, prevention of mother-child HIV transmission, and increased access to antiretroviral drugs, safe drinking water, and sanitation have all contributed to the decline.

Child mortality is increasingly concentrated in Sub-Saharan Africa and South Asia, where under-5 mortality rates were 109 and 62 per 1,000, respectively, in 2011. In high-income countries the mortality rate is less than one-tenth those. Half of all child deaths occurred in only five countries—India, Nigeria, Democratic Republic of Congo, Pakistan, and China. India and Nigeria together account for one-third of all under-5 deaths worldwide. Under-5 mortality is higher among children living in rural areas and in poorer households. These children are less likely to have access to good-quality health care or to avail themselves of these services.

Good childcare practices such as early and exclusive breastfeeding, and low-cost treatments and interventions such as antibiotics for respiratory infections, oral rehydration for diarrhea, immunization, and the use of insecticide-treated bednets and appropriate drugs in malarial regions, can prevent many unnecessary deaths. However, only 34 percent of children sleep under insecticide-treated bednets in Sub-Saharan

Child mortality rates have declined over four decades

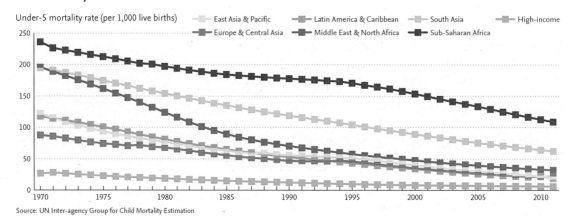

Under-5 mortality rate (per 1,000 live births)   East Asia & Pacific   Latin America & Caribbean   South Asia   High-income
                                                    Europe & Central Asia   Middle East & North Africa   Sub-Saharan Africa

Source: UN Inter-agency Group for Child Mortality Estimation

52

Children of a slum-dwelling family have a high risk of dying before the age of 5

Africa, where 90 percent of malaria deaths occur. More than 30 percent of children in South Asia with respiratory infections are not taken to health providers and 16 percent of children in developing countries lack immunization against measles. Improved public services, such as safe water and sanitation and education, especially for girls and mothers, can help save children's lives. Greater effort is needed to make sure these services reach poor families and people in rural areas, because they suffer the most and are the hardest to reach.

Nutrition and child mortality

More than one-third of child deaths are attributable to malnutrition, which weakens children's immune systems and reduces resistance to diseases. The process often begins at birth, when poorly nourished mothers give birth to underweight babies. Improper feeding and childcare practices worsen malnutrition. In developing countries, nearly 30 percent of children under 5 are stunted (that is, too short for their age) as a result of chronic malnutrition. Breast milk alone is the ideal nourishment for infants for the first six months, providing all of the nutrients as well as antibodies that help to prevent disease. However, exclusive breastfeeding is often stopped in favor of commercial breast milk substitutes or early introduction of solid or soft foods. Fewer than 40 percent of infants under six months in developing countries enjoy the benefit of exclusive breastfeeding.

Except in Sub-Saharan Africa, the number of under-5 deaths has fallen significantly

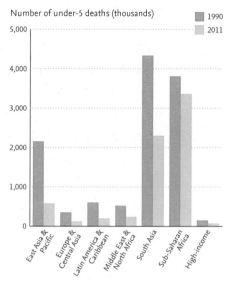

Number of under-5 deaths (thousands)

Source: UN Inter-agency Group for Child Mortality Estimation

Children in poor households are more likely to die than children in rich households

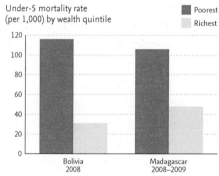

Under-5 mortality rate (per 1,000) by wealth quintile

Source: Demographic and Health Surveys

Children living in rural areas are more likely to die than children in urban areas

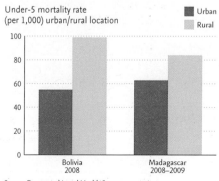

Under-5 mortality rate (per 1,000) urban/rural location

Source: Demographic and Health Surveys

CHILD MORTALITY

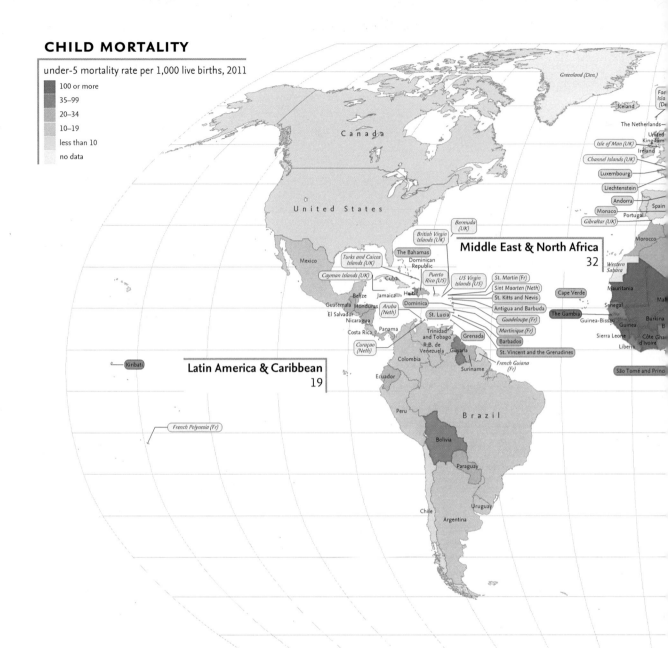

under-5 mortality rate per 1,000 live births, 2011

- 100 or more
- 35–99
- 20–34
- 10–19
- less than 10
- no data

Middle East & North Africa
32

Latin America & Caribbean
19

Canada

United States

Greenland (Den.)

Iceland

Faroe Islands (Den.)

The Netherlands

United Kingdom

Isle of Man (UK)

Ireland

Channel Islands (UK)

Luxembourg

Liechtenstein

Andorra

Spain

Monaco

Portugal

Gibraltar (UK)

Morocco

Western Sahara

Mauritania

Mali

Mexico

Bermuda (UK)

British Virgin Islands (UK)

The Bahamas

Dominican Republic

Turks and Caicos Islands (UK)

Puerto Rico (US)

Cayman Islands (UK)

Cuba

US Virgin Islands (US)

St. Martin (Fr)

Sint Maarten (Neth)

St. Kitts and Nevis

Cape Verde

Senegal

Belize

Jamaica

Haiti

Dominica

Antigua and Barbuda

Guadeloupe (Fr)

The Gambia

Guinea-Bissau

Guinea

Burkina Faso

Guatemala

Honduras

Aruba (Neth)

El Salvador

Nicaragua

St. Lucia

Martinique (Fr)

Sierra Leone

Côte d'Ivoire

Ghana

Costa Rica

Panama

Barbados

Liberia

Curaçao (Neth)

Trinidad and Tobago

Grenada

St. Vincent and the Grenadines

Colombia

R.B. de Venezuela

Guyana

Suriname

French Guiana (Fr)

São Tomé and Principe

Kiribati

Ecuador

Peru

Brazil

French Polynesia (Fr)

Bolivia

Paraguay

Chile

Uruguay

Argentina

Man with sick child in waiting room of local hospital in Africa

Highest under-5 mortality rate, 2011

Rank	Country	Under-5 mortality rate (per 1,000 live births)
1	Sierra Leone	185
2	Somalia	180
3	Mali	176
4	Chad	169
5	Congo, Dem. Rep.	168
6	Central African Republic	164
7	Guinea-Bissau	161
8	Angola	158
9	Burkina Faso	146
10	Burundi	139

Europe & Central Asia
21

R u s s i a n   F e d e r a t i o n

Sweden
Finland
Estonia
Latvia
Lithuania
Germany
Poland
Belarus
Czech Republic
Slovak Republic
Slovenia
Croatia
Ukraine
Serbia
Austria
Hungary
Moldova
Romania
Bosnia and Herzegovina
FYR Macedonia
Montenegro
Bulgaria
Georgia
Kosovo
Albania Greece
Armenia
Azerbaijan
San
Marino
Cyprus
Turkey
Tunisia
Malta
Lebanon
Syrian
Arab Rep.
Israel
Jordan
West Bank and Gaza
Libya
Arab Rep.
of Egypt
Saudi Arabia
Qatar

Kazakhstan

Mongolia

Uzbekistan
Kyrgyz Republic
Turkmenistan
Tajikistan
Islamic Republic
of Iran
Afghanistan

Iraq
Kuwait
Bahrain
United Arab
Emirates
Oman

Pakistan

C h i n a

Dem. People's
Rep. of Korea
Rep. of
Korea
Japan

Nepal Bhutan
India Bangladesh
Myanmar

Niger
Chad
Sudan
Eritrea
Rep. of
Yemen
Djibouti
Central
African
Republic
South
Sudan
Ethiopia
Cameroon
Equatorial Guinea
Gabon
Rep. of
Congo
Uganda
Kenya
Somalia
Dem. Rep.
of Congo
Rwanda
Burundi
Tanzania
Seychelles
Comoros
Angola
Zambia Malawi
Mozambique
Namibia Botswana
Zimbabwe
Madagascar
Mayotte
(Fr)
Réunion (Fr) Mauritius
Swaziland
South Africa Lesotho

Sri Lanka

Lao
P.D.R.
Thailand
Vietnam
Cambodia
Brunei Darussalam
Malaysia
Singapore
Maldives

N. Mariana Islands (US)
Guam (US)
Palau
Federated States of Micronesia
Nauru

Philippines

Indonesia

Papua New
Guinea
Timor-Leste

A u s t r a l i a

New
Caledonia
(Fr)

Vanuatu
Solomon Islands
Tuvalu
Fiji
American Samoa (US)
Samoa
Tonga

New Zealand

East Asia & Pacific
21

Marshall Islands

South Asia
62

Sub-Saharan Africa
109

Facts

▶ 6.9 million children a year die before their fifth birthday, approximately 40 percent of them during their first four weeks of life.

▶ Substantial progress has been made toward reducing child mortality. In 2011, 14,000 fewer children under age 5 died every day compared with 1990, and the rate of decline in under-5 mortality increased between 2000 and 2011.

▶ Four diseases—pneumonia, diarrhea, malaria, and AIDS—accounted for 38 percent of all deaths in children under 5 worldwide in 2010.

▶ The number of child deaths has significantly decreased since 1990 in all regions except Sub-Saharan Africa.

Internet links

▶ UNICEF Childinfo—Child Mortality	www.childinfo.org/mortality.html
▶ World Health Organization—Maternal, Newborn, Child and Adolescent Health	www.who.int/child_adolescent_health/data/child/en
▶ World Bank HNPstats	go.worldbank.org/N2N84RDV00
▶ Demographic and Health Surveys	www.measuredhs.com
▶ UN Millennium Development Goals	unstats.un.org/unsd/mdg
▶ Inter-agency Group for Child Mortality Estimation database (CME Info)	www.childmortality.org/

MALNOURISHED CHILDREN

proportion of children under 5
who are underweight, 2005–2011,
most recent year available

- 30.0% or more
- 20.0–29.9%
- 10.0–19.9%
- less than 10.0%
- no data

Middle East & North Africa
6%

Latin America & Caribbean
3%

Malnourished children are vulnerable to diseases

Highest rates of malnutrition, 2005–2011

Rank	Country	Prevalence of child stunting (%)
1	Burundi	58
2	Timor-Leste	58
3	Niger	55
4	Madagascar	49
5	Guatemala	48
6	India	48
7	Malawi	48
8	Lao P.D.R.	48
9	Congo, Dem. Rep.	46
10	Zambia	46

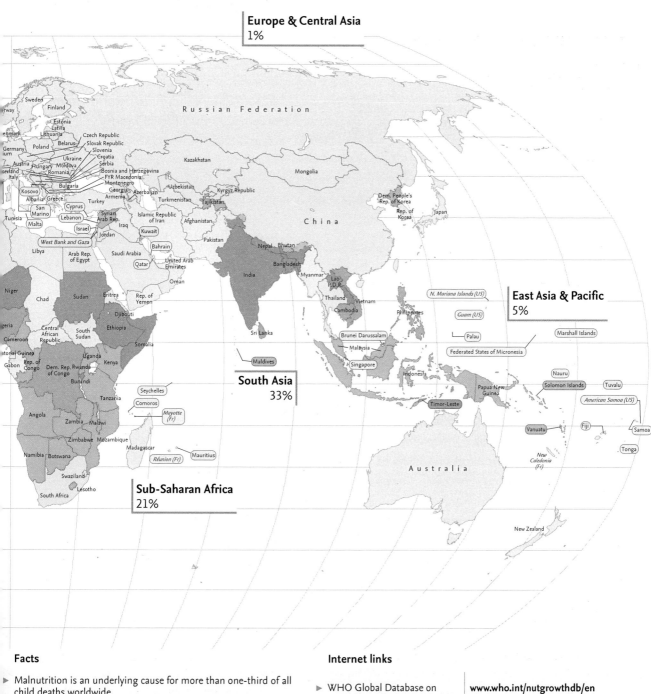

Europe & Central Asia
1%

East Asia & Pacific
5%

South Asia
33%

Sub-Saharan Africa
21%

Facts

▶ Malnutrition is an underlying cause for more than one-third of all child deaths worldwide.

▶ Nearly one-fifth of children under 5 (about 100 million) in developing countries are underweight.

▶ South Asia has the highest prevalence of underweight children. One-third of children under 5 are underweight. Latin America and the Caribbean has the lowest prevalence of underweight children at 3 percent.

▶ Children in rural areas are nearly twice as likely to be underweight as those in urban areas, and poor children are more than twice as likely to be underweight as rich children.

Internet links

▶ WHO Global Database on Child Growth and Nutrition	**www.who.int/nutgrowthdb/en**
▶ UNICEF Childinfo— Undernutrition	**www.childinfo.org/ undernutrition.html**
▶ UNICEF Health Statistics	**www.unicef.org/health/index_ statistics.html**
▶ FAO Food Security Statistics	**www.fao.org/publications/ sofi/en/**

Improving the health of mothers

Having a baby is a happy event. But for many mothers, it is also life-threatening. More than 280,000 women die each year from pregnancy-related causes. Over 99 percent of all maternal deaths occur in developing countries— 85 percent in poor countries in Sub-Saharan Africa and South Asia. Most of these deaths are avoidable with access to health care and prompt medical procedures.

The risk of maternal death is often rooted in a poor childhood. When malnourished girls become mothers, they are more vulnerable to complications or death during delivery. These mothers often do not have adequate access to health care before, during, and after pregnancy, resulting in untreated complications and higher risk of death. The majority of all maternal deaths occur just before, during, or immediately after delivery. Care by skilled health staff is crucial for handling normal deliveries safely, recognizing the onset of complications, and referring the mother for emergency care as needed. Less than half of births in South Asia and Sub-Saharan Africa are attended by skilled health staff, compared with 99 percent in high-income countries.

Prenatal care during pregnancy is important for the health and wellbeing of mothers and their infants. The World Health Organization recommends that every woman have at least four prenatal visits during pregnancy. But only 56 percent of women in developing countries receive such a level of care, and 19 percent receive no prenatal care. In any country, poor women are much less likely to receive care during pregnancy and childbirth from skilled health staff.

Maternal deaths are both caused by poverty and a cause of it. A mother's death is not just a human tragedy but also an economic and social catastrophe for the family. Her children lose the opportunity of a mother's nurture and too often the chance of education, leading the family even further into poverty.

Women in South Asia and Sub-Saharan Africa are at higher risk of dying during childbirth

Maternal mortality ratio (per 100,000 live births)

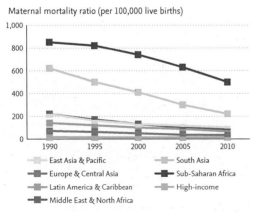

Source: WHO, UNICEF, UNFPA, and World Bank, 2012,
Trends in maternal mortality: 1990 to 2010

Mothers in South Asia and Sub-Saharan Africa still lack adequate health care during childbirth

Births attended by skilled health staff (%)

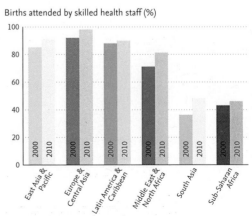

Source: UNICEF, *The state of the world's children 2012*

Compounding the risks of poor reproductive health care are poorly timed and inadequately spaced births, which expose women to frequent pregnancies in short intervals. Although cheap and easy methods of preventing unwanted pregnancies are available, every year more than 100 million couples, or 17 percent of married women, wanting to avoid pregnancy do not use contraception. As a result, 50 percent of all pregnancies are unplanned and 25 percent are unwanted— and a quarter of pregnant women seek abortions. Many of these abortions are performed by untrained providers, and 47,000 women die every year because of them. Contraceptive use among women in developing countries has risen, from less than 10 percent in 1960 to 61 percent in 2008. But there is much variation—in Sub-Saharan Africa, only about 22 percent of women plan their pregnancies.

Teenage pregnancies are high risk for both mother and child. They are more likely to result in premature delivery, low birth weight, delivery complications, and death. About 16 million girls ages 15–19 give birth each year, accounting for more than 10 percent of all births. In addition to the risk of death during pregnancy and childbirth, which is twice as high as for older pregnant women, adolescent mothers often give up opportunities for education and future employment and earnings.

In the long run, promoting girls' and women's education and offering them opportunities for success are just as important for reducing birth rates as promoting contraception and family planning. Education and greater gender equity

become a form of social contraception for women. A woman's education provides knowledge and skills to improve the nutritional and health status of the family and build job skills that allow her to join the workforce and marry later in life. Education also gives her the power to say how many children she wants and when. These are enduring qualities she will hand down to her daughters.

Contraceptive use is particularly low in Sub-Saharan Africa

Contraceptive prevalence (% of married women ages 15–49), 2010

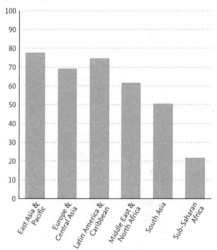

Source: World Development Indicators database

Adolescent fertility is decreasing everywhere, but large regional differences remain

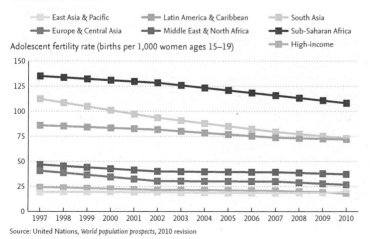

Source: United Nations, *World population prospects*, 2010 revision

Poor women receive less care during pregnancy

Pregnant women receiving prenatal care by wealth quintile (%)

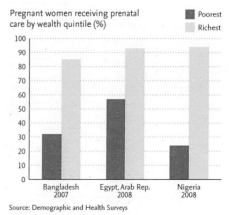

Source: Demographic and Health Surveys

HEALTH OF MOTHERS

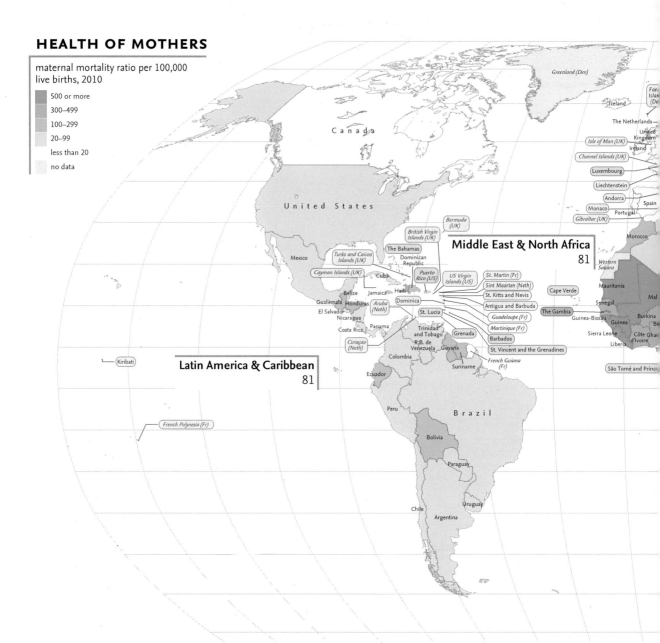

maternal mortality ratio per 100,000
live births, 2010

- 500 or more
- 300–499
- 100–299
- 20–99
- less than 20
- no data

Greenland (Den)

Iceland

Faer
Isla
(De

The Netherlands

United
Kingdom

Isle of Man (UK)

Ireland

Channel Islands (UK)

Luxembourg

Liechtenstein

Andorra

Spain

Monaco

Portugal

Gibraltar (UK)

Canada

United States

Morocco

Western
Sahara

Mauritania

Mal

Mexico

Bermuda (UK)

British Virgin Islands (UK)

The Bahamas

Dominican Republic

Cayman Islands (UK)

Cuba

Turks and Caicos Islands (UK)

Puerto Rico (US)

US Virgin Islands (US)

St. Martin (Fr)

Sint Maarten (Neth)

St. Kitts and Nevis

Antigua and Barbuda

Guadeloupe (Fr)

Martinique (Fr)

Barbados

St. Vincent and the Grenadines

Cape Verde

The Gambia

Senegal

Guinea-Bissau

Guinea

Burkina

Be

Sierra Leone

Côte Ghar
d'Ivoire

Liberia

Middle East & North Africa
81

Belize

Jamaica

Haiti

Guatemala

Honduras

El Salvador

Nicaragua

Costa Rica

Panama

Dominica

Aruba (Neth)

St. Lucia

Grenada

Trinidad and Tobago

R.B. de Venezuela

Guyana

Colombia

Suriname

Curaçao (Neth)

French Guiana (Fr)

São Tomé and Princi

Kiribati

Latin America & Caribbean
81

Ecuador

Peru

Brazil

Bolivia

French Polynesia (Fr)

Paraguay

Chile

Uruguay

Argentina

Fertility and mortality are highest in Sub-Saharan Africa with low levels of contraceptive use and inadequate delivery care

Countries with low contraceptive prevalence rate, 2005–2010

Rank	Country	Contraceptive prevalence rate (% of married women ages 15–49)
1	Chad	5
2	Sudan	8
3	Sierra Leone	8
4	Mali	8
5	Guinea	9
6	Mauritania	9
7	Liberia	11
8	Senegal	12
9	Côte d'Ivoire	13
10	Macedonia, FYR	14

Europe & Central Asia
32

East Asia & Pacific
83

South Asia
220

Sub-Saharan Africa
500

Facts

▶ 287,000 women die each year because of pregnancy-related causes. For every woman who dies, at least 20 others suffer injuries, infection, and disability. Almost all maternal deaths are preventable.

▶ Sub-Saharan Africa and South Asia, which bear the greatest burden of maternal mortality, also have the lowest levels of skilled birth attendance, at 46 percent and 48 percent, respectively.

▶ Eighty percent of women in the developing world receive antenatal care from a skilled health provider at least once during pregnancy. But only 56 percent of all pregnant women benefit from four antenatal visits.

▶ Of 44 million abortions performed every year, nearly half are unsafe. Forty-seven thousand of them result in death.

Internet links

▶ UNICEF—Maternal and Newborn Health	**www.unicef.org/health/index_ maternalhealth.html**
▶ UNICEF Childinfo— Maternal Health	**www.childinfo.org/ health.html**
▶ World Health Organization— Maternal Health	**www.who.int/topics/ maternal_health/en**
▶ World Bank HNPstats	**go.worldbank.org/N2N84RDV00**
▶ Maternal Mortality Estimation Inter-agency Group database (MME Info)	**www.maternalmortalitydata.org/**
▶ UN MDG Indicators	**unstats.un.org/unsd/mdg**

Communicable diseases

Communicable diseases such as HIV/AIDS, tuberculosis, and malaria kill millions of people each year. They exact a terrible toll on society and the economies of developing countries. Although international awareness and funding to fight epidemic diseases have increased, much remains to be done. Meanwhile, the burden of non-communicable diseases is also increasing.

Every day, over 7,400 people are infected with HIV, and about 5,000 die from AIDS. The number of people living with HIV reached 34 million in 2010. Although the global prevalence rate of HIV appears to have leveled off in the late 1990s, the number of infected people continues to rise because better care and antiretroviral therapy, which suppresses the virus and stops the progression of HIV to AIDS, are keeping more people alive for longer. Access to antiretroviral therapy has expanded by

a factor of 17 over the past seven years. In 2010, 6.7 million people in developing countries received antiretroviral therapy. Almost 70 percent of people living with HIV are in Sub-Saharan Africa, where women and children are especially vulnerable to the disease. Women constitute 58 percent of adults (ages 15 and older) living with HIV in Sub-Saharan Africa whereas they constitute 37 percent of adults living with HIV worldwide. More than 90 percent of all HIV-positive children live in the region. Infants are often at high risk of infection through mother-to-child transmission.

Tuberculosis, still a major cause of illness and death worldwide, is becoming more dangerous with the spread of drug-resistant strains of the bacteria. Drug-resistance is caused by inconsistent or partial treatment, wrong treatment regimens, or unavailability of appropriate drugs. Twenty-nine out of 30 countries with the highest tuberculosis incidence rates are located in Sub-Saharan Africa and East Asia and the Pacific. Together they account for 85 percent of all tuberculosis cases. Poor people are especially vulnerable to the disease because of underlying health problems and limited

HIV prevalence is concentrated in Sub-Saharan Africa

HIV prevalence rate, adults ages 15–49 (%)

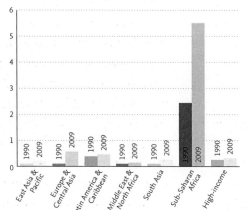

Source: UNAIDS, *Report on the global AIDS epidemic, 2010*

In low- and middle-income countries, nearly half of people eligible for antiretroviral therapy were covered in 2010

Antiretroviral therapy coverage (%), 2010

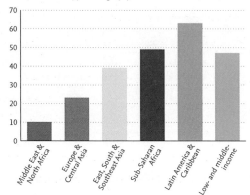

Source: WHO, *Global HIV/AIDS response progress report, 2011*

Tuberculosis incidence is leveling off, but remains high in Sub-Saharan Africa

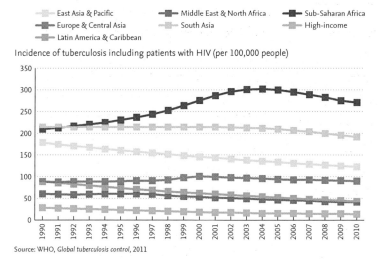

East Asia & Pacific · Europe & Central Asia · Latin America & Caribbean · Middle East & North Africa · South Asia · Sub-Saharan Africa · High-income

Incidence of tuberculosis including patients with HIV (per 100,000 people)

Source: WHO, *Global tuberculosis control*, 2011

Many more children are sleeping under insecticide-treated bednets

Children sleeping under ITN (% of children under 5)

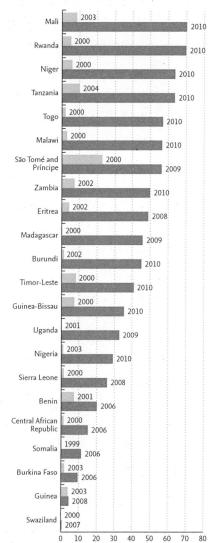

Source: UNICEF, *The state of the world's children*, 2012

access to treatment. Tuberculosis is a leading killer of people living with HIV. At least one-third of the people living with HIV worldwide are infected with tuberculosis, and about one in four deaths among people with HIV is caused by tuberculosis.

Malaria causes approximately 700,000 deaths each year, primarily among children below age 5 and pregnant women. Ninety percent of all malaria deaths occur in Sub-Saharan Africa. Insecticide-treated bednets are one of the most effective ways to prevent malaria transmission as these nets provide a physical barrier against the bite of an infected mosquito. In addition, a net treated with insecticide provides additional protection by repelling or killing mosquitoes that rest on the net—an important protective effect that extends beyond the individual to the community. The percentage of households owning at least one insecticide-treated bednet in Sub-Saharan Africa has increased from 3 percent in 2000 to 50 percent in 2011, although it is still too low to cover everybody at risk. In addition to the use of insecticide-treated bednets, malaria control depends on surveillance, efficient public health measures, education, and access to medications.

Increase in non-communicable diseases

Urbanization, aging populations, tobacco use, unhealthy diet, physical inactivity, and harmful use of alcohol have combined to make chronic and non-communicable diseases—such as diabetes, cancer, cardiovascular diseases, and injuries—increasingly important causes of mortality and morbidity in developing countries. The rise of chronic, non-communicable diseases comes on top of an unfinished agenda on communicable diseases. The increase in non-communicable diseases, accompanied by a shift in the distribution of disease and death from younger to older people as the population ages, will result in many developing countries, especially low-income countries, struggling to provide adequate health care for their people.

HIV/AIDS

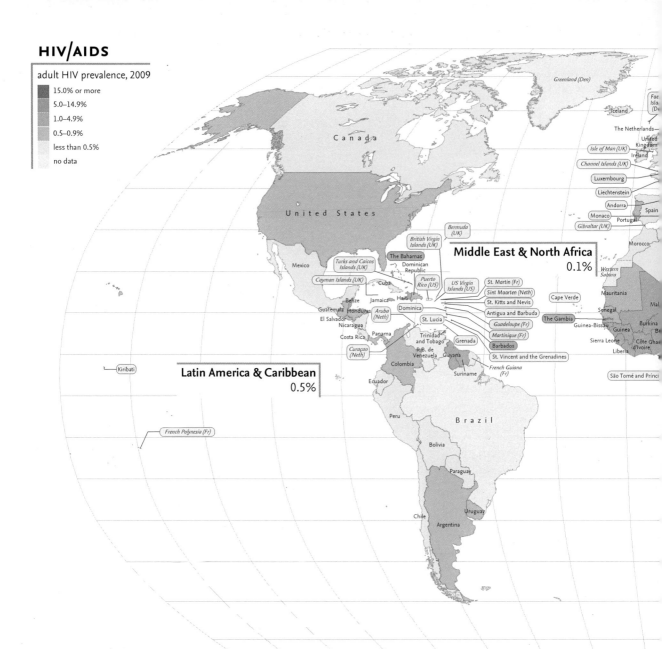

adult HIV prevalence, 2009

- 15.0% or more
- 5.0–14.9%
- 1.0–4.9%
- 0.5–0.9%
- less than 0.5%
- no data

Greenland (Den)

Canada

United States

Mexico

Middle East & North Africa
0.1%

Bermuda (UK)
British Virgin Islands (UK)
The Bahamas
Dominican Republic
Turks and Caicos Islands (UK)
Cayman Islands (UK)
Cuba
Puerto Rico (US)
US Virgin Islands (US)
St. Martin (Fr)
Sint Maarten (Neth)
St. Kitts and Nevis
Cape Verde
Belize
Jamaica
Haiti
Guatemala
Honduras
Aruba (Neth)
Dominica
Antigua and Barbuda
The Gambia
El Salvador
Nicaragua
Guadeloupe (Fr)
St. Lucia
Martinique (Fr)
Costa Rica
Panama
Trinidad and Tobago
Grenada
Barbados
Curaçao (Neth)
R.B. de Venezuela
Guyana
St. Vincent and the Grenadines
Colombia
Suriname
French Guiana (Fr)
Ecuador
Peru
Brazil
Bolivia
Paraguay
Chile
Uruguay
Argentina

Kiribati

Latin America & Caribbean
0.5%

French Polynesia (Fr)

Iceland
Fae Isla (De
The Netherlands
United Kingdom
Isle of Man (UK)
Ireland
Channel Islands (UK)
Luxembourg
Liechtenstein
Andorra
Spain
Monaco
Portugal
Gibraltar (UK)
Morocco
Western Sahara
Mauritania
Mali
Senegal
Burkina
Guinea-Bissau
Guinea
Sierra Leone
Côte d'Ivoire
Liberia
São Tomé and Princi

A campaigner holds a candle for HIV/AIDS victims at a rally in Cambodia

Countries with the highest HIV prevalence rates, 2009

Rank	Country	Prevalence of HIV (% of population ages 15–49)
1	Swaziland	25.9
2	Botswana	24.8
3	Lesotho	23.6
4	South Africa	17.8
5	Zimbabwe	14.3
6	Zambia	13.5
7	Namibia	13.1
8	Mozambique	11.5
9	Malawi	11.0
10	Uganda	6.5

Europe & Central Asia
0.6%

R u s s i a n   F e d e r a t i o n

Sweden
Finland
Estonia
Latvia
Lithuania
Germany
Poland
Belarus
Czech Republic
Slovak Republic
Slovenia
Ukraine
Croatia
Austria
Hungary
Moldova
Serbia
Italy
Romania
Bosnia and Herzegovina
FYR Macedonia
Bulgaria
Montenegro
Kosovo
Greece
Georgia
Albania
Azerbaijan
San Marino
Cyprus
Turkey
Armenia
Malta
Lebanon
Israel
Syrian Arab Rep.
Jordan
West Bank and Gaza
Tunisia
Libya
Arab Rep. of Egypt
Saudi Arabia
Qatar
Bahrain
Kuwait
Iraq
Islamic Republic of Iran
Afghanistan
United Arab Emirates
Oman
Rep. of Yemen
Djibouti

Kazakhstan
Uzbekistan
Kyrgyz Republic
Turkmenistan
Tajikistan
Mongolia

C h i n a

Dem. People's Rep. of Korea
Rep. of Korea
Japan

Pakistan
Nepal
Bhutan
India
Bangladesh
Myanmar
Lao P.D.R.
Thailand
Vietnam
Cambodia

Sri Lanka

Maldives

South Asia
0.3%

N. Mariana Islands (US)
Guam (US)

East Asia & Pacific
0.2%

Philippines

Brunei Darussalam
Malaysia
Singapore
Indonesia

Palau
Federated States of Micronesia
Marshall Islands

Nauru
Solomon Islands
Tuvalu

Papua New Guinea
Timor-Leste

American Samoa (US)

Vanuatu
Fiji
Samoa

New Caledonia (Fr)
Tonga

A u s t r a l i a

New Zealand

Niger
Chad
Sudan
Eritrea
geria
Cameroon
Central African Republic
South Sudan
Ethiopia
Somalia
atonal Guinea
Gabon
Rep. of Congo
Uganda
Kenya
Dem. Rep. of Congo
Rwanda
Burundi
Tanzania
Seychelles
Comoros
Angola
Zambia
Malawi
Mayotte (Fr)
Zimbabwe
Mozambique
Namibia
Botswana
Madagascar
Réunion (Fr)
Mauritius
Swaziland
South Africa
Lesotho

Sub-Saharan Africa
5.5%

Facts

▶ 34 million people were living with HIV in 2010; 2.1 million of them were children under 15 years, and 16 million were women. Every day, about 7,400 persons become infected with HIV and about 5,000 persons die from AIDS.

▶ Over 90 percent of children living with HIV are in Sub-Saharan Africa.

▶ 90 percent of all malaria deaths occur in Sub-Saharan Africa, and most of these deaths are among children under 5.

▶ One-third of the world's population has latent tuberculosis infections. One in every 10 of those people will become sick with active tuberculosis in his or her lifetime.

▶ Chronic and non-communicable diseases such as heart disease and stroke, cancer, and diabetes are increasing because of aging and unhealthy lifestyles including consumption of unhealthy food, lack of exercise, and smoking. They account for 60 percent of all deaths.

Internet links

▶ World Health Organization on Tuberculosis, Malaria, and HIV/AIDS	www.who.int/topics/tuberculosis www.who.int/topics/malaria www.who.int/topics/hiv_aids
▶ UNAIDS	www.unaids.org
▶ World Bank HNPstats	go.worldbank.org/N2N84RDV00
▶ UNICEF Childinfo on Malaria and HIV/AIDS	www.childinfo.org/malaria.html www.childinfo.org/hiv_aids.html
▶ UNICEF on Malaria and HIV/AIDS	www.unicef.org/health/index_malaria.html www.unicef.org/aids/index_documents.html

Structure of the world economy

Services, the most rapidly growing sector of the global economy, now account for almost 70 percent of world output. Developing economies are also becoming important producers of manufactured goods; others already specialize in services. However, for many of these economies, the natural resource sectors, especially agriculture and mining, continue to be the main source of income.

Gross domestic product (GDP) measures the overall output of an economy. It is the sum of value added in agriculture (including forestry and fisheries), industry (including mining and manufacturing), and the service sector (including government and private services). As economies develop, they typically shift from the production and export of agricultural and mining commodities to manufactured goods, and later to services. In many high-income economies more than 70 percent of GDP is produced in the service sector.

Services now account for 55 percent of the output of middle-income economies, although some countries—such as Jordan, Panama, and South Africa—have maintained large service sectors for some time. In low-income economies, the service sectors are growing and now produce 50 percent of GDP. East Asia and the Pacific, led by China, and South Asia, led by India, have increased their service output in real terms by more than 300 percent since 1990.

Although the service sector is growing everywhere, agriculture remains very

Services now account for two-thirds of global output

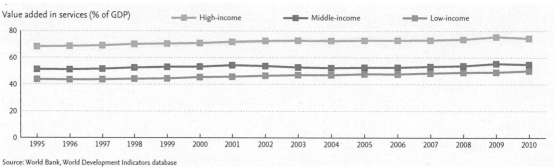

Source: World Bank, World Development Indicators database

Service sectors are growing rapidly in both East Asia and the Pacific and South Asia

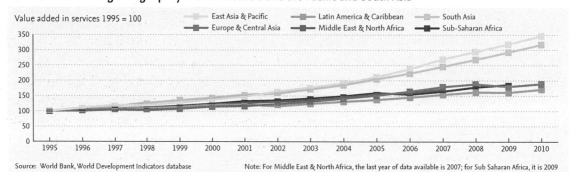

Source: World Bank, World Development Indicators database   Note: For Middle East & North Africa, the last year of data available is 2007; for Sub Saharan Africa, it is 2009

Many countries are still dependent on agricultural employment

Agricultural employment as a share of total employment (%), 2007–2011

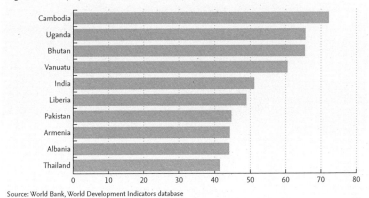

Source: World Bank, World Development Indicators database

...agriculture is still of major importance in developing countries

important to developing economies. Agriculture not only feeds a growing population, it produces raw materials for industries such as rubber and timber. Increases in oil prices have resulted in additional demand for food crops, such as corn and sugar cane, used to produce biofuels. Higher prices for agricultural products raise the incomes of producers, but higher food prices also reduce the welfare of consumers.

In 2011, value added in agriculture as a share of GDP was over 40 percent in four low-income economies, three of them in Africa. Agriculture is also an important source of employment. It employs over 35 percent of the labor force in 17 countries, over 50 percent in five countries, and as much as 72 percent in Cambodia. Not only low-income economies but also some middle-income economies remain highly dependent on agriculture. In Bhutan, agriculture accounts for 65 percent of total employment. In comparison, agricultural employment made up 3.7 percent of total employment in Japan, 1.6 percent in Germany and in the United States, and 1.2 percent in the United Kingdom and Argentina.

While the shift toward services describes the general trend of industrial development, there are many variations. Economies grow fastest when they develop in ways that make best use of their factor endowments.

Countries differ in their factor endowments (natural resources, labor, human capital, and physical capital), but the relative importance of those factors evolves along with the optimal industrial structure at each stage of development. Government can play an important role by facilitating the development of markets, directing growth toward industries

that make best use of current endowments, and encouraging industries that are likely to evolve in line with its future endowments. In planning their development path, a country can look toward other countries with similar endowment structures and two to four times their current average income (approximately 10 to 30 years ahead of them) and encourage industries that have already gained an entry in international trade with the possibility of overtaking existing suppliers. This is the path followed by China and other fast-growing economies and can serve as a model for many more.

AGRICULTURAL OUTPUT

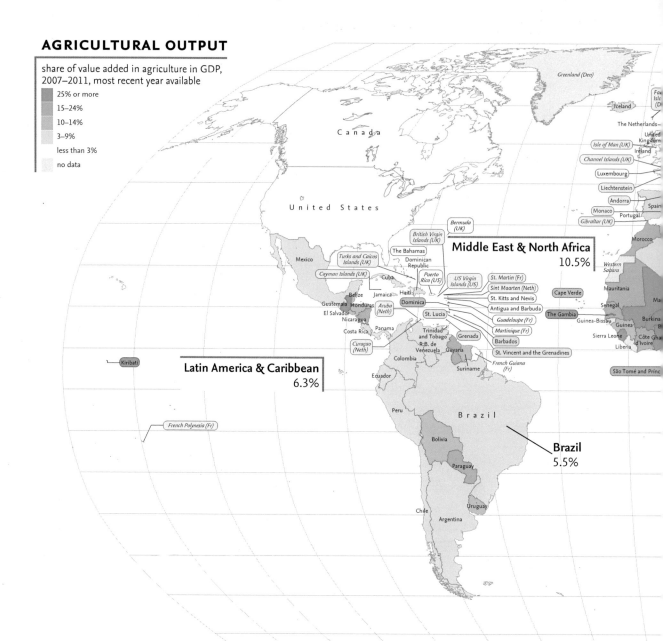

share of value added in agriculture in GDP,
2007–2011, most recent year available

- 25% or more
- 15–24%
- 10–14%
- 3–9%
- less than 3%
- no data

Middle East & North Africa
10.5%

Latin America & Caribbean
6.3%

Brazil
5.5%

Family tending potato fields in northeast Brazil

Countries most dependent on agriculture, 2010–2011 (most recent year available)

Rank	Country	Agricultural value added as share of GDP (%)
1	Central African Republic	56.5
2	Comoros	46.3
3	Sierra Leone	44.4
4	Togo	43.2
5	Congo, Dem. Rep.	42.9
6	Ethiopia	41.9
7	Guatemala	40.5
8	Solomon Islands	38.9
9	Nepal	38.1
10	Mali	36.5

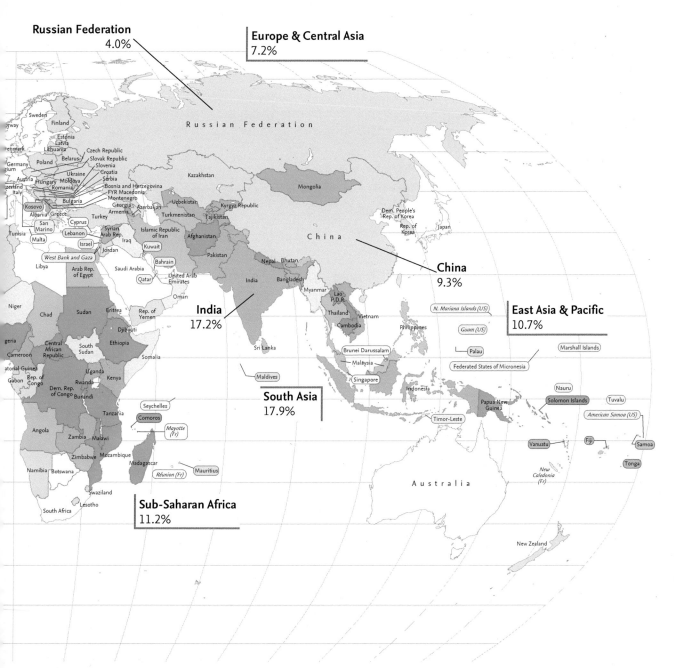

Russian Federation
4.0%

Europe & Central Asia
7.2%

China
9.3%

East Asia & Pacific
10.7%

India
17.2%

South Asia
17.9%

Sub-Saharan Africa
11.2%

Facts

▶ The global agricultural sector grew by 2.5 percent a year from 2000 to 2010. The service sector grew by 2.7 percent and the industrial sector by 2.5 percent over the same period.

▶ In Sub-Saharan Africa the agricultural sector grew by 3.3 percent a year from 2000 to 2010, while the service sector grew by 4.8 percent and the industrial sector by 4.7 percent.

▶ In East Asia and Pacific the industrial sector was the fastest growing with 10.2 percent annual growth over the period 2000 to 2010. Services were second with 10 percent growth. Agriculture grew by 4.1 percent.

▶ In South Asia the dominant sectors were services with annual growth of 8.6 percent and industry with 8.1 percent annual growth, while agriculture grew by 3.2 percent over the same period.

▶ On average, services have grown faster than other parts of the economy, except in East Asia and the Pacific and Europe and Central Asia.

Internet links

▶ World Bank data	data.worldbank.org/data-catalog/world-development-indicators
▶ Organisation for Economic Co-operation and Development	www.oecd.org/
▶ United Nations— National Accounts Main Aggregates Database	unstats.un.org/unsd/snaama
▶ New Structural Economics: A Framework for Rethinking Development and Policy	go.worldbank.org/QZK6IM4GO0
▶ "Demystifying Success: The New Structural Economics Approach"	wbi.worldbank.org/wbi/devoutreach/article/1048/demystifying-success-new-structural-economics-approach

Governance

Governance describes the way public officials and institutions acquire and exercise authority to provide public goods and services including education, health care, infrastructure, and a sound investment climate. Good governance is associated with citizen participation and improved accountability of public officials. It is fundamental to development and economic growth.

Governance has several dimensions:
- the process by which governments are selected, monitored, and replaced;
- the capacity of government to effectively formulate and implement sound policies;
- the respect of citizens and the state for the institutions that govern interactions between them.

Features of good governance—such as free and fair elections, respect for individual liberties and property rights, a free and vibrant press, an open and impartial judiciary, and well-informed and effective legislative structures—all contribute to strong and capable institutions of the state.

Although bad governance is often equated with corruption, the two concepts, while related, are different. Corruption—the abuse of public office for private gain—is an outcome of poor governance, reflecting the breakdown of accountability. A capable and accountable state creates opportunities for poor people, provides better services, and improves development outcomes—which is why the World Bank includes a governance and anticorruption strategy as part of its effort to reduce poverty. There are now several global collaborative governance initiatives, such as the Stolen Asset Recovery (StAR) Initiative, the Extractive Industries Transparency Initiative (EITI), the Construction Sector Transparency Initiative (CoST), and the Business Fighting Corruption Through Collective Action Initiative.

The links among weak institutions, poor development outcomes, and the risk

Countries of the former Soviet Union rank lowest on control of corruption

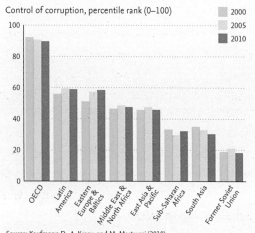

Source: Kaufmann D., A. Kraay, and M. Mastruzzi (2010),
The Worldwide Governance Indicators: Methodology and Analytical Issues

Informal payments to public officials 'to get things done' are more common in South Asia and the Middle East and North Africa

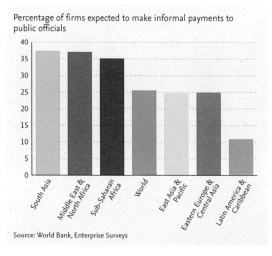

Source: World Bank, Enterprise Surveys

Parliament in session in Tajikistan

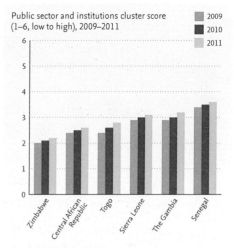

Several Sub-Saharan African countries improved their performance

Public sector and institutions cluster score (1–6, low to high), 2009–2011

■ 2009
■ 2010
■ 2011

Source: World Bank, Country Policy and Institutional Assessment

of conflict are often evident in countries that are in fragile situations. Some 1.5 billion people live in areas affected by fragility, conflict, or large-scale organized criminal violence, and no fragile or conflict-affected country has achieved a single Millennium Development Goal. A major episode of violence can wipe out an entire generation of economic progress. *World Development Report 2011: Conflict, Security, and Development* found that countries and areas with the weakest institutional legitimacy (both formal and informal) and poor governance are the most vulnerable to violence and instability and the least able to respond to internal and external stresses.

Measuring the quality of institutions and governance outcomes is difficult and often subject to large margins of error. Data for one dimension of governance—control of corruption—are presented in the map on pages 72–73. The data are aggregate measures derived from several sources of informed views of individuals in both the private and the public sectors. The map represents data on control of corruption by percentile ranges, from the best performing (90th to 100th percentile) to the poorest performing (0 to 9th percentile). Some developing countries have better scores on some governance measures than developed countries.

The World Bank's Country Policy and Institutional Assessment (CPIA) is an annual staff effort to measure the extent to which a country's policy and institutional framework supports sustainable growth and poverty reduction. Scores of these assessments are disclosed only for low-income countries that are eligible for lending by the World Bank's International Development Association (IDA). CPIA indicators examine policies and institutions, not development outcomes, which can depend on forces outside a country's control. There are 16 criteria grouped into four clusters; one of the clusters (shown in the bottom right chart on page 70) is the public sector management and institutions cluster. This cluster includes five criteria: property rights and rule-based governance; quality of budgetary and financial management; efficiency of revenue mobilization; quality of public administration; and transparency, accountability, and corruption in the public sector. The median value for all low-income economies was 2.9 in 2011.

CONTROLLING CORRUPTION

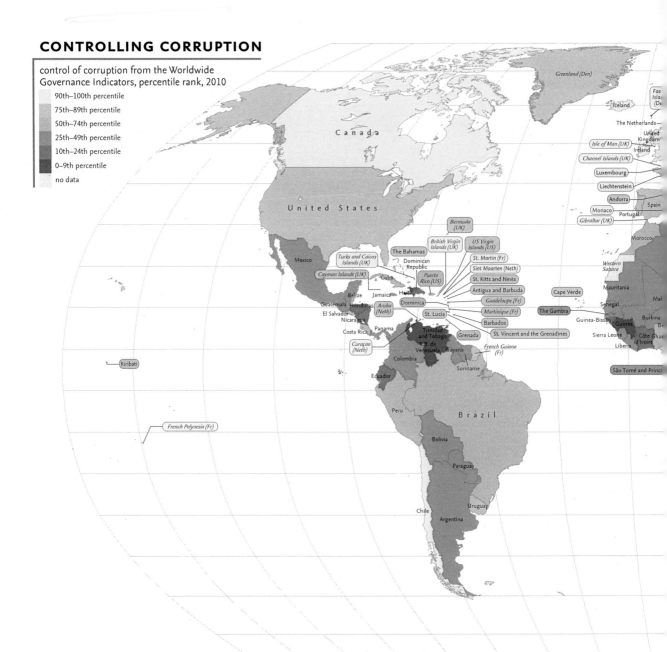

control of corruption from the Worldwide
Governance Indicators, percentile rank, 2010

- 90th–100th percentile
- 75th–89th percentile
- 50th–74th percentile
- 25th–49th percentile
- 10th–24th percentile
- 0–9th percentile
- no data

Anticorruption billboard in Zambia

Control of corruption

Approximate rank	Developing country with population over 1 million	Percentile rank, 2010	Lower percentile range
1	Chile	91	85
2	Uruguay	86	80
3	Botswana	80	73
4	Mauritius	73	69
5	Costa Rica	73	67
6	Cuba	72	62
7	Rwanda	71	62
8	Lithuania	66	61
9	Namibia	64	58
10	Latvia	63	58

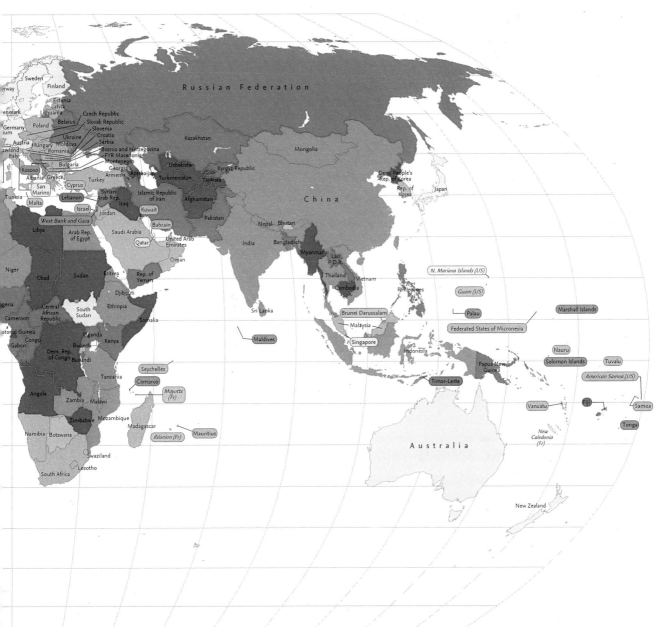

Facts

► Eleven Sub-Saharan African countries rank in the 50th percentile or higher in the Worldwide Governance Indicators measure of control of corruption.

► There is a positive correlation between higher levels of income and lower levels of corruption. Nine out of 10 countries in the ranking table are upper-middle-income economies. Only Rwanda is a low-income economy.

► Three key principles for promoting good governance include transparency, accountability, and participation. Participation implies that people have rights that are recognized and they have a voice in the decisions that affect them.

Internet links

► World Bank—Worldwide Governance Indicators	www.govindicators.org
► World Bank— Enterprise Surveys	www.enterprisesurveys.org
► World Bank— Doing Business	www.doingbusiness.org
► United Nations Development Programme (UNDP)— Democratic Governance	www.undp.org/governance
► Transparency International	www.transparency.org
► World Bank—Public Sector Governance	www.worldbank.org/ publicsector

Upper
rcentile
range

93
92
86
80
80
76
75
72
72
70

Infrastructure for development

Infrastructure—the basic systems for delivering energy, transport, water and sanitation, and information and communications services to people—directly or indirectly affects lives everywhere. Increased productivity and incomes and improvements in health and education outcomes require investment in infrastructure.

Infrastructure services play a key role in the most important development objective—reducing poverty and improving the lives of billions of people in developing countries. These services affect people in many ways: what they consume and produce; how they heat and light their homes; how they travel to work, to school, or to visit family and friends; and how they communicate. Access to clean water and sanitation reduces infant mortality. Electricity powers hospitals and refrigerators for vaccines. Roads in rural areas boost school attendance and use of medical clinics. And information and communication technologies can improve teacher training and promote better health practices.

The global supply of infrastructure services is not able to meet today's needs. Developing countries require about $900 billion (7–9 percent of GDP) to maintain existing infrastructure and to build new infrastructure, but only half that amount is available. The continuing global recession will curtail maintenance and new investments in infrastructure as governments face shrinking budgets and declining private financial flows.

Water and sanitation infrastructure has barely kept pace with population growth in the developing world. Further improvements will require more public and private investment. Measured in 2010 constant price dollars, investment commitments in water and sanitation projects with private participation remained low: $29 billion over the last decade compared with $58 billion during the previous one. Since 2001, average annual investment commitments have ranged between $2 billion and $3 billion.

Private investment goes primarily to energy and telecommunications

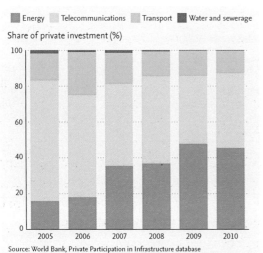

Source: World Bank, Private Participation in Infrastructure database

Access to clean water and sanitation remains low in Sub-Saharan Africa

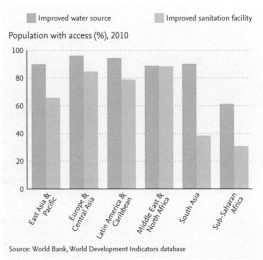

Source: World Bank, World Development Indicators database

Global mobile penetration reached 86 percent while fixed telephone line subscriptions remained below 20 percent in 2011

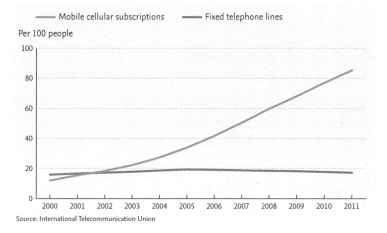

——— Mobile cellular subscriptions　　——— Fixed telephone lines

Per 100 people

Source: International Telecommunication Union

Pastoralist in a Nigerian village using a mobile phone

Infrastructure is typically an enabler, but rarely the sole solution to development challenges. Reducing disease transmission, for example, requires better water and sanitation facilities, but it also requires good hygiene practices such as routine hand washing.

Physical isolation is a strong contributor to poverty. People living in remote places have reduced access to health and education services, employment opportunities, and markets. Problems are particularly severe in rural areas that lack good transportation facilities. Transport infrastructure—the roads, bridges, railroads, waterways, ports, and the services they provide—can eliminate growth-constraining bottlenecks and shortages, increase agricultural productivity, improve poor rural farmers' incomes and nutrition, and expand nonfarm employment. In Vietnam, a World Bank project provided financing for ethnic minority women to undertake road maintenance in rural areas. As a result, 13,470 kilometers of road are being maintained and 1,533 ethnic minority women from four communes were trained as rural transportation managers; many more eagerly await the opportunity.

Information and communications technology has vast potential for fostering growth in developing countries by helping to increase productivity in a wide range of economic activities from agriculture to manufacturing and services. Mobile phones keep families and communities in contact and provide market information for farmers and businesspeople. According to the International Telecommunication Union, by the end of 2011 there were almost 6 billion mobile cellular subscriptions in the world, or about 86 per 100 people. The

Internet users in developing countries have tripled since 2005

■ Developed countries　　■ Developing countries

Individuals using the Internet (millions)

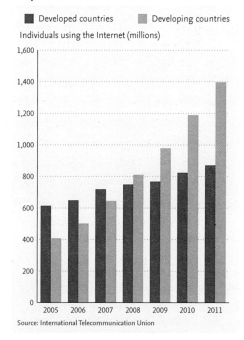

Source: International Telecommunication Union

Internet delivers information to schools and hospitals, and computers improve public and private services as well as increase productivity and participation. Over the last five years, developing countries have increased their number of Internet users from 501 million in 2006 to 1.4 billion in 2011.

MOBILE CELLULAR SUBSCRIPTIONS

mobile cellular subscriptions per 100 people,
2011 or latest available data

- less than 30
- 30–69
- 70–99
- 100–129
- 130 or more
- no data

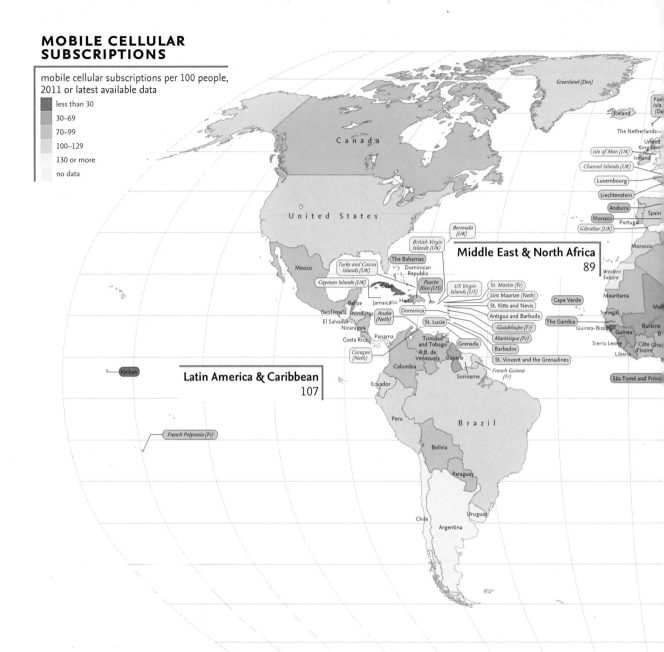

Greenland (Den)

Faeroe Islands (De)

Iceland

The Netherlands

United Kingdom

Isle of Man (UK)

Ireland

Channel Islands (UK)

Luxembourg

Liechtenstein

Andorra

Spain

Monaco

Portugal

Gibraltar (UK)

Morocco

Western Sahara

Mauritania

Mali

Senegal

Cape Verde

The Gambia

Guinea-Bissau

Guinea

Burkina

Sierra Leone

Côte d'Ivoire

Liberia

São Tomé and Príncipe

Canada

United States

Mexico

Bermuda (UK)

British Virgin Islands (UK)

The Bahamas

Dominican Republic

Turks and Caicos Islands (UK)

Cayman Islands (UK)

Cuba

Puerto Rico (US)

US Virgin Islands (US)

St. Martin (Fr)

Sint Maarten (Neth)

St. Kitts and Nevis

Antigua and Barbuda

Guadeloupe (Fr)

Martinique (Fr)

Barbados

St. Vincent and the Grenadines

French Guiana (Fr)

Belize

Jamaica

Haiti

Dominica

St. Lucia

Grenada

Guatemala

Honduras

Aruba (Neth)

El Salvador

Nicaragua

Costa Rica

Panama

Curaçao (Neth)

Trinidad and Tobago

R.B. de Venezuela

Guyana

Colombia

Suriname

Ecuador

Peru

Brazil

Bolivia

Paraguay

Chile

Uruguay

Argentina

Middle East & North Africa
89

Latin America & Caribbean
107

Kiribati

French Polynesia (Fr)

A food vendor talking on her mobile phone in Armenia

Most mobile cellular subscriptions, 2011

Rank	Economies with population over 1 million	Subscriptions per 100 people
1	Hong Kong SAR, China	210
2	Panama	204
3	Saudi Arabia	191
4	Russian Federation	179
5	Oman	169
6	Finland	166
7	Libya	156
8	Austria	155
9	Italy	152
10	Lithuania	151

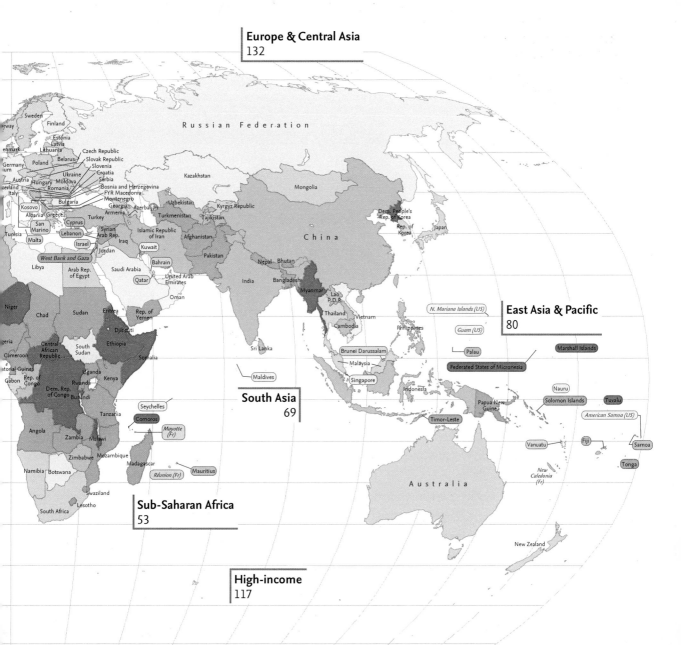

Europe & Central Asia
132

East Asia & Pacific
80

South Asia
69

Sub-Saharan Africa
53

High-income
117

Facts

▶ Developing countries accounted for more than 80 percent of the 660 million new mobile cellular subscriptions added in 2011.

▶ By the end of 2011, there were more than 1 billion mobile-broadband subscriptions worldwide.

▶ The number of people using the Internet continues to grow worldwide. By the end of 2011, 2.3 billion people were online.

▶ In 2011, India added 142 million mobile cellular subscriptions, twice as many as in all of Africa.

Internet links

▶ International Telecommunication Union	www.itu.int
▶ World Bank—Information and Communications Technologies	www.worldbank.org/ict
▶ International Road Federation	www.irfnet.org
▶ World Resources Institute—Water	insights.wri.org/topic/water
▶ World Bank—Climate Change	data.worldbank.org/climate-change
▶ WHO—Water, Sanitation, and Health	www.who.int/water_sanitation_health/en

Investment for growth

Sustainable economic growth is impossible without investment. Investment replenishes assets used up in production and increases the total capital stock. A good investment climate is one in which government policies encourage firms and entrepreneurs to invest productively, create jobs, and contribute to growth and poverty reduction. On average, 22 percent of the world's output is invested for production purposes. High rates of investment alone do not ensure rapid economic growth.

Physical investment takes many forms: buildings, machinery and equipment, improvements to property, and additions to inventories. Investment is financed out of domestic savings or external savings. However, external financing is limited and generally more volatile than domestic savings.

Countries that have high savings and investment rates are likely to have high rates of economic growth. Growth is also spurred by improved efficiency as a result of technological advances and investments in people, through better education and health care. To sustain growth, government policies must create a climate that encourages productive investment.

In most recent years, the East Asia and the Pacific region has had the highest investment rate, averaging 40 percent of gross domestic product (GDP). South Asia invested between 30 and 34 percent of its output. Even Sub-Saharan Africa, at 20 percent the lowest investment rate among developing regions, exceeded the rate of 18 percent in high-income economies. Total investment in developing regions in 2010 was $6.4 trillion, about 80 percent of the level of investment in high-income economies.

Government policies play a key role in shaping the investment climate. They influence the security of property rights, the effectiveness of regulation, the impact of taxation, the quality and accessibility of infrastructure, and the functioning of

Investment has grown rapidly in the East Asia and Pacific region

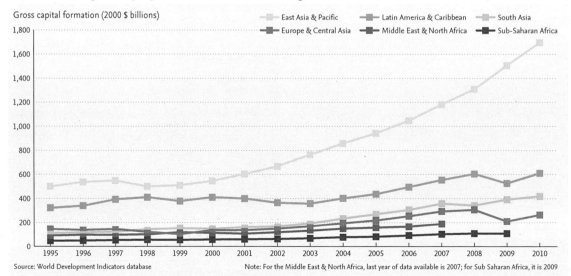

Gross capital formation (2000 $ billions)

East Asia & Pacific — Latin America & Caribbean — South Asia
Europe & Central Asia — Middle East & North Africa — Sub-Saharan Africa

Source: World Development Indicators database

Note: For the Middle East & North Africa, last year of data available is 2007; for Sub Saharan Africa, it is 2009

Sub-Saharan Africa had the second-highest percentage of countries with positive business reform in 2010–2011

Countries in the region that made at least one positive reform (%)

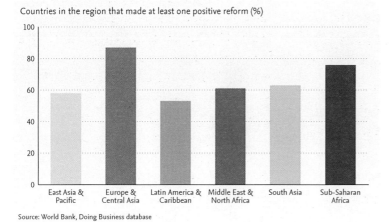

Source: World Bank, Doing Business database

financial and labor markets. The quality of the investment climate also contributes strongly to increased productivity and employment creation, both necessary for poverty reduction. Poor governance increases transaction costs, encourages unproductive activities such as lobbying, and reduces transparency. Hence, it leads to misallocation of resources and discourages new investment.

Countries in Sub-Saharan Africa made rapid changes to their economies' regulatory environment. Regulatory reforms were implemented in 36 of the 46 economies between 2010 and 2011, representing 78 percent of countries in the region. Europe and Central Asia was the most active reformer for the eighth year in a row: 88 percent of countries in the region

made at least one positive reform to make doing business easier.

Although China and some of the other 'tigers' in the East Asia and the Pacific region have obtained spectacular growth rates, high levels of investment do not guarantee high growth rates. Investment produces growth, but investment also chases growth. More investment is likely in places where high returns are possible.

Over 1995–2010, most developing regions invested an average of 19 to 36 percent of their GDP each year. The results obtained have varied, from Latin America and the Caribbean, where an investment ratio of 20 percent produced growth of only 3.1 percent, to South Asia, where an investment ratio of 28 percent resulted in annual growth of 6.5 percent. Sub-Saharan Africa is an interesting exception: an investment ratio of 19 percent led to an annual growth rate of 4.3 percent, as good as or better than several regions with higher investment ratios.

Asian countries have invested heavily and grown rapidly, but other regions have not obtained the same results

Annual average GDP growth rate (%), 1995–2010

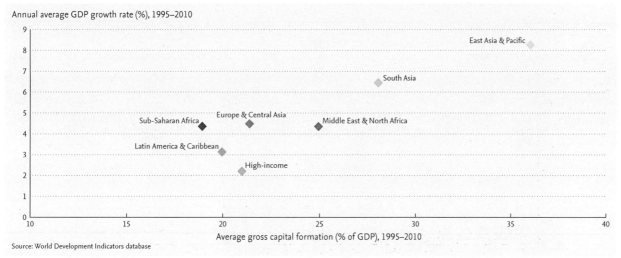

Average gross capital formation (% of GDP), 1995–2010

Source: World Development Indicators database

INVESTMENT FOR GROWTH

gross capital formation as a share of GDP, 2009–2011, most recent year available

- less than 15%
- 15–19%
- 20–24%
- 25–29%
- 30% or more
- no data

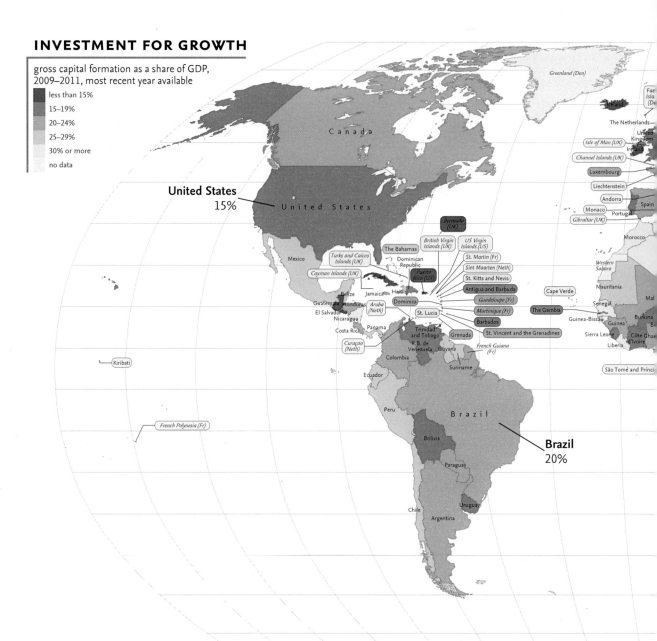

United States
15%

Brazil
20%

China's rapidly growing economy has benefited from foreign investment

Highest average gross capital formation

Rank	Country with population over 1 million	% of GDP 1995–2010
1	China	41
2	Lesotho	40
3	Turkmenistan	35
4	Vietnam	34
5	Iran, Islamic Rep.	33
6	Qatar	33
7	Mongolia	32
8	Algeria	31
9	Korea, Rep.	31
10	Azerbaijan	30

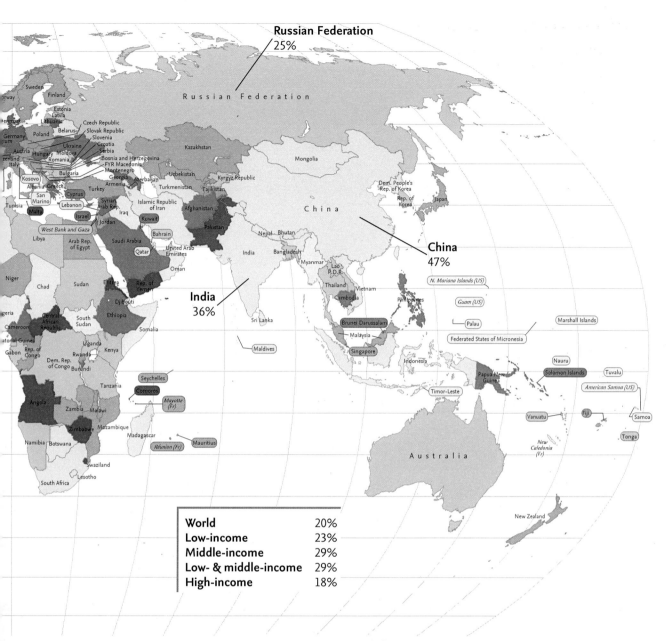

Russian Federation
25%

China
47%

India
36%

World	20%
Low-income	23%
Middle-income	29%
Low- & middle-income	29%
High-income	18%

Facts

▶ Capital formation has grown fastest in South Asia. Between 2000 and 2010, it increased at an average rate of 12.4 percent a year.

▶ Capital formation has been slowest in Latin America and the Caribbean, averaging 5.3 percent a year between 2000 and 2010.

▶ Investment declined in six countries between 2000 and 2010.

▶ Of the top 10 countries with the highest average investment rate between 1995 and 2010, three were from Sub-Saharan Africa.

▶ In China, investment grew at an average of 13.3 percent a year between 2000 and 2010.

Internet links

▶ World Bank Data and Statistics	**data.worldbank.org/indicator/ NG.GDI.TOTL.CD**
▶ Organisation for Economic Co-operation and Development—Statistics	**www.oecd.org** (click on 'Statistics')
▶ United Nations data	**data.un.org**
▶ International Monetary Fund— World Economic Outlook	**www.imf.org/weo**
▶ UNCTAD World Investment Report Series	**unctad.org/en/pages/ DIAE/World%20Investment %20Report/WIR-Series.aspx**

STARTING A BUSINESS

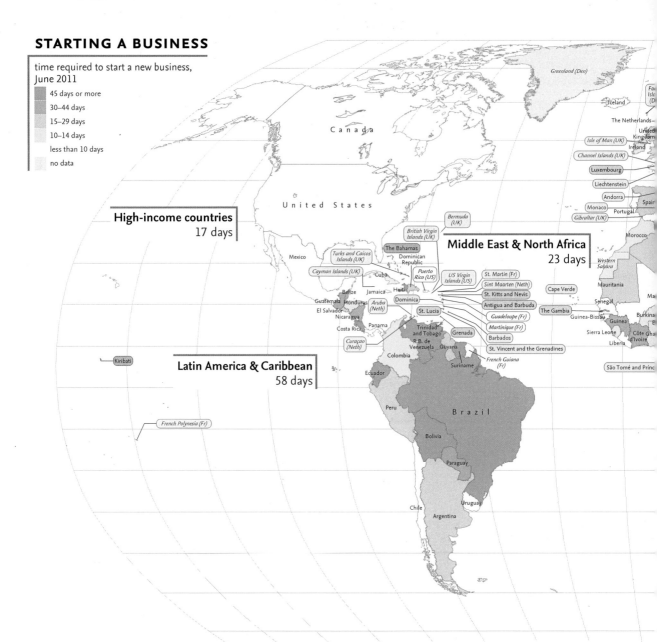

time required to start a new business, June 2011

- 45 days or more
- 30–44 days
- 15–29 days
- 10–14 days
- less than 10 days
- no data

High-income countries
17 days

Middle East & North Africa
23 days

Latin America & Caribbean
58 days

Business meeting, Mozambique

Best performers based on number of days to start a business in developing countries

Rank	Country	Days (as of June 2011)
1	Georgia	2
2	Macedonia, FYR	3
3	Rwanda	3
4	Albania	5
5	Belarus	5
6	Senegal	5
7	Liberia	6
8	Malaysia	6
9	Mauritius	6
10	Turkey	6

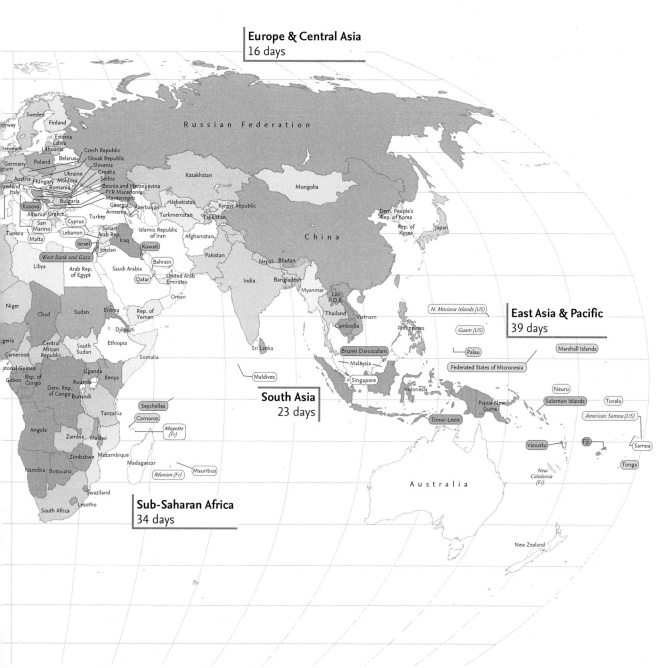

Europe & Central Asia
16 days

East Asia & Pacific
39 days

South Asia
23 days

Sub-Saharan Africa
34 days

Facts

▶ In the past six years, policy makers in 163 economies made domestic regulations more business friendly.

▶ Fifty-three economies made it easier to start a business between 2010 and 2011.

▶ In 2010–2011, Bhutan launched a public credit registry and streamlined business start-up procedures.

▶ In Colombia, new firm registrations increased by 5.2 percent after the creation of a one-stop shop for businesses in 2010–2011.

▶ In 2010–2011, FYR Macedonia streamlined the filing and payment of taxes, introduced an electronic cadastre for property registration, and started an operation of the online system for business registration.

▶ In 2010–2011, Malawi improved its credit information system by passing a new law allowing the creation of a private credit bureau.

Internet links

▶ World Bank—
Doing Business database   **www.doingbusiness.org**

▶ World Bank—
Enterprise Surveys   **www.enterprisesurveys.org**

▶ World Bank—
Private Participation in   **ppi.worldbank.org/**
Infrastructure database

▶ World Bank—
Privatization database   **rru.worldbank.org/
                                 Privatization/**

The integrating world

Economies have become more dependent on each other for goods, services, labor, and capital. Although many barriers remain, advances in information and communications technology, expanding financial markets, and cheaper transportation systems enable easier movement of inputs and outputs among economies, accelerating global integration. Global integration creates many opportunities, but the benefits need to be shared equitably both among and within economies.

Traditional patterns of production and employment have given way to new modes of production and distribution, which are often spread over multiple locations. Developing economies offering lower costs and new markets are attracting foreign investment in manufacturing. Skilled as well as unskilled workers are seeking employment in economies that offer higher wages. High-income economies are looking at the developing world to meet their increasing demand for service and technology workers.

International trade is a critical channel for integration. Despite a drop in global trade in 2009, goods equivalent to 48 percent of global gross domestic product (GDP) were traded in 2010, up from 32 percent in 1990. Over the same period, trade in services increased from 8 percent to 12 percent of global GDP. These trends are likely to continue as globally diversified production processes require more trade in intermediate goods.

After a sharp decline in 2009, global trade rebounded in 2010

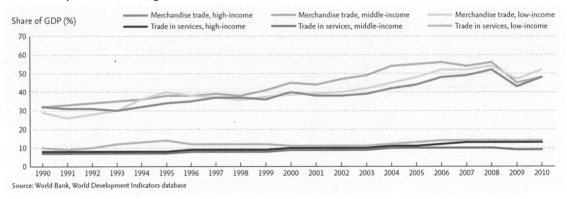

Source: World Bank, World Development Indicators database

Developing economies are trading more with other developing economies

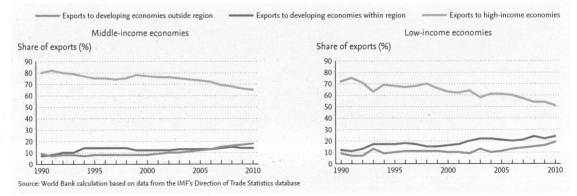

Source: World Bank calculation based on data from the IMF's Direction of Trade Statistics database

Agricultural and textile products are subject to higher trade restrictions

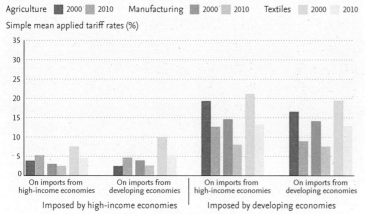

Agriculture ■ 2000 ■ 2010 Manufacturing ■ 2000 ■ 2010 Textiles ■ 2000 ■ 2010

Simple mean applied tariff rates (%)

Imposed by high-income economies | Imposed by developing economies

On imports from high-income economies | On imports from developing economies | On imports from high-income economies | On imports from developing economies

Source: World Bank, World Integrated Trade Solution, based on data from the UN Conference on Trade and Development's Trade Analysis and Information System database and the UN Statistics Division's Comtrade database

Foreign direct investment and portfolio equity flows to developing economies continue to increase

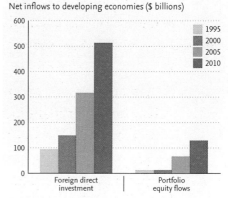

Net inflows to developing economies ($ billions)

■ 1995 ■ 2000 ■ 2005 ■ 2010

Foreign direct investment | Portfolio equity flows

Source: World Bank, World Development Indicators database

High-income economies remain the principal source and destination of international trade, but more developing economies are participating, and trade with other developing economies is growing.

Developing economies now account for almost 30 percent of world trade. Some, such as China, Mexico, and Thailand, are specializing in manufactured goods, but many remain primary exporters of food, fuel, and raw materials. Between 2000 and 2010, trade (in nominal terms) among developing economies grew at an annual average rate of 21.7 percent—over 14 percentage points faster than trade among high-income economies—while trade between high-income economies and low- and middle-income economies grew by 14 percent during the period. As of 2010, almost half of merchandise exports from low-income economies and a third from middle-income economies now go to other developing economies, but demand from high-income economies remains the driving force of international trade.

Reductions in tariff and nontariff barriers have helped to spur trade, but many trade barriers remain. The poorest countries impose higher barriers across a broad range of goods to protect their producers and raise revenues for their governments. Rich countries often impose their highest barriers selectively on the exports of developing countries, especially agricultural and textile products. In addition to tariff protection, they provide subsidies and other forms of support to their farmers, enabling them to sell agricultural products at very low prices that developing country producers cannot match. Total agricultural support in OECD countries exceeded $366 billion in 2010,

representing a 3.1 percent increase from 2009, in nominal terms.

During the past decade, flows of foreign direct investment (FDI) toward developing economies have increased substantially. It has long been recognized that FDI flows can carry with them benefits of knowledge and technology transfer to domestic firms and the labor force, productivity spillover, enhanced competition, and improved access for exports abroad. Moreover, they are the preferred source of capital for financing a current account deficit because FDI is non-debt-creating. Although slowed by the financial crisis, FDI inflows to developing economies recovered significantly from $400 billion in 2009 to $587 billion in 2010. Emerging economies, particularly in East Asia and the Pacific, experienced a robust increase in economic growth supported by foreign investment. China received 79 percent of the regional inflows and commanded one-quarter of all FDI inflows in the developing economies.

MERCHANDISE TRADE

exports and imports as a share of GDP, 2010

less than 40%

	40–59%
	60–74%
	75–99%
	100% or more
	no data

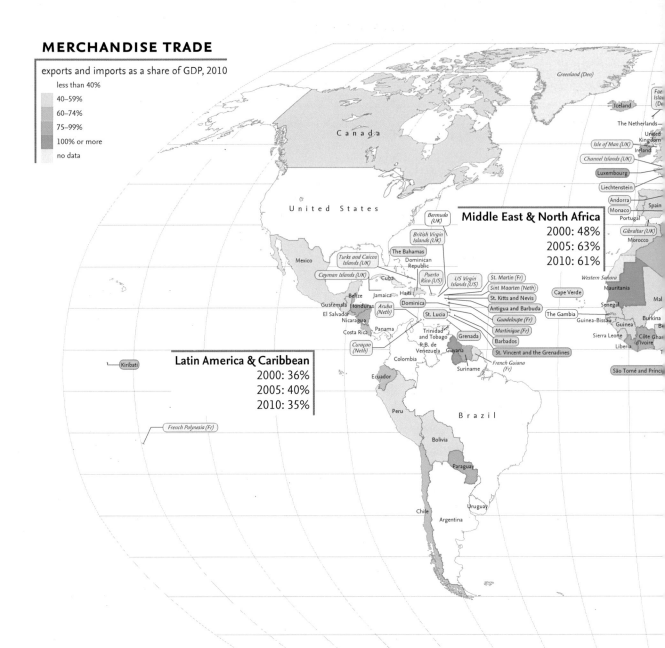

Middle East & North Africa
2000: 48%
2005: 63%
2010: 61%

Latin America & Caribbean
2000: 36%
2005: 40%
2010: 35%

Mexico is a major importer

Merchandise trade

	Largest merchandise exporters, 2010			Largest merchandise importers, 2010	
Rank	Developing country	$ billions	Rank	Developing country	$ billions
1	China	1,578	1	China	1,395
2	Russian Federation	400	2	India	350
3	Mexico	298	3	Mexico	310
4	India	220	4	Russian Federation	249
5	Brazil	202	5	Brazil	191

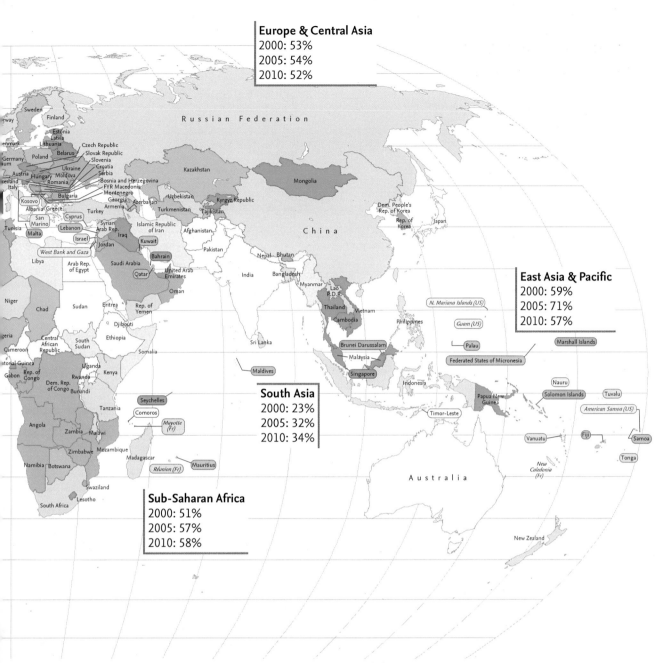

Europe & Central Asia
2000: 53%
2005: 54%
2010: 52%

East Asia & Pacific
2000: 59%
2005: 71%
2010: 57%

South Asia
2000: 23%
2005: 32%
2010: 34%

Sub-Saharan Africa
2000: 51%
2005: 57%
2010: 58%

Facts

▶ The five largest exporters in 2010 accounted for more than half the merchandise exports of developing economies.

▶ World trade in services as a percentage of GDP grew from 7 percent in 1990 to over 12 percent in 2008, but after the global financial crisis, it declined to 11 percent in 2009 and 2010.

▶ Average tariffs imposed by high-income economies have declined, but high barriers to some exports of developing countries remain, especially agricultural and textile products. For instance, simple mean applied tariff on imported agricultural products from developing countries rose to 4.7 percent in 2010 from 2.5 percent in 2000.

▶ Starting in 2009, China replaced Germany as the second-ranking importer of the world, with only the United States importing more goods.

Internet links

▶ Organisation for Economic Co-operation and Development (OECD)—Trade	**www.oecd.org/trade**
▶ International Monetary Fund— Statistics	**www.imfstatistics.org** (select 'BOPS' or 'DOTS')
▶ World Trade Organization— Statistics Database	**www.wto.org** (go to 'Documents and resources', select 'Statistics Database')
▶ United Nations Conference on Trade and Development— Statistics	**www.unctad.org** (go to 'Statistics', select 'UNCTADstat')
▶ United Nations— Trade Statistics	**unstats.un.org/unsd/trade** **unstats.un.org/unsd/ servicetrade**

FOREIGN DIRECT INVESTMENT

foreign direct investment net inflows as a
share of GDP, 2010 or latest available data

- less than 1.0%
- 1.0–1.9%
- 2.0–3.9%
- 4.0–5.9%
- 6.0% or more
- no data

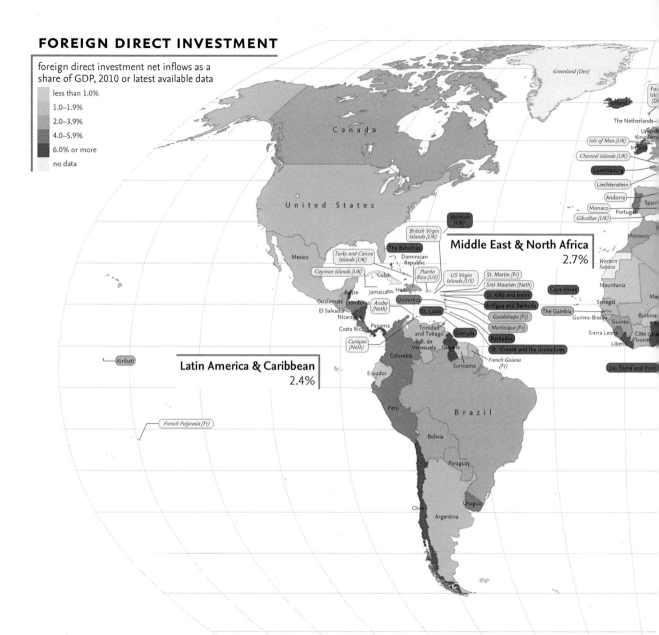

Middle East & North Africa
2.7%

Latin America & Caribbean
2.4%

China received over 80 percent of FDI inflows to East Asia and the Pacific in 2010

Developing countries that attracted the largest FDI net inflows, 2010

Rank	Developing country	$ billions
1	China	185.1
2	Brazil	48.5
3	Russian Federation	43.3
4	India	24.2
5	Mexico	20.2
6	Chile	15.1
7	Indonesia	13.8
8	Kazakhstan	10.8
9	Thailand	9.7
10	Malaysia	9.2

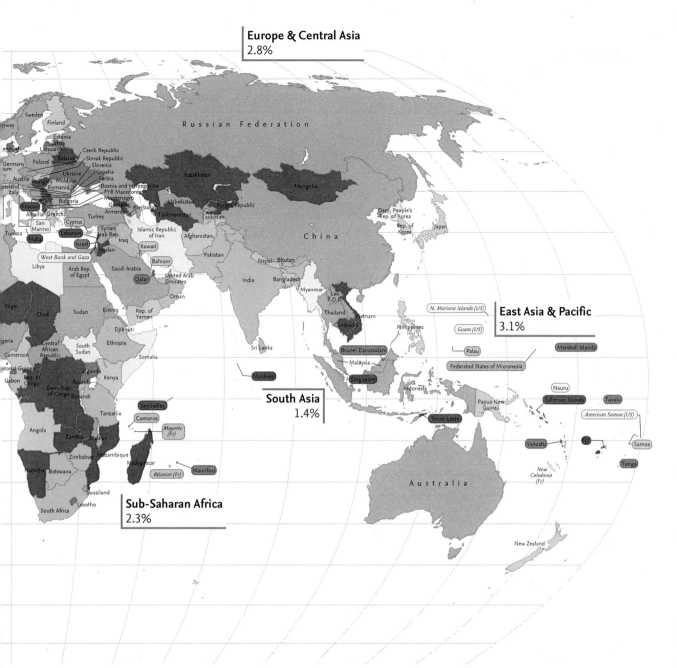

Europe & Central Asia
2.8%

East Asia & Pacific
3.1%

South Asia
1.4%

Sub-Saharan Africa
2.3%

Facts

▶ Luxembourg's net outward direct investment in foreign economies in 2010 was nearly 3.5 times its GDP. Hong Kong S.A.R., China was the second-highest with FDI outflows accounting for 42 percent of its GDP.

▶ Mexico, the second-largest recipient of FDI in Latin America and the Caribbean, received US$19 billion FDI in 2010, up 25 percent over the 2009 level.

▶ Low-income countries as a group saw FDI inflows increase by almost 40 percent in 2010, largely due to rising South-South investment in extractive industries and infrastructure development. But an overwhelming share of FDI inflows went to China, where they increased by 62 percent to $185 billion.

▶ FDI net flows to high-income countries accounted for nearly 65 percent of the world total in 2010. Among developing regions, East Asia and the Pacific received the largest amount in 2010 ($231.3 billion), having grown fivefold since 2000.

Internet links

▶ International Monetary Fund— Balance of Payments Statistics — **www.imfstatistics.org** (select 'BOPS')

▶ World Bank Group—Data — **data.worldbank.org**

▶ United Nations Conference on Trade and Development— Statistics — **www.unctad.org** (go to 'Statistics', then select 'UNCTADstat')

People on the move

The movement of people across national borders is a visible and increasingly important aspect of global integration. Three percent of the world's population—more than 213 million people—now live in countries in which they were not born. The forces driving the flow of migrants from poor economies to rich economies are likely to grow stronger in the future.

Migration is on the rise, especially from poor economies to rich economies. Wage differences and demographic trends encourage migration. In many high-income economies, the population is aging and growing slowly, while in many developing countries the population is young and growing rapidly. This imbalance creates a strong demand for developing-economy workers, especially to provide services that can be supplied only locally. Immigrants in high-income economies have increased to 12 percent of the population, up from 8 percent two decades before. There can be other reasons for immigration. After the breakup of the Soviet Union in 1991, many people moved between the newly independent states, raising the number of migrants recorded in middle-income economies.

Migration is often accompanied by a flow of remittances—transfers of gifts and wages and salaries earned abroad—from migrants to their countries of origin. The direction of the remittances is related to the geographical movement of the labor force and the relative economic positions of sending and receiving countries, as well as the impact these flows have on the receiving economies. Over the past decade, international migration has intensified and this is reflected in remittances becoming an increasing source of financial flows to low- and middle-income and even some

Most migrants reside in high-income economies

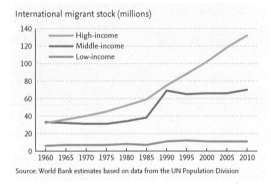

International migrant stock (millions)

Source: World Bank estimates based on data from the UN Population Division

A larger share of remittance flows are now going to developing economies

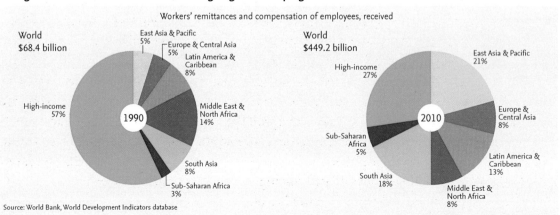

Workers' remittances and compensation of employees, received

Source: World Bank, World Development Indicators database

Remittances to developing countries have fallen slightly since 2008

Remittances received (% of GDP)

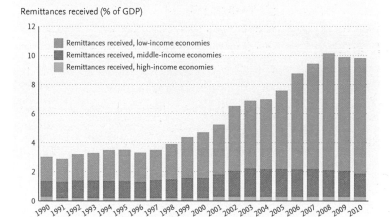

Source: World Bank estimates based on the International Monetary Fund's Balance of Payments Statistics and OECD DAC's International Development Statistics

Among developing regions, Sub-Saharan Africa was the highest net migrant sender during 2005–2010

Net out-migration (millions)

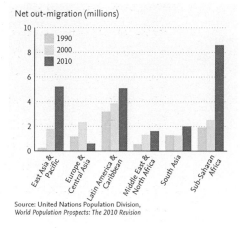

Source: United Nations Population Division, *World Population Prospects: The 2010 Revision*

high-income economies. Unlike other kinds of financial flows, remittances do not create liabilities and are often received by people who need financing the most. From 2000 to 2010, remittance inflows to developing economies more than quadrupled. Global remittance flows almost reached $450 billion in 2010, with 72 percent going to developing economies.

In 2010, the largest share of remittances went to Asia: East Asia and the Pacific received $94.0 billion in remittances and South Asia received $82.0 billion. The top remittance-receiving developing economies in 2010 were India ($54.0 billion), China ($53.0 billion), Mexico ($22.0 billion), and the Philippines ($21.4 billion). Among the high-income economies, France ($15.6 billion), Germany ($11.3 billion), Spain ($10.5 billion), and the Republic of Korea ($8.7 billion) received the largest amount of remittances in the form of compensation of employees.

Empirical studies have found that remittances can raise income levels, especially among the poor. Evidence from some countries suggests that a large proportion of remittances received are invested, which should lead to improvements in the overall economy. Migration opportunities may also encourage higher levels of educational attainment. And increases in income from remittances along with the transfer of knowledge through migrants result in better health outcomes for other household members.

Migration may also have negative effects. Among international migrants are millions of highly educated people who have moved to developed countries from developing countries. By migrating they improve their own prospects and provide valuable services in high-income economies, but the loss of human capital, so-called brain drain, from developing countries, may increase the concentration of poverty and reduce the social benefits of migration.

Remittances have remained fairly resilient during the global financial crisis. The slowdown of the global economy during the second half of 2008 affected remittance flows in all regions. Remittance flows to developing countries dropped from $323 billion in 2008 to $306 billion in 2009, but increased in 2010 to $325 billion, above the 2008 level. Even though remittances fell 5.2 percent in 2009, other financial flows to developing countries, such as foreign direct investment, fell much more drastically in response to the financial crisis (36.3 percent from 2008 to 2009).

MIGRATION

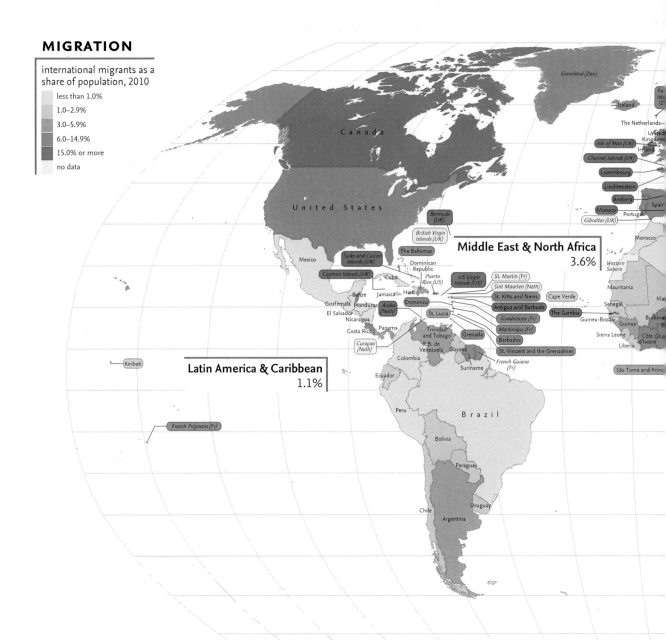

international migrants as a
share of population, 2010

- less than 1.0%
- 1.0–2.9%
- 3.0–5.9%
- 6.0–14.9%
- 15.0% or more
- no data

Greenland (Den)

Canada

Iceland

Fa
Isle
(C

The Netherlands
United
Kingdom
Ireland

Isle of Man (UK)

Channel Islands (UK)

Luxembourg

Liechtenstein

Andorra
Spain
Monaco
Portugal
Gibraltar (UK)

United States

Bermuda
(UK)

British Virgin
Islands (UK)

Middle East & North Africa
3.6%

Morocco

Mexico

The Bahamas

Turks and Caicos
Islands (UK)

Dominican
Republic

Cayman Islands (UK)

Cuba

Puerto
Rico (US)

US Virgin
Islands (US)

St. Martin (Fr)
Sint Maarten (Neth)

Western
Sahara

Mauritania

Belize

Jamaica

Haiti

Guatemala Honduras

Aruba
(Neth)

Dominica

St. Kitts and Nevis

Cape Verde

Ma

Senegal

El Salvador

St. Lucia

Antigua and Barbuda

The Gambia

Nicaragua

Guadeloupe (Fr)

Guinea-Bissau

Guinea

Burkina

Costa Rica

Panama

Curaçao
(Neth)

Trinidad
and Tobago

Grenada

Martinique (Fr)

Barbados

Sierra Leone

Côte Gha
d'Ivoire

R.B. de
Venezuela

Guyana

St. Vincent and the Grenadines

Liberia

Kiribati

Colombia

Suriname

French Guiana
(Fr)

São Tomé and Prínc

Latin America & Caribbean
1.1%

Ecuador

Peru

B r a z i l

French Polynesia (Fr)

Bolivia

Paraguay

Chile

Uruguay

Argentina

Immigrants becoming U.S. citizens at a naturalization oath ceremony

Countries with highest migrations, 2005–2010

Rank	Country	Net in-migration (thousands)
1	United States	4,955
2	United Arab Emirates	3,077
3	Spain	2,250
4	Italy	1,999
5	Russian Federation	1,136

Rank	Country	Net out-migration (thousands)
1	India	3,000
2	Bangladesh	2,908
3	Pakistan	2,000
4	China	1,884
5	Mexico	1,805

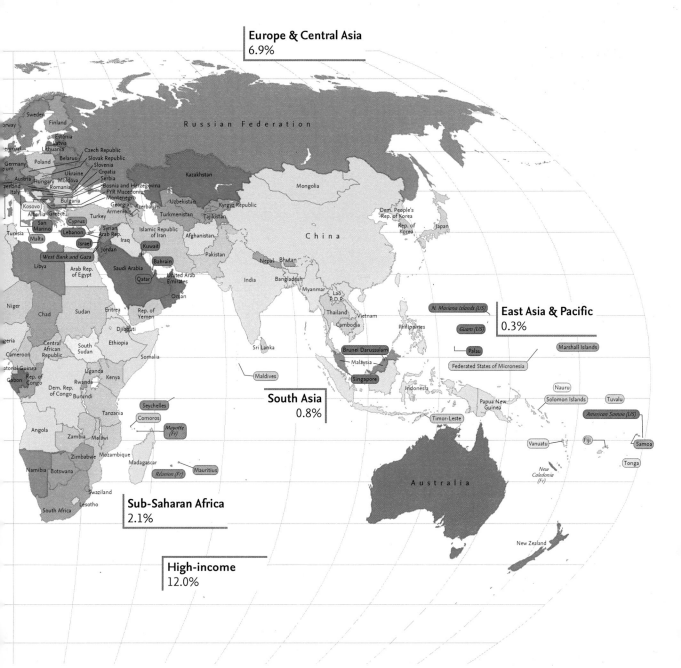

Europe & Central Asia
6.9%

East Asia & Pacific
0.3%

South Asia
0.8%

Sub-Saharan Africa
2.1%

High-income
12.0%

Facts

▶ In the 1960s, the majority of migrants lived in developing countries. In 2010, nearly two-thirds resided in high-income countries.

▶ The number of migrants in the world grew from about 72 million in 1960 to more than 213 million in 2010. This represents about 3 percent of the world's population.

▶ As of 2010, 81 million migrants lived in developing countries (about 1.4 percent of their population), compared to 132 million in high-income countries (about 12 percent of their population).

▶ Refugees are an important component of the migrant stock. At the end of 2010, the number of refugees, including those under the mandate of the United Nations Relief and Works Agency for Palestine Refugees in the Near East (UNRWA), stood at 15.4 million, accounting for approximately 7 percent of the migrants in the world.

Internet links

▶ United Nations Population Division— International Migration — www.un.org/esa/population/migration

▶ United Nations Refugee Agency—Statistics — www.unhcr.org/statistics.html

▶ OECD—Migration — www.oecd.org/migration

▶ International Organization for Migration — www.iom.int

▶ International Labour Organization— Labour Migration — www.ilo.org (go to 'Topics', select 'Labour Migration')

REMITTANCES

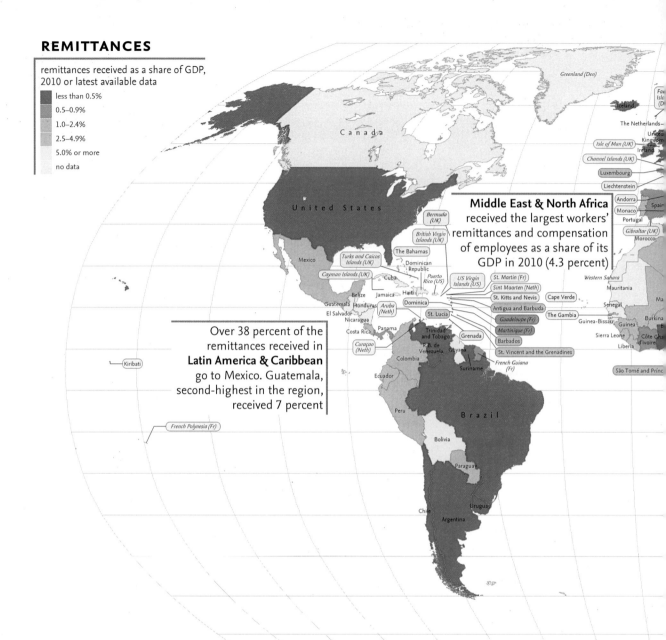

remittances received as a share of GDP,
2010 or latest available data

- less than 0.5%
- 0.5–0.9%
- 1.0–2.4%
- 2.5–4.9%
- 5.0% or more
- no data

Middle East & North Africa
received the largest workers'
remittances and compensation
of employees as a share of its
GDP in 2010 (4.3 percent)

Over 38 percent of the
remittances received in
Latin America & Caribbean
go to Mexico. Guatemala,
second-highest in the region,
received 7 percent

India has the world's largest migrant outflow

Top recipients of workers' remittances and compensation of employees, 2010

Rank	Developing country	$ billions
1	India	54.0
2	China	53.0
3	Mexico	22.0
4	Philippines	21.4
5	Bangladesh	10.9
6	Nigeria	10.0
7	Pakistan	9.7
8	Vietnam	8.3
9	Egypt, Arab Rep.	7.7
10	Lebanon	7.6

Outflows of remittances from **high-income economies** were $245 billion in 2010, up from $61 billion in 1990

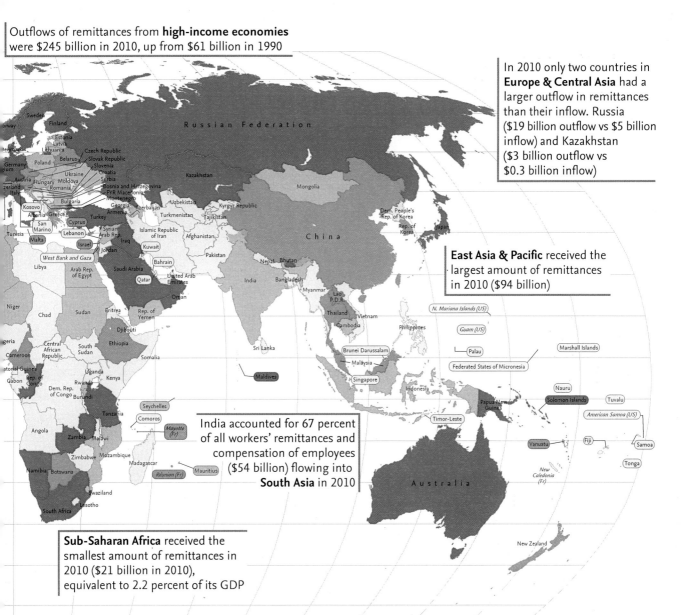

In 2010 only two countries in **Europe & Central Asia** had a larger outflow in remittances than their inflow. Russia ($19 billion outflow vs $5 billion inflow) and Kazakhstan ($3 billion outflow vs $0.3 billion inflow)

East Asia & Pacific received the largest amount of remittances in 2010 ($94 billion)

India accounted for 67 percent of all workers' remittances and compensation of employees ($54 billion) flowing into **South Asia** in 2010

Sub-Saharan Africa received the smallest amount of remittances in 2010 ($21 billion in 2010), equivalent to 2.2 percent of its GDP

Facts

▶ As a share of GDP, Tajikistan (40 percent), Lesotho (34 percent), the Kyrgz Republic (27 percent), and Samoa (24 percent) were the largest recipients of remittances in 2010. Chile (0.001 percent), Japan (0.03 percent), R.B. Venezuela (0.04 percent), and the United States (0.04 percent) were the lowest.

▶ At the beginning of the 1990s, more than half of remittances went to high-income economies. In 2010, middle-income economies received nearly 67 percent of all remittances, and low-income economies received 5.5 percent.

▶ Remittances to developing countries increased from 1.1 percent of GDP in 1990 to 1.7 percent in 2010. In high-income countries they remained constant at 0.3 percent.

▶ High-income economies are the principal source of outward remittance flows. The United States is the largest, with $51.6 billion in 2010. Saudi Arabia ($27.1 billion) is the second, followed by Switzerland ($21.7 billion).

Internet links

▶ World Bank— Migration and Remittances	**www.worldbank.org/prospects/migrationandremittances**
▶ OECD—Migration	**www.oecd.org/migration**
▶ International Monetary Fund—Balance of Payments Statistics	**www.imf.org/** (go to 'Data and Statistics', then select 'Balance of Payments Statistics')
▶ Development Research Centre on Migration, Globalisation and Poverty	**www.migrationdrc.org**
▶ Migration Information Source	**www.migrationinformation.org**

Aid for development

The global economy is more integrated than ever. Countries are exchanging more goods and services, international financial flows have increased, and private investors are active in many developing countries. But even in an expanding world economy, many countries cannot finance their own development. Aid helps to fill the gap.

Development is a partnership between developing and donor countries. Donor countries help recipient countries build the capacity to foster change; recipient countries invest in their people and create an environment that sustains growth. Countries that have difficulty tapping financial markets must rely on aid flows from wealthier countries to fund development programs. Net official development assistance (ODA) to developing countries reached $131.1 billion in 2010, the highest ever in nominal terms—representing a 3.2 percent increase in real terms from the 2009 level.

According to the Organisation for Economic Co-operation and Development's Development Assistance Committee (DAC), the top 10 donors in 2010 contributed 84 percent of all aid provided by DAC members. The top four—the United States, the European Commission, France, and Germany—contributed 53 percent.

Aid increased sharply in 2005, as donor countries followed through on promises made at the 2002 United Nations

Net ODA received in per capita terms has increased for most regions

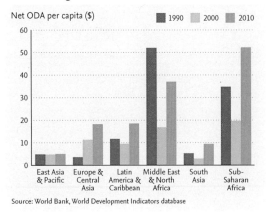

Source: World Bank, World Development Indicators database

Who were the largest donors in 2010?

| | | DAC donors | |
| | | Net bilateral ODA disbursements in 2010 | |
Rank	Country	$ millions	% of total
1	United States	26,586	25.7
2	European Commission	12,428	12.0
3	France	8,036	7.8
4	Germany	8,017	7.8
5	United Kingdom	7,787	7.5
6	Japan	7,337	7.1
7	Netherlands	4,841	4.7
8	Spain	3,999	3.9
9	Norway	3,926	3.8
10	Canada	3,561	3.4
	Other DAC members	16,867	16.3
	All DAC members	103,385	100.0

Source: OECD DAC

The social sector received the most DAC donor bilateral aid in 2010

Aid by sector as share of donors' bilateral commitments, 2010

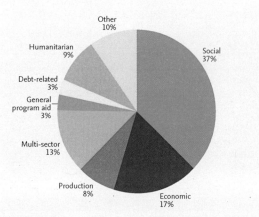

Source: OECD DAC

International Conference on Financing for Development, in Monterrey, Mexico, and reinforced at the 2005 Group of Eight (G8) summit at Gleneagles, Scotland. But a large part of this increase came as debt relief, not new aid flows. Aid in absolute terms and measured as a share of donors' gross national income declined between 2005 and 2007, but has increased since then. Still, a significant increase in donor commitment is required to meet the targets set at Gleneagles.

The form of aid and purpose for which it is given make a difference. Debt-related aid provides relief from liabilities that recipient countries have difficulty servicing, and can free up public resources for other purposes, but it may not result in an equivalent expansion of development activities. Humanitarian assistance provides relief for sudden disasters and emergency situations, but it does not generally contribute to financing long-term development. Furthermore, the administrative costs of providing aid are mainly spent in the donor economy.

Aid is not the only source of development finance or, for many countries, the most important. Remittances and private capital flows are a growing source of financing for some. Remittances received worldwide more than tripled in the past decade, from $136 billion in 2000 to $449 billion in 2010. But extremely poor countries, especially in Sub-Saharan Africa, still require substantial increases in aid to reach their development goals.

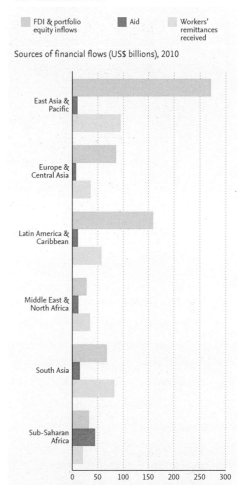

Aid is the biggest source of financing for Sub-Saharan Africa

FDI & portfolio equity inflows   Aid   Workers' remittances received

Sources of financial flows (US$ billions), 2010

Source: World Bank's *Global Development Finance*; World Bank estimates based on data from International Monetary Fund's Balance of Payments Statistics; OECD DAC's International Development Statistics

In 2010, DAC aid to recipient countries increased, but the amount of aid received as a percentage of GNI decreased

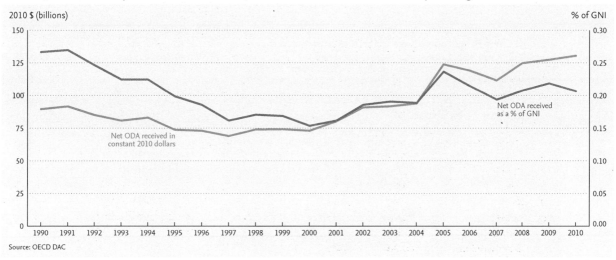

Source: OECD DAC

AID

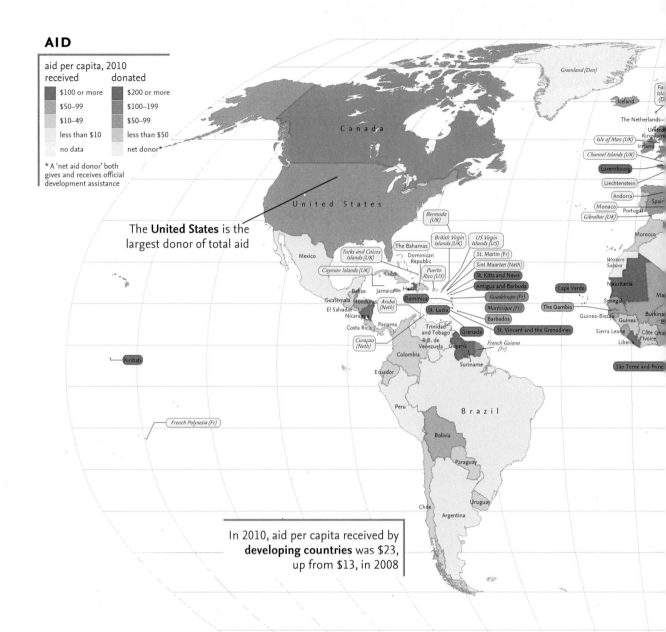

aid per capita, 2010

received	donated
$100 or more	$200 or more
$50–99	$100–199
$10–49	$50–99
less than $10	less than $50
no data	net donor*

* A 'net aid donor' both gives and receives official development assistance

The **United States** is the largest donor of total aid

In 2010, aid per capita received by **developing countries** was $23, up from $13, in 2008

A British Chinook helicopter takes UNHCR relief items to the Leepa Valley, in Pakistan-administered Kashmir

Net ODA received as a share of GNI, 2010

Rank	Developing country	%
1	Liberia	175.5
2	Solomon Islands	61.4
3	Marshall Islands	45.9
4	Haiti	45.5
5	Afghanistan	42.4
6	Federated States of Micronesia	40.2
7	Burundi	31.0
8	Democratic Republic of Congo	29.0
9	Tuvalu	26.2
10	Samoa	25.5

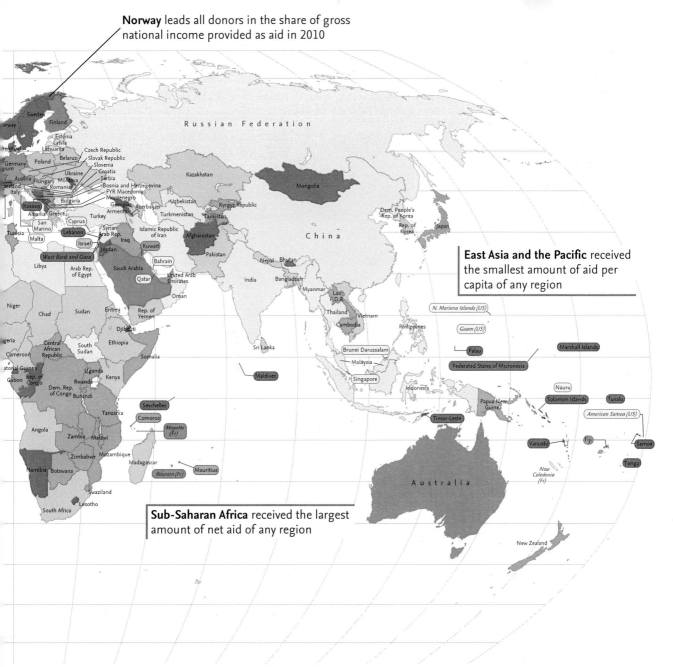

Norway leads all donors in the share of gross national income provided as aid in 2010

East Asia and the Pacific received the smallest amount of aid per capita of any region

Sub-Saharan Africa received the largest amount of net aid of any region

Facts

▶ Many donor countries pledged to provide aid equivalent to at least 0.7 percent of GNI, but the average remains around 0.31 percent. In 2010, only five countries—Denmark, Luxembourg, the Netherlands, Norway, and Sweden—fulfilled their pledge.

▶ Since 1990, aid per capita has increased by $17 in Sub-Saharan Africa, from $35 to $52. Aid per capita to the Middle East and North Africa decreased by more than half in recent years, from $76 in 2008 to $37 in 2010.

▶ Aid received by low-income countries in 2010 constituted 9.5 percent of their GNI. In middle-income countries, aid was only 0.3 percent of GNI.

▶ The top non-DAC donor that reports aid is Saudi Arabia, which provided $3.5 billion in 2010. This would rank 11th among the top DAC donors behind Norway's 3.6 billion. Turkey is the second-highest non-DAC donor, providing less than a billion in aid in 2010.

Internet links

▶ Organisation for Economic Co-operation and Development (OECD), Development Assistance Committee (DAC)	www.oecd.org/dac
▶ Statistics on aid from OECD DAC	www.oecd.org/dac/stats
▶ The European Commission, Development and Cooperation—Europeaid	ec.europa.eu/europeaid/index_en.htm
▶ World Bank Group, International Development Association	www.worldbank.org/ida
▶ International Monetary Fund, Extended Credit Facility	www.imf.org (go to 'About the IMF', then select 'Factsheet')

External debt

Many countries borrow from abroad to finance development, but when debt exceeds a country's capacity to service it, the debt burden becomes unsustainable and hinders development. Making debt manageable for poor countries frees up resources that can be used to support economic growth and social development.

Developing countries borrow because at early stages of development they have small stocks of capital and are likely to have investment opportunities that may be risky but have high returns. Often these investment projects have a significant public good component, such as transportation, infrastructure, education, and public health. Because government budgets and domestic savings are low, many countries must turn to external sources of funding. Poor and less creditworthy countries may qualify for concessional lending by official creditors, such as the multilateral development banks and other governments; creditworthy middle-income countries can borrow at market rates from official and private lenders.

By the end of 2010, developing countries' external debt was $4 trillion, with the 10 largest debtors owing 73 percent of the total. External debt from private creditors to developing countries increased from $1.3 trillion in 2000 to $3 trillion in 2010. Short-term debt was the fastest growing component. Multilateral creditors, the World Bank Group in particular, were important sources of financing to public sector borrowers. In 2010 alone the World

Debt service continued to decline for most regions in 2010

Total debt service (% of exports of goods, services, and income)

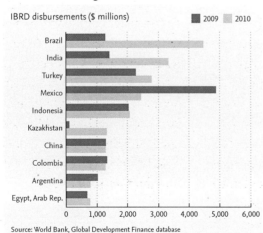

Source: World Bank, Global Development Finance database

Eighty-five percent of IBRD disbursements in 2010 went to the 10 largest borrowers

IBRD disbursements ($ millions)

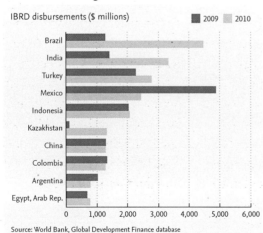

Source: World Bank, Global Development Finance database

India was the largest recipient of IDA disbursements in 2010

IDA loans and grants disbursement ($ millions)

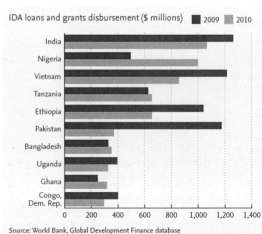

Source: World Bank, Global Development Finance database

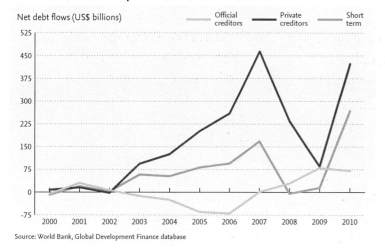

Net debt inflows from private creditors rebounded in 2010

Net debt flows (US$ billions)

Legend: Official creditors · Private creditors · Short term

Source: World Bank, Global Development Finance database

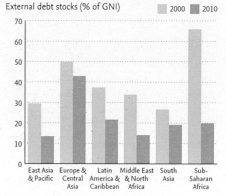

Sub-Saharan Africa saw significant reductions in its external debt stocks over the last decade, mostly due to HIPC and MDRI

External debt stocks (% of GNI)   ■ 2000 ■ 2010

Source: World Bank, Global Development Finance database

Bank Group made $43 billion in new commitments and disbursements of $34 billion. This included commitments of $32 billion made through the International Bank for Reconstruction and Development (IBRD) at market rates and $11 billion in grants and concessional lending made by the International Development Association (IDA).

Debt burdens and debt relief

Overborrowing and unexpected events such as terms-of-trade shocks, natural disasters, or civil conflict can turn ordinary debt burdens into unmanageable ones. Oil price increases in the 1980s precipitated a debt crisis among middle-income countries. For many poor countries, especially those in Africa, debt burdens became unsustainable after a decade of slow growth in the 1990s. In 1996, the World Bank and the International Monetary Fund (IMF) launched the Heavily Indebted Poor Countries (HIPC) initiative to provide relief to low-income countries with recurring debt repayment problems. The initiative aimed to provide permanent relief from unsustainable debt and to redirect the resources going to debt service to social expenditures aimed at poverty reduction. By the end of 2011, 36 countries had participated in the initiative and received debt relief of $76.4 billion. Since 2006, the World Bank, the IMF, the African Development Fund, and the Inter-American Development Bank have provided additional debt relief under the Multilateral Debt Relief Initiative (MDRI). As of September 2011, 32 HIPC countries, primarily in Sub-Saharan Africa, had received additional assistance of $47.1 billion under the MDRI.

All developing regions have improved their external debt position. Measured against gross national income (GNI), the stock of external debt was 21 percent in 2010, compared to 37.8 percent in 2000. The ratio of debt service (principal and interest payments) to exports fell to 9.8 percent. And the ratio of external debt outstanding to exports fell from 128.5 percent in 2000 to 68.7 percent in 2010. East Asia and the Pacific and the Middle East and North Africa had the lowest external debt ratios. Europe and Central Asia was the most indebted region in 2010: the ratios of external debt outstanding to GNI (43 percent) and to export earnings (121 percent) were three times those of the East Asian countries. The debt-to-export ratio in Sub-Saharan African countries declined to 54 percent at the end of 2010, compared with 185.1 percent in 2000, and the debt service to export ratio fell to 3.3 percent, less than one-third its 2000 level.

EXTERNAL DEBT

external debt as a share of GNI, 2010

- 60% or more
- 45–59%
- 30–44%
- 15–29%
- less than 15%
- no data

Nicaragua
2000: 181%
2010: 77%

Guinea-Bissau
2000: 467%
2010: 125%

Liberia
2000: 719%
2010: 28%

India is among the 10 most indebted developing economies

Highest debtors in 2010

Rank	Developing country	Total external debt (US$ billions) [Total debt (% of GNI)]
1	China	548 [9%]
2	Russian Federation	384 [27%]
3	Brazil	346 [17%]
4	Turkey	293 [40%]
5	India	290 [17%]
6	Mexico	200 [20%]
7	Indonesia	179 [26%]
8	Argentina	127 [36%]
9	Romania	121 [76%]
10	Kazakhstan	118 [94%]

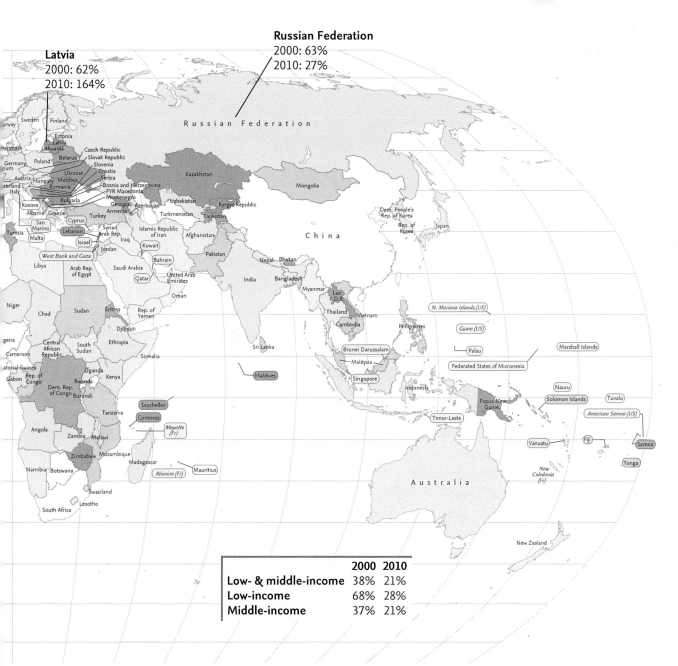

Latvia
2000: 62%
2010: 164%

Russian Federation
2000: 63%
2010: 27%

	2000	2010
Low- & middle-income	38%	21%
Low-income	68%	28%
Middle-income	37%	21%

Facts

▶ In Sub-Saharan Africa, the ratio of debt to GNI fell from an average 65 percent in 2000 to 20 percent in 2010.

▶ Net debt inflows from private creditors surged to $424 billion in 2010, from $86 billion in 2009.

▶ The ratio of debt service to exports for developing countries fell from 21 percent in 2000 to 9.8 percent in 2010.

▶ Short-term debt inflow to the top 10 borrowers was $220 billion, 80 percent of the total short-term inflow of $269 billion in 2010. Half of this went to China, where imports rose 34 percent in U.S. dollar terms in 2010.

▶ In 2010 the World Bank committed over $43 billion in loan, credits, and grants, equivalent to 53 percent of the commitments from all multilateral institutions to public sector borrowers in 2010.

Internet links

▶ World Bank Data	**data.worldbank.org**
▶ Bank for International Settlements	**www.bis.org** (go to 'Statistics', then select 'External debt')
▶ Quarterly External Debt Statistics	**www.worldbank.org/qeds**
▶ External Debt Statistics and the IMF	**www.imf.org/external/ np/sta/ed/ed.htm**
▶ Joint External Debt Hub	**www.jedh.org**

The urban environment

Cities will continue to grow as people seek the economic and social opportunities they offer. Cities can be efficient providers of water and sanitation services and access to health care, education, and other social and cultural services, but they also face increasing costs of congestion and pollution, and they make demands on the environment and natural resources.

Cities, now home to more than half of the world's people, are growing rapidly in size and number, especially in developing countries. People flock to cities for work, access to public services, and a higher standard of living. The world's urban population is expected to almost double by 2050, rising to 6.4 billion from 3.5 billion in 2010. Sub-Saharan Africa will experience a drastic increase in its urban population, from 315 million to more than a billion over the next four decades.

Among developing regions, urbanization has gone farthest in Latin America and the Caribbean, where 79 percent of the people now live in urban areas; this number is expected to increase to 88 percent by 2050. By 2050, 70 percent of the world's population will live in urban areas, in some countries placing tremendous pressure on the capacity of the natural and human-made environment to support them. The consequences could be further deterioration of living conditions, the growth of slums, the destruction of habitat, and increased air and water pollution.

East Asia now has the largest number of people living in cities

Population living in urban areas (millions)

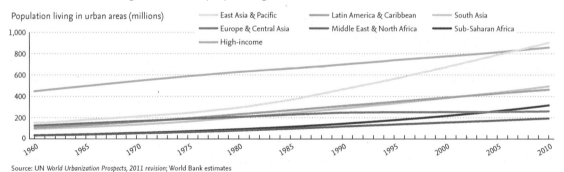

Source: UN *World Urbanization Prospects, 2011 revision*; World Bank estimates

Pollution from particulate matter in cities is decreasing

Urban-population-weighted particulate matter (PM10 per cubic meter)

Source: World Bank estimates based on the study *Ambient Particulate Matter Concentration in Residential and Pollution Hotspot Areas of the World Cities*; New estimates based on the *Global Model of Ambient Particulates (GMAPS)*, 2011

Cities house more than half the world's population, but basic services are often lacking in poor areas

Sub-Saharan Africa is urbanizing more rapidly than other regions

Average annual growth in urban population (%), 1990–2010

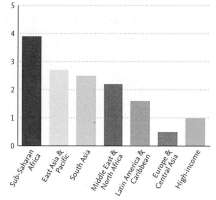

Source: United Nations Population Division; World Bank estimates

UN Habitat defines a slum dwelling as a household that lacks one or more of the following:

- Durable housing of a permanent nature
- Sufficient living space
- Easy access to safe water
- Access to adequate sanitation
- Security of tenure that prevents forced evictions.

By this definition, more than 900 million people in developing regions live in slums—about one in three people living in urban areas or one of every six people worldwide. To achieve significant improvements in the lives of slum dwellers, public and private investment in durable, affordable housing is required.

Sub-Saharan Africa and South Asia have the lowest access to improved sanitation in urban areas

Proportion of urban population with access to improved sanitation facilities (%)

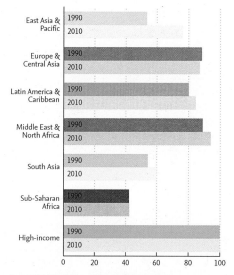

Source: World Health Organization; World Bank estimates

Urbanization and the environment

The cost of urbanization to human health comes from a variety of sources. The proximity to industrial works and roadways and the use of inefficient and polluting sources of energy can result in exposure to high levels of soot and small, airborne particles (designated 'PM10'—fine, suspended particles less than 10 microns in diameter) that contribute to lung cancer, other respiratory diseases, and heart disease.

Air and water pollution in many of the world's major cities cause moderate to severe sickness and death and cost billions of dollars in lost productivity and damages. Although all the world's large cities share these problems, water pollution tends to be most serious in South, Southeast, and Central Asia. Air pollution has the biggest impact in China, Latin America and the Caribbean, and Eastern Europe. Not only are the human and financial costs of pollution high, they tend to fall disproportionately on poor people. Therefore addressing pollution is justified on equity, economic, and environmental grounds.

URBANIZATION

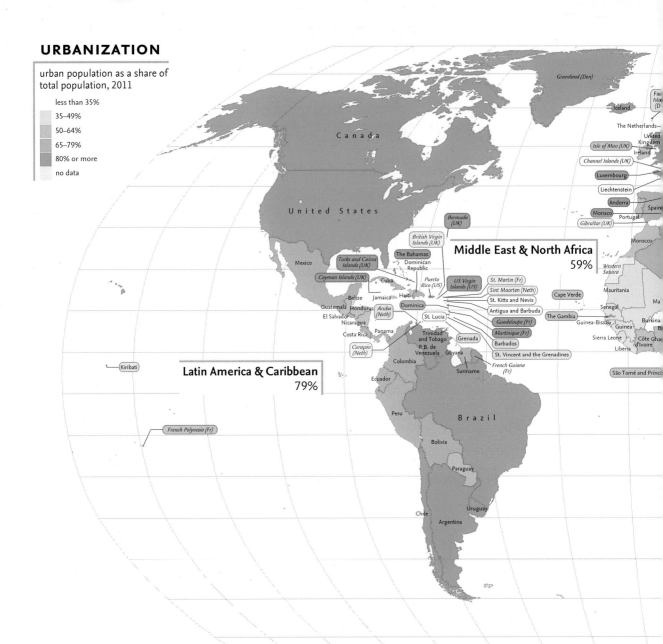

urban population as a share of total population, 2011

- less than 35%
- 35–49%
- 50–64%
- 65–79%
- 80% or more
- no data

Middle East & North Africa
59%

Latin America & Caribbean
79%

Canada

United States

Mexico

Greenland (Den)

Iceland

The Netherlands

United Kingdom

Ireland

Isle of Man (UK)

Channel Islands (UK)

Luxembourg

Liechtenstein

Andorra

Monaco   Portugal   Spain

Gibraltar (UK)

Morocco

Western Sahara

Mauritania

Ma

Senegal

The Gambia

Guinea-Bissau   Guinea

Sierra Leone   Côte d'Ivoire

Liberia

Burkina
Fa

São Tomé and Princi

Cape Verde

Bermuda (UK)

British Virgin Islands (UK)

The Bahamas

Dominican Republic

Turks and Caicos Islands (UK)

Cayman Islands (UK)

Cuba

Puerto Rico (US)

US Virgin Islands (US)

St. Martin (Fr)

Sint Maarten (Neth)

St. Kitts and Nevis

Antigua and Barbuda

Guadeloupe (Fr)

Martinique (Fr)

Barbados

St. Vincent and the Grenadines

Grenada

French Guiana (Fr)

Belize   Jamaica   Haiti

Guatemala   Honduras

El Salvador

Nicaragua

Aruba (Neth)

Dominica

St. Lucia

Costa Rica

Panama

Curaçao (Neth)

Trinidad and Tobago

R.B. de Venezuela

Guyana

Colombia

Suriname

Ecuador

Peru

Brazil

Bolivia

Paraguay

Chile

Uruguay

Argentina

Kiribati

French Polynesia (Fr)

Dhaka, Bangladesh, is one of the fastest-growing cities in the developing world

Largest urban agglomerations in developing countries, 2011

Rank	Country	Urban agglomeration	Population (millions)
1	India	Delhi	22.7
2	Mexico	Mexico City	20.4
3	China	Shanghai	20.2
4	Brazil	São Paulo	19.9
5	India	Mumbai	19.7
6	China	Beijing	15.6
7	Bangladesh	Dhaka	15.4
8	India	Calcutta	14.4
9	Pakistan	Karachi	13.9
10	Argentina	Buenos Aires	13.5

Europe & Central Asia
64%

R u s s i a n   F e d e r a t i o n

Sweden
Finland
Estonia
Latvia
Lithuania
Germany
Belarus
Czech Republic
Slovak Republic
Poland
Slovenia
Croatia
Austria
Ukraine
Serbia
Hungary Moldova
Bosnia and Herzegovina
Italy
Romania
FYR Macedonia
Montenegro
Bulgaria
Kosovo
Georgia
Albania Greece
Armenia
San
Marino
Turkey
Azerbaijan
Cyprus
Tunisia
Lebanon
Syrian
Arab Rep.
Malta
Israel
Iraq
Jordan
West Bank and Gaza
Kuwait
Libya
Arab Rep.
of Egypt
Saudi Arabia
Bahrain
Qatar
United Arab
Emirates
Oman

Kazakhstan

Uzbekistan
Kyrgyz Republic
Turkmenistan
Tajikistan
Islamic Republic
of Iran
Afghanistan
Pakistan

Mongolia

C h i n a

Dem. People's
Rep. of Korea
Rep. of
Korea
Japan

Nepal Bhutan
India
Bangladesh
Myanmar
Lao
P.D.R.
Thailand
Cambodia
Vietnam
Philippines

East Asia & Pacific
48%

N. Mariana Islands (US)
Guam (US)
Palau
Marshall Islands
Federated States of Micronesia

Niger
Chad
Sudan
Eritrea
Rep. of
Yemen
Djibouti
Central
African
Republic
South
Sudan
Ethiopia
Cameroon
Somalia
Sri Lanka
Maldives
Equatorial Guinea
Rep. of
Gabon
Congo
Uganda
Rwanda
Kenya
Dem. Rep.
of Congo Burundi
Tanzania

Brunei Darussalam
Malaysia
Singapore
Indonesia
Nauru
Solomon Islands
Tuvalu
Papua New
Guinea
American Samoa (US)
Timor-Leste

South Asia
31%

Seychelles
Comoros
Angola
Zambia Malawi
Mayotte
(Fr)
Mozambique
Zimbabwe
Madagascar
Namibia Botswana
Réunion (Fr)
Mauritius

Vanuatu
Fiji
Samoa
Tonga
New
Caledonia
(Fr)

A u s t r a l i a

Swaziland
South Africa Lesotho

Sub-Saharan Africa
36%

New Zealand

Facts

▶ Latin America and the Caribbean has the highest share of people living in urban areas.

▶ An estimated 1 billion people live in urban slums in developing countries.

▶ The urban population of Sub-Saharan Africa is growing at an average annual rate of 3.9 percent, faster than any other region.

▶ In 1800, 3 percent of the world's people lived in urban areas; by 1900, 14 percent did; and today more than 50 percent do.

▶ Over 90 percent of urbanization is taking place in the developing world.

▶ A total of 227 million people in the world have moved out of slum conditions since 2000.

Internet links

▶ United Nations Population Information Network	**www.un.org/popin**
▶ Population Reference Bureau	**www.prb.org**
▶ World Bank Urban Development	**www.worldbank.org/urban**
▶ United Nations, *World Urbanization Prospects, 2011 Revision*	**esa.un.org/unpd/wup/ CD-ROM/Urban-Rural-Population.htm**
▶ World Bank Open Data	**data.worldbank.org/**
▶ United Nations—Habitat	**www.unhabitat.org/ documents/SOWC10/ R1.pdf**

Feeding a growing world

The world's food supply has expanded faster than its population, but increasing consumption in middle- and high-income economies and industrial demand for agricultural outputs have led to higher prices and local shortages. One billion people lack adequate nutrition to meet their daily needs— a situation that climate change could make worse.

In recent years, the world has had difficulty producing enough food to feed all at affordable prices, causing 1 billion people to lack sufficient food to meet their daily energy needs. Inadequate calorie intake and diets that do not supply vital nutrients take a pervasive toll on early childhood development, impairing children's cognitive development and adversely affecting health and productivity.

The demand for agricultural outputs will continue to grow because of population growth, rising incomes, changes in dietary preferences, and industrial demand for commodities such as maize and oilseeds. By 2050, there will be 9 billion people living on Earth, almost 2 billion more than today. Most will live in cities, but all will depend on agricultural areas around the world to feed them.

Meeting the growing demand for food requires producing more food and moving it, often across borders, from surplus to deficit areas. Improving the quality of life of those who produce it requires a continuously increasing productivity and sustainable use of land. In recent decades, about two-thirds of growth of the world agricultural output has come from higher agricultural productivity and only one-third from the expansion of agricultural land. Agricultural output has grown more rapidly than population, but so has the demand for agricultural products. For the past 50 years, production in the developing regions of Asia and South America has grown even faster, around 2 percent a year. But in Sub-Saharan Africa, with some of the highest rates of

Over the past two decades, world food production has increased by 18 percent

Food production index, 2002–2004 = 100

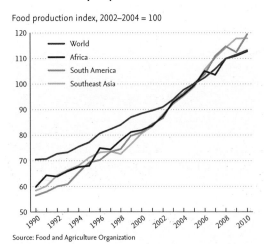

Source: Food and Agriculture Organization

World food prices rose sharply in 2008 and 2011, reaching their highest levels in 30 years

Real food price index, 2002–2004 = 100

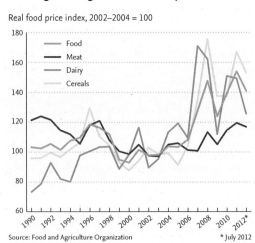

Source: Food and Agriculture Organization   * July 2012

Land degradation costs an estimated $40 billion annually worldwide. Overgrazing is one of many causes of land degradation

undernourishment, food production has barely kept pace with population increase, and it remains expensive to import food from Latin America, Eastern Europe, and other surplus regions.

Producing more affordable food entails more efficient use of the agricultural inputs. Intensified cultivation through the use of fertilizers, pesticides, irrigation, and new plant varieties can make limited land more productive. Such practices, however, may also cause further environmental degradation. Moreover, agricultural inputs are becoming costlier along with rising crude oil prices. The effects of climate change that causes more frequent droughts and floods as well as more erratic weather patterns represent another challenge to efforts to raise agricultural productivity.

Many poor farmers subsist on fragile lands, not always well suited to intensive farming. Even on lands suitable for intensive farming practices, the farmers often lack fertilizers, farm equipment, irrigation systems, and high-yielding plant varieties and are poorly linked to markets for their produce. Overgrazing, deforestation, improper crop rotation, and poor soil and water management contribute to land degradation. The degradation of land reduces its productivity, encouraging growing populations to move on to new and poorer land, converting forests and fragile, semiarid areas into low-productivity cultivated areas.

Sustainable production methods, based on environmentally sound practices, along with the development of more efficient markets for farm inputs and outputs and off-farm activities, are the keys to improving rural livelihoods and expanding the global food supply.

Cereal yields have improved in most developing regions but still trail high-income producers

Cereal yield (kilograms per hectare)

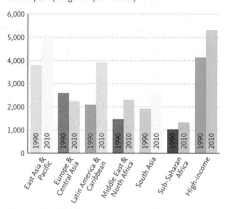

Source: Food and Agriculture Organization and World Bank estimates

Land under cereal production has expanded...

Land under cereal production (million hectares)

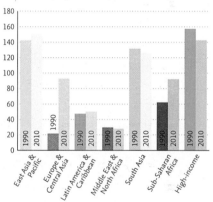

Source: Food and Agriculture Organization and World Bank estimates

...and cereal production has increased

Cereal production (million metric tons)

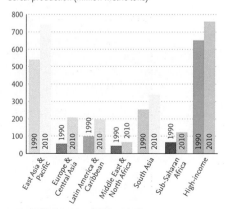

Source: Food and Agriculture Organization and World Bank estimates

AGRICULTURAL LAND

agricultural land (% of land area),
2007–2009, most recent year available

- less than 15.0%
- 15.0–29.9%
- 30.0–44.9%
- 45.0–59.9%
- 60.0% or more
- no data

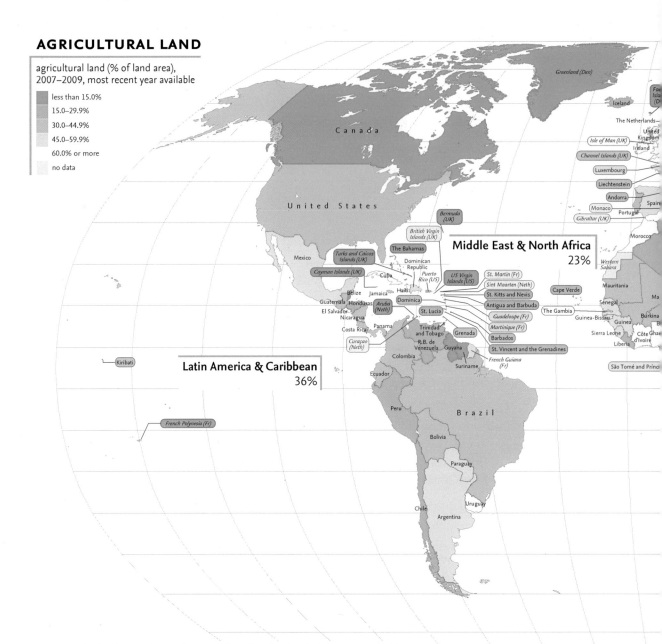

Middle East & North Africa
23%

Latin America & Caribbean
36%

Agriculture is the main user of land and water, but to remain viable,
it must also maintain the quality and quantity of these resources

Countries with highest cereal yield, 2010

Rank	Country	Kilograms per hectare
1	Oman	18,987
2	Mauritius	10,000
3	Belgium	9,231
4	Netherlands	8,574
5	Ireland	7,409
6	New Zealand	7,387
7	France	7,093
8	United States	6,988
9	United Kingdom	6,957
10	Chile	6,822

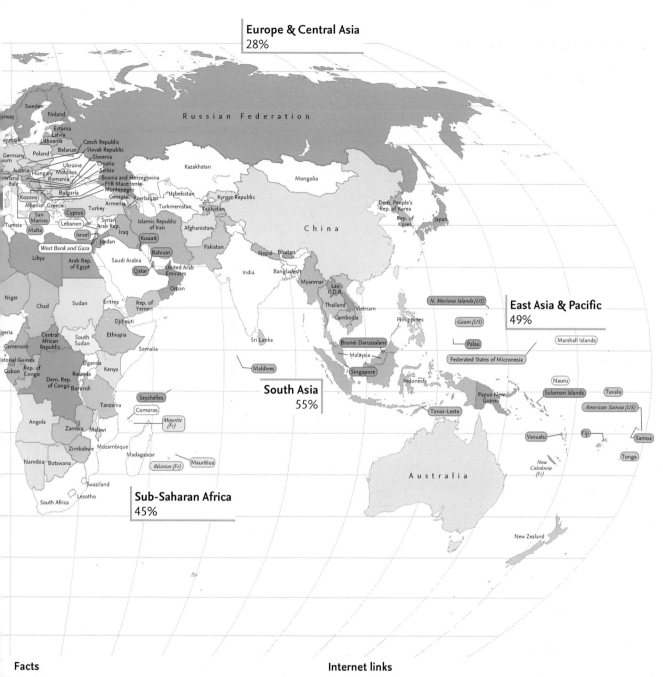

Europe & Central Asia
28%

East Asia & Pacific
49%

South Asia
55%

Sub-Saharan Africa
45%

Facts

▶ To meet the demand of a larger and more affluent population, annual cereal production will have to grow from 2.1 billion tons to 3 billion tons by 2050.

▶ Thirty percent of the Earth's land is used for growing crops and pastureland; another 30 percent is covered by forests.

▶ Seventy percent of freshwater withdrawals are used for irrigating crops.

▶ Only 0.2 hectare of arable land is available per person, less than half the amount 50 years ago.

Internet links

▶ Food and Agriculture Organization of the United Nations—Statistics — **www.fao.org/corp/statistics/en/**

▶ FAO Statistical Yearbook 2012 — **www.fao.org/docrep/015/ i2490e/i2490e00.htm**

▶ International Fund for Agricultural Development— Water and Food Security — **www.ifad.org/english/water/ pub/water_food.pdf**

A thirsty planet gets thirstier

Water is crucial to economic growth and development—and to the survival of terrestrial and aquatic ecosystems. Demand for water is increasing for food production, industrial uses, and human consumption. Meanwhile, over 800 million people lack convenient access to safe drinking water.

With the projected growth in population and economic activity, the share of the world's population facing water shortages will increase more than fivefold by 2050. Human needs for water in daily life compete with demands from agriculture, energy production, and other industrial uses. Urbanization and changes in lifestyle have led to higher per capita use. Climate change is also expected to influence the availability and distribution of freshwater supplies. These trends pose a significant challenge for meeting the Millennium Development Goals and sustaining the growth of developing countries.

Although the Earth's water resources are estimated at about 1.4 billion cubic kilometers, only a fraction is available for human needs. Freshwater makes up only 2.5 percent of total water resources, or about 35 million cubic kilometers. Most freshwater occurs in the form of permanent ice or snow, locked up in Antarctica and Greenland, or in deep groundwater aquifers. The principal sources of water for human use are lakes, rivers, soil moisture, and relatively shallow groundwater basins. The usable

South Asia and Middle East and North Africa face severe water conditions

Renewable internal freshwater resources per capita (1,000 cubic meters), 2009

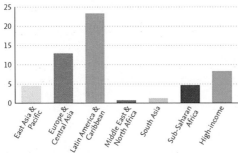

Source: World Resources Institute; Food and Agriculture Organization's AQUASTAT database

Most freshwater in developing countries is used for agriculture

Share of freshwater withdrawals (%), MRY 1999–2009

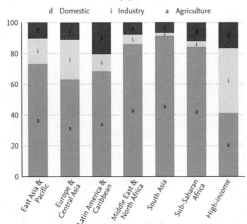

Source: World Resources Institute; Food and Agriculture Organization's AQUASTAT database

Irrigated lands are increasing, putting more pressure on water resources

Irrigated land (million hectares)

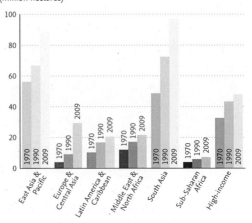

Source: Food and Agriculture Organization and World Bank estimates

Increasing water scarcity increases the competition for water by different sectors of the economy, and agriculture accounts for 70 percent of global water withdrawal

portion is less than 1 percent of all freshwater and only 0.03 percent of all water on Earth. Much of that is located far from human populations.

Humans compete with natural systems in the use of freshwater. Extraction of water for human needs diminishes the amount available to maintain the integrity of terrestrial and marine ecosystems. The three major factors leading to increased water demand over the past century have been population growth, industrial development, and the expansion of irrigated land in agriculture. Agriculture accounts for more than 70 percent of freshwater withdrawals in the world and 90 percent in low-income countries. Most of this water is used for irrigation to provide about 40 percent of world food production. Pollution of water bodies causes further degradation of natural systems and reduces the supply fit for human consumption.

Although domestic use of water for drinking and washing is the smallest part of the demand for water— usually less than 5 percent of the total—providing safe water for human consumption is of great importance for health and wellbeing. Water supplies should be free of chemical and biological contaminants and delivered in such a way that their cleanliness is protected. They should also be regularly and conveniently available.

Despite progress, almost 40 percent of the population of Sub-Saharan Africa lacks access to an improved water source

Access to an improved water source (% of population)

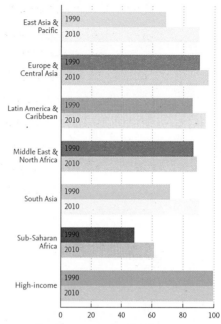

Source: World Health Organization and World Bank estimates

People in rural areas are more likely to lack access to improved water sources

People without access to improved water (millions), 2010

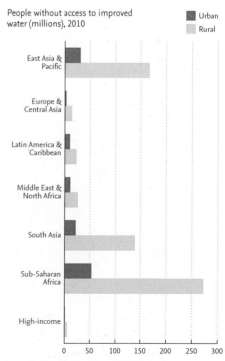

Source: World Health Organization and World Bank estimates

ACCESS TO WATER

share of population with access to
an improved water source, 2010

- less than 50%
- 50–69%
- 70–89%
- 90–99%
- 100%
- no data

Middle East & North Africa
89%

Latin America & Caribbean
94%

Many people still lack access to a convenient and reliable water source

Lowest access to clean water sources, 2010

Rank	Country	Access to an improved water source (% of population)
1	Somalia	29
2	Papua New Guinea	40
3	Ethiopia	44
4	Congo, Dem. Rep.	45
5	Madagascar	46
6	Mozambique	47
7	Niger	49
8	Afghanistan	50
9	Mauritania	50
10	Angola	51

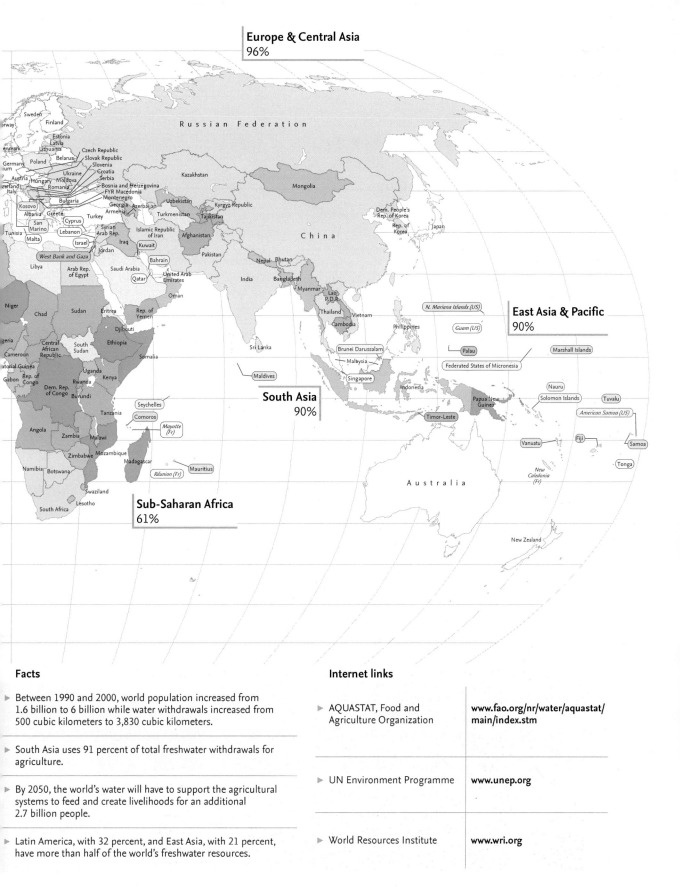

Europe & Central Asia
96%

R u s s i a n   F e d e r a t i o n

Sweden
Finland
Estonia
Latvia
Lithuania
Germany
Poland
Belarus
Czech Republic
Slovak Republic
Slovenia
Croatia
Serbia
Austria
Hungary
Moldova
Ukraine
Romania
Bosnia and Herzegovina
FYR Macedonia
Montenegro
Bulgaria
Kosovo
Albania
Greece
San
Marino
Cyprus
Lebanon
Turkey
Georgia
Armenia
Azerbaijan
Turkmenistan
Tajikistan
Kyrgyz Republic
Uzbekistan
Kazakhstan
Mongolia

Tunisia
Malta
Israel
Syrian
Arab Rep.
Jordan
Iraq
Kuwait
Bahrain
Islamic Republic
of Iran
Afghanistan
Pakistan
West Bank and Gaza
Libya
Arab Rep.
of Egypt
Saudi Arabia
Qatar
United Arab
Emirates
Oman

Niger
Chad
Sudan
Eritrea
Rep. of
Yemen
Djibouti
Ethiopia
South
Sudan
Central
African
Republic
Somalia
Cameroon
Equatorial Guinea
Gabon
Rep. of
Congo
Dem. Rep.
of Congo
Uganda
Rwanda
Burundi
Kenya
Tanzania
Seychelles
Comoros
Mayotte
(Fr)
Angola
Zambia
Malawi
Mozambique
Zimbabwe
Madagascar
Mauritius
Réunion (Fr)
Namibia
Botswana
Swaziland
South Africa
Lesotho

C h i n a
Dem. People's
Rep. of Korea
Rep. of
Korea
Japan
Nepal
Bhutan
India
Bangladesh
Myanmar
Lao
P.D.R.
Thailand
Vietnam
Cambodia
Sri Lanka
Maldives
Brunei Darussalam
Malaysia
Singapore
Indonesia
Philippines
N. Mariana Islands (US)
Guam (US)
Palau
Federated States of Micronesia
Marshall Islands
Nauru
Solomon Islands
Tuvalu
American Samoa (US)
Papua New
Guinea
Timor-Leste
Vanuatu
Fiji
Samoa
Tonga
New
Caledonia
(Fr)
A u s t r a l i a
New Zealand

East Asia & Pacific
90%

South Asia
90%

Sub-Saharan Africa
61%

Facts

▶ Between 1990 and 2000, world population increased from
1.6 billion to 6 billion while water withdrawals increased from
500 cubic kilometers to 3,830 cubic kilometers.

▶ South Asia uses 91 percent of total freshwater withdrawals for
agriculture.

▶ By 2050, the world's water will have to support the agricultural
systems to feed and create livelihoods for an additional
2.7 billion people.

▶ Latin America, with 32 percent, and East Asia, with 21 percent,
have more than half of the world's freshwater resources.

Internet links

▶ AQUASTAT, Food and Agriculture Organization	**www.fao.org/nr/water/aquastat/ main/index.stm**
▶ UN Environment Programme	**www.unep.org**
▶ World Resources Institute	**www.wri.org**

Protecting forests

Forests contribute to the livelihood of poor people and nourish the natural systems on which many more people depend. More than 31 percent of the world's land area is forested, which accounts for as much as 90 percent of terrestrial biodiversity. In most countries, however, forests are shrinking.

Forest loss is taking a terrible toll on both the natural and the economic resources of many countries. Forests meet many people's basic, everyday needs, providing food, fuel, building materials, and clean water. Forests also provide essential public goods of global value. They facilitate the hydrological and nutrient cycles and act as carbon sinks, reducing the accumulation of greenhouse gases in the atmosphere.

Deforestation is the main cause of biodiversity loss. Biodiversity refers to the variety of plants and animal species on Earth, the genetic variability within each species, and the variety of ecosystems in

Forests cover more than 31 percent of all land worldwide

Forest coverage (% of land area)

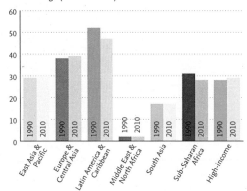

Source: Food and Agriculture Organization and World Bank estimates

Protected areas conserve habitat for plants and animals

Nationally protected terrestrial areas (% of total area), 2010

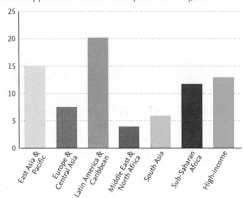

Source: United Nations Environment Programme;
World Conservation Monitoring Centre and World Bank estimates

Among developing regions, Latin America and the Caribbean and Sub-Saharan Africa have the largest areas of protected land

Regional distribution of protected land area (1,000 sq. km), 2010

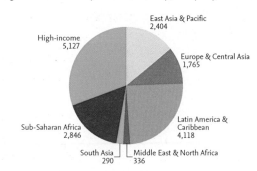

East Asia & Pacific 2,404
High-income 5,127
Europe & Central Asia 1,765
Sub-Saharan Africa 2,846
Latin America & Caribbean 4,118
South Asia 290
Middle East & North Africa 336

Source: United Nations Environment Programme;
World Conservation Monitoring Centre and World Bank estimates

Nearly 75 percent of all forest areas are in developing economies

Regional forest coverage (1,000 sq. km), 2010

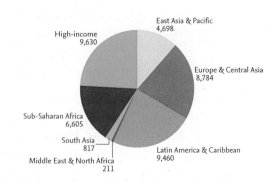

East Asia & Pacific 4,698
High-income 9,630
Europe & Central Asia 8,784
Sub-Saharan Africa 6,605
South Asia 817
Middle East & North Africa 211
Latin America & Caribbean 9,460

Source: Food and Agriculture Organization and World Bank estimates

A bend in the Ganga River, India

which they live. Tropical forests are particularly rich in diversity of life. In addition, forest loss in the tropics is responsible for 10 to 30 percent of global greenhouse gas emissions.

Deforestation is largely driven by human action. Because many services provided by forests are not valued, forests are subject to destructive and unsustainable exploitation that is not economically or environmentally justified. Forests are cleared to expand agricultural land or allow the exploitation of minerals. Timber is used to provide fuel and raw material for manufacturing and construction. In many cases, a proper accounting would show that forests are more valuable than these destructive uses.

Global deforestation is proceeding at 13 million hectares a year, but because of reforestation in some regions, net forest losses will average 5 million hectares a year between 2000 and 2010. New incentives and careful regulation are needed to stop deforestation. Forest areas may be designated as protected areas to prevent illegal and unsustainable exploitation. About 13 percent of the world's forest area is under protection, including some lower-density forest areas. Generally, the least well-protected forests are located in Africa.

Rainforest protected from destruction within the Argentinian sector of Iguazú National Park

FOREST LOST AND GAINED

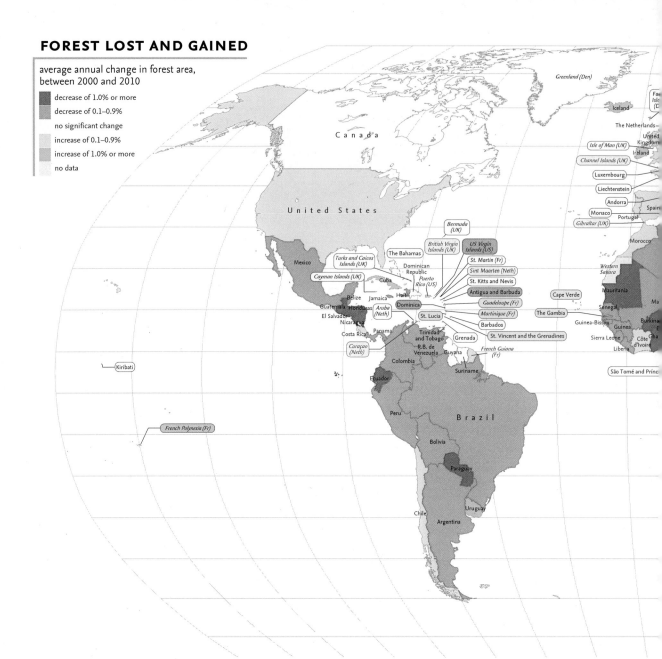

average annual change in forest area,
between 2000 and 2010

- decrease of 1.0% or more
- decrease of 0.1–0.9%
- no significant change
- increase of 0.1–0.9%
- increase of 1.0% or more
- no data

Indonesia is among the top 10 countries with the largest forest area

Countries with the largest forest area, 2010

Rank	Country	Forest area (1,000 sq. km)
1	Russian Federation	8,091
2	Brazil	5,195
3	Canada	3,101
4	United States	3,040
5	China	2,069
6	Congo, Dem. Rep.	1,541
7	Australia	1,493
8	Indonesia	944
9	Sudan	699
10	India	684

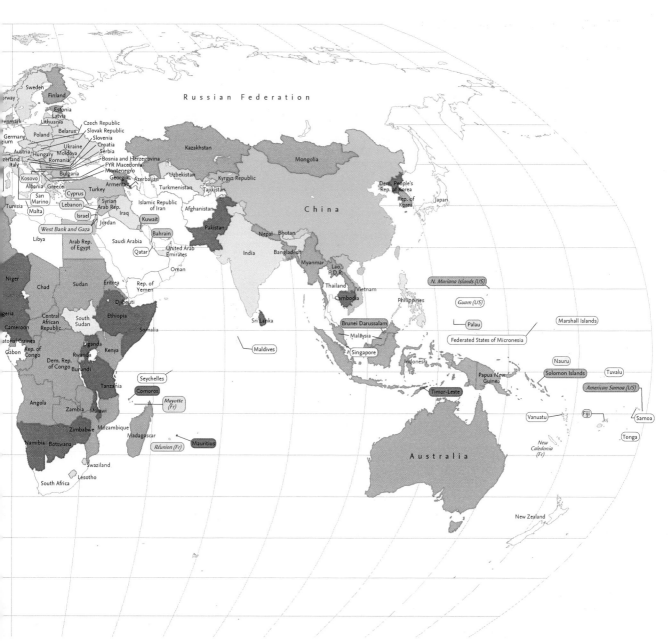

Russian Federation
China
Mongolia
Kazakhstan
Australia
New Zealand

Facts

▶ Between 1990 and 2010, the world lost about 138 million hectares of forest, almost 7 million hectares per year.

▶ China added an average of about 2.5 million hectares of forest each year from 1990 to 2010.

▶ The forest area in Brazil decreased by more than 55 million hectares, more than 40 percent of the world's forest loss, between 1990 and 2010.

▶ At the global level, deforestation seems to be slowing: the estimate of forest cover change indicates an annual loss of 5.3 million hectares during the years 2000 to 2010, compared with 13.8 million hectares annually between 1990 and 2010.

Internet links

▶ Food and Agriculture Organization—Forestry	**www.fao.org** (click on Forestry)
▶ International Union for Conservation of Nature	**www.iucn.org**
▶ Food and Agriculture Organization's Global Forest Resources Assessment 2010 database	**www.fao.org/forestry/fra2010**

PROTECTED AREAS

nationally protected terrestrial and marine areas
as a share of total land area, 2010

- less than 1.0%
- 1.0–4.9%
- 5.0–9.9%
- 10.0–19.9%
- 20.0% or more
- no data

Middle East & North Africa
4.0%

Latin America & Caribbean
19.8%

The Cara, one of the many species of fish found in the
Amazon region of Brazil near Manaus

Economies with the highest proportion of
protected terrestrial and marine areas, 2010

Rank	Economy	Terrestrial and marine protected areas (% of total territorial area)
1	Venezuela, RB	50
2	Liechtenstein	42
3	Germany	42
4	Hong Kong SAR, China	42
5	Greenland	40
6	Ecuador	38
7	Nicaragua	37
8	Zambia	36
9	Botswana	31
10	Saudi Arabia	30

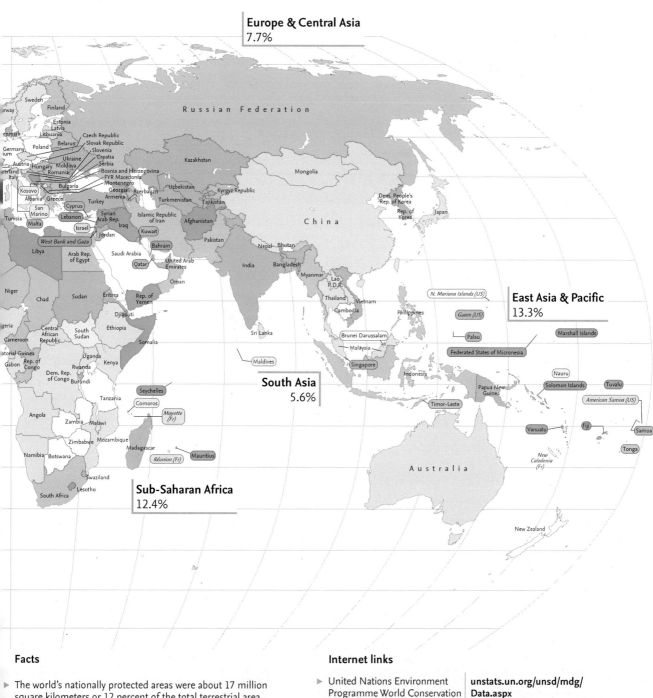

Europe & Central Asia
7.7%

East Asia & Pacific
13.3%

South Asia
5.6%

Sub-Saharan Africa
12.4%

Facts

▶ The world's nationally protected areas were about 17 million square kilometers or 12 percent of the total terrestrial area in 2010.

▶ Global marine protected areas were about 1.4 million square kilometers or 10 percent of the world's territorial waters up to 12 nautical miles in 2010.

▶ There were 130,709 nationally and 27,188 internationally designated marine and terrestrial protected areas in 2011.

▶ About 10 percent, or about 400 million hectares, of the world's forest area has been declared protected.

Internet links

▶ United Nations Environment Programme World Conservation Monitoring Centre	**unstats.un.org/unsd/mdg/ Data.aspx**
▶ International Union for Conservation of Nature	**www.iucn.org**
▶ World Database on Protected Areas	**www.wdpa.org/Default.aspx**
▶ Food and Agriculture Organization's Global Forest Resources Assessment 2010 database	**www.fao.org/forestry/fra2010**

Energy security and climate change

World demand for energy is surging. The share of energy production from alternative sources has increased slightly since 1990, but fossil fuels supplied more than 80 percent of the world's total energy production in 2009. Fossil fuels are the primary source of carbon dioxide emissions, which, along with the other greenhouse gases, are believed to be the principal cause of global climate change. Producing the energy needed for growth while mitigating its effects on the world's climate is a global challenge for everyone.

Developing countries contain more than five-sixths of the world's population and use more than half the world's energy, and their demand is growing faster than richer countries'. Energy use around the globe decreased by about 1 percent during the recession from 2007 to 2008, but in fast-growing East Asia and the Pacific, it grew by 5.3 percent.

As economies develop, technological progress and a shift away from energy-intensive activities help to increase energy efficiency, but rising incomes and growing populations increase the demand for energy. As a result, between 1990 and 2009, worldwide energy use increased by about 38 percent while the population rose by only 29 percent.

The way energy is generated determines its environmental consequences. The extensive use of fossil fuels in recent decades has boosted emissions of carbon dioxide,

Carbon dioxide emissions are highest in high-income economies, and still growing

Carbon dioxide emissions per capita (metric tons)

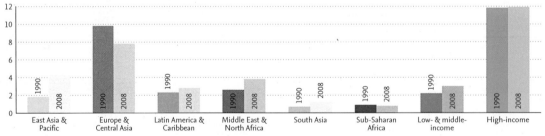

Source: Carbon Dioxide Information Analysis Center (CDIAC) and World Bank estimates

The four largest emitters account for about half of all carbon dioxide emissions produced in 2008, but average emissions per person in China and India are still quite low

Carbon dioxide emissions (billion metric tons)

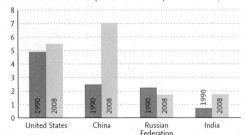

Source: Carbon Dioxide Information Analysis Center (CDIAC) and World Bank estimates

Carbon dioxide emissions per capita (metric tons)

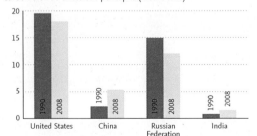

Source: Carbon Dioxide Information Analysis Center (CDIAC) and World Bank estimates

the principal greenhouse gas that traps heat in the atmosphere. Burning coal releases twice as much carbon dioxide as burning the equivalent amount of natural gas. It is estimated that half the amount of carbon released each year by human activities stays in the atmosphere, contributing to climate change; half the remaining carbon is being dissolved in the ocean and the other half is absorbed on land by vegetation and soils. Clearing of forests has reduced their ability to trap carbon dioxide.

The level of carbon dioxide in the atmosphere has increased by more than 30 percent since the beginning of the industrial revolution. According to the Intergovernmental Panel on Climate Change, the rate and duration of global warming in the 20th century are unprecedented in the past thousand years. The global average surface temperature has increased by about 0.6 degrees Celsius since 1861, the year instrument records became available, and the 1990s were the warmest decade yet recorded. A recent study found that average summer temperatures in the northern hemisphere are now about 0.5–0.6 degrees Celsius warmer than during a 1950–1980 base period. An important change in recent years is the emergence of extremely hot outliers. These hot extremes, which covered much less than 1 percent of Earth's surface during the base period, now typically cover about 10 percent of the land area. Warming is expected to continue, with increases in the range of 1.4–5.8 degrees Celsius over the next 100 years.

Global warming shrinks glaciers, changes the frequency and intensity of rainfall, shifts growing seasons, advances the flowering of trees and emergence of insects, and causes the sea level to rise. The magnitude and effect of climate change vary across regions, but developing countries are likely to suffer most because of their dependence on climate-sensitive activities such as agriculture and fishing. They also have more limited capacity to respond to the effects of climate change.

High-income economies use almost 50 percent of the world's energy, but developing countries' demand is rising

Energy use (million kilotons of oil equivalent)

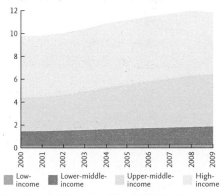

Low-income | Lower-middle-income | Upper-middle-income | High-income

Source: International Energy Agency (IEA) and World Bank estimates

Using solar energy to generate electricity has changed the lives of hundreds of rural families

Fossil fuels are the source of more than 80 percent of the world's energy supply

Global primary energy supply by sources, 2009

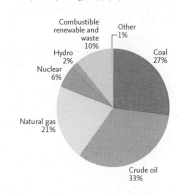

Combustible renewable and waste 10%
Other 1%
Hydro 2%
Nuclear 6%
Coal 27%
Natural gas 21%
Crude oil 33%

Source: International Energy Agency's World Energy Balance database

ENERGY USE

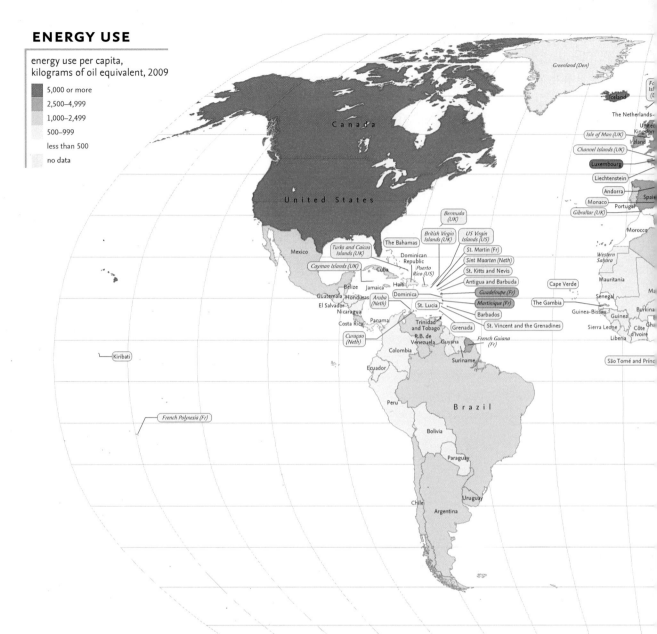

energy use per capita,
kilograms of oil equivalent, 2009

- 5,000 or more
- 2,500–4,999
- 1,000–2,499
- 500–999
- less than 500
- no data

Water pipes at mini hydroelectric plant

Countries with highest energy consumption, 2009

Rank	Country	Million metric tons of oil equivalent
1	China	2,257
2	United States	2,163
3	India	676
4	Russian Federation	647
5	Japan	472
6	Germany	319
7	France	256
8	Canada	254
9	Brazil	240
10	Korea, Rep.	229

Facts

- In 2009, petroleum, coal, and natural gas were the top sources of the world's energy supply, accounting for 33, 26, and 21 percent, respectively.

- Renewable energy from nuclear, hydro, and solar sources constituted less than 10 percent of the world's energy consumption in 2009.

- Sub-Saharan Africa still gets more than half of its energy from traditional combustible renewable sources and waste.

- China, Brazil, Canada, the United States, and the Russian Federation produce more than half of the world's hydropower energy.

- Latin America and the Caribbean produces more than 55 percent of its electricity from hydropower.

- About 1.8 billion people in the world live without access to electricity.

- In Sub-Saharan Africa, almost 68 percent of people live without access to electricity.

Internet links

▶ International Energy Agency	**www.iea.org**
▶ The World Bank Group Energy Program	**www.worldbank.org/energy**
▶ International Energy Agency's *World Energy Outlook*	**www.iea.org/publications/ worldenergyoutlook/resources**

GREENHOUSE GASES

carbon dioxide emissions per capita, 2008

- 15.0 metric tons or more
- 10.0–14.9 metric tons
- 5.0–9.9 metric tons
- 1.0–4.9 metric tons
- less than 1.0 metric tons
- no data

Greenland (Den)

Iceland

Fa
Isle
(D

The Netherlands

Isle of Man (UK)
United
Kingdom
Ireland

Channel Islands (UK)

Luxembourg

Liechtenstein

Andorra

Monaco

Gibraltar (UK)

Portugal

Spain

Morocco

Canada

United States

Bermuda (UK)

British Virgin Islands (UK)

The Bahamas

Middle East & North Africa
3.8 metric tons

Western Sahara

Mauritania

Mexico

Dominican Republic

Puerto Rico (US)

Cuba

Cayman Islands (UK)

Turks and Caicos Islands (UK)

US Virgin Islands (US)

St. Martin (Fr)

Sint Maarten (Neth)

St. Kitts and Nevis

Antigua and Barbuda

Guadeloupe (Fr)

Martinique (Fr)

Barbados

St. Vincent and the Grenadines

Cape Verde

Senegal

The Gambia

Guinea-Bissau

Guinea

Mali

Burkina

Sierra Leone

Côte d'Ivoire

Liberia

Gha

Belize
Jamaica
Haiti
Guatemala Honduras
El Salvador
Nicaragua
Costa Rica
Panama

Aruba (Neth)
Dominica
St. Lucia
Grenada

Trinidad and Tobago

R.B. de Venezuela

Guyana

Colombia

Curaçao (Neth)

French Guiana (Fr)

São Tomé and Princ

Latin America & Caribbean
2.8 metric tons

Ecuador

Suriname

Kiribati

Peru

Brazil

French Polynesia (Fr)

Bolivia

Paraguay

Chile

Uruguay

Argentina

Use of biomass energy increases health risks for many poor people who depend on biomass energy from plant materials or animal wastes for cooking and heating

Greatest increase in emissions between 1990 and 2008

Rank	Country	Increase in carbon dioxide emissions (million metric tons of oil equivalent)
1	China	4,571
2	India	1,052
3	United States	582
4	Iran, Islamic Rep.	311
5	Korea, Rep.	265
6	Indonesia	256
7	Saudi Arabia	219
8	Thailand	190
9	Brazil	184
10	Malaysia	152

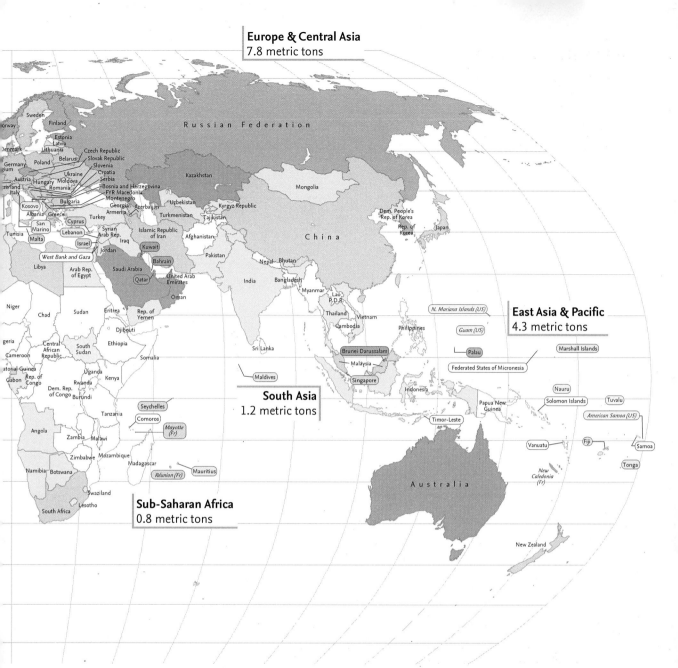

Europe & Central Asia
7.8 metric tons

East Asia & Pacific
4.3 metric tons

South Asia
1.2 metric tons

Sub-Saharan Africa
0.8 metric tons

Facts

▶ Between 1990 and 2008, the world's carbon dioxide energy-related emissions rose by 36 percent to 30.2 billion metric tons. They are projected to rise to 35.2 billion metric tons in 2020 and 43.2 billion metric tons in 2035.

▶ High-income economies emit more than four times as much carbon dioxide per person as developing economies.

▶ Developing countries emitted nearly half the world's 32 billion metric tons of total carbon dioxide emissions in 2008.

▶ Carbon dioxide concentrations in the atmosphere have increased from 280 parts per million in preindustrial times to 390.4 in 2011 —an increase of more than 39 percent—and will likely reach 400 by 2016.

▶ Carbon dioxide constitutes about 75 percent of global greenhouse gas emissions.

Internet links

▶ U.S. Energy Information Administration	**www.eia.gov/**
▶ Intergovernmental Panel on Climate Change	**www.ipcc.ch**
▶ Carbon Dioxide Information Analysis Center	**cdiac.ornl.gov**
▶ National Oceanic and Atmospheric Administration (NOAA)	**www.noaa.gov/**
▶ The IEA Greenhouse Gas R&D Programme	**www.ieaghg.org**

Key indicators of development

Economy	Total population millions 2011	Life expectancy at birth years 2010	Under-5 mortality rate per 1,000 live births 2011	Access to an improved water source % of population 2010	Gross national income (GNI)[a]	
					$ billions 2011	per capita $ 2011
Afghanistan	35.32	48	101	50	14.3	410
Albania	3.22	77	14	95	12.8	3,980
Algeria	35.98	73	30	83	160.8	4,470
American Samoa	0.07	..	..	..	..	.. d
Andorra	0.09	..	3	100	..	.. e
Angola	19.62	51	158	51	79.7	4,060
Antigua and Barbuda	0.09	..	8	..	1.1	12,060
Argentina	40.76	76	14	..	397.2	9,740
Armenia	3.10	74	18	98	10.4	3,360
Aruba	0.11	75	..	100	..	.. e
Australia	22.62	82	5	100	1,030.3	46,200
Austria	8.42	80	4	100	406.6	48,300
Azerbaijan	9.17	71	45	80	48.5	5,290
Bahamas, The	0.35	75	16	..	7.5	21,970
Bahrain	1.32	75	10	..	20.1	15,920
Bangladesh	150.49	69	46	81	116.4	770
Barbados	0.27	77	20	100	3.5	12,660
Belarus	9.47	70	6	100	55.3	5,830
Belgium	11.01	80	4	100	508.1	46,160
Belize	0.36	76	17	98	1.3	3,690
Benin	9.10	56	106	75	7.1	780
Bermuda	0.06	79	..	..	..	.. e
Bhutan	0.74	67	54	96	1.5	2,070
Bolivia	10.09	66	51	88	20.5	2,040
Bosnia and Herzegovina	3.75	75	8	99	18.0	4,780
Botswana	2.03	53	26	96	15.2	7,480
Brazil	196.66	73	16	98	2,107.6	10,720
Brunei Darussalam	0.41	78	7	..	12.5	31,800
Bulgaria	7.48	74	12	100	48.9	6,550
Burkina Faso	16.97	55	146	79	9.7	570
Burundi	8.58	50	139	72	2.2	250
Cambodia	14.31	63	43	64	11.8	830
Cameroon	20.03	51	127	77	24.2	1,210
Canada	34.48	81	6	100	1,570.9	45,560
Cape Verde	0.50	74	21	88	1.8	3,540
Cayman Islands	0.06	..	..	96	..	.. e
Central African Republic	4.49	48	164	67	2.1	470
Chad	11.53	49	169	51	8.0	690
Channel Islands	0.15	80	..	..	..	.. e
Chile	17.27	79	9	96	212.0	12,280
China	1,344.13	73	15	91	6,644.3	4,940
Hong Kong SAR, China	7.07	83	..	..	248.7	35,160
Macao SAR, China	0.56	81	..	..	24.7	45,460
Colombia	46.93	73	18	92	286.5	6,110
Comoros	0.75	61	79	95	0.6	770
Congo, Dem. Rep.	67.76	48	168	45	13.1	190
Congo, Rep.	4.14	57	99	71	9.4	2,270
Costa Rica	4.73	79	10	97	36.2	7,660
Côte d'Ivoire	20.15	55	115	80	22.1	1,100
Croatia	4.41	76	5	99	61.0	13,850
Cuba	11.25	79	6	94	..	.. d
Curaçao	0.15	..	..	..	..	.. e
Cyprus	1.12	79	3	100	23.7 f	29,450 f
Czech Republic	10.55	77	4	100	195.3	18,520
Denmark	5.57	79	4	100	336.6	60,390
Djibouti	0.91	58	90	88	1.1	1,270
Dominica	0.07	..	12	..	0.5	7,090
Dominican Republic	10.06	73	25	86	52.6	5,240
Ecuador	14.67	75	23	94	60.7	4,140
Egypt, Arab Rep.	82.54	73	21	99	214.7	2,600
El Salvador	6.23	72	15	88	21.7	3,480
Equatorial Guinea	0.72	51	118	..	10.5	14,540
Eritrea	5.42	61	68	..	2.3	430
Estonia	1.34	75	4	98	20.4	15,200
Ethiopia	84.73	59	77	44	33.8	400
Faeroe Islands	0.05	..	..	..	..	.. e
Fiji	0.87	69	16	98	3.2	3,680
Finland	5.39	80	3	100	260.8	48,420
France	65.44	81	4	100	2,775.7	42,420
French Polynesia	0.27	75	..	100	..	.. e
Gabon	1.53	62	66	87	12.2	7,980
Gambia, The	1.78	58	101	89	1.1	610
Georgia	4.49	73	21	98	12.8 g	2,860 g
Germany	81.73	80	4	100	3,594.3	43,980
Ghana	24.97	64	78	86	35.1	1,410
Greece	11.30	80	4	100	283.0	25,030

Total debt service % of exports of goods, services and income[b] 2010	Merchandise trade % of GDP 2010	Foreign direct investment net inflows, % of GDP 2010	Starting a business time required in days June 2011	Mobile cellular subscriptions[c] per 100 people 2011	Carbon dioxide emissions per capita metric tons 2008	Economy
..	28	0.4	7	54	0.0	Afghanistan
11.1	52	9.4	5	96	1.3	Albania
1.0	60	1.4	25	99	3.2	Algeria
..	..	..	..	..	..	American Samoa
..	..	..	..	75	6.5	Andorra
4.5	91	-3.9	68	48	1.4	Angola
..	55	8.4	21	182	5.1	Antigua and Barbuda
16.7	34	1.6	26	135	4.8	Argentina
33.4	51	6.5	8	104	1.8	Armenia
..	..	..	..	123	21.7	Aruba
..	37	2.7	2	108	18.6	Australia
..	83	3.3	28	155	8.1	Austria
1.4	63	2.3	8	109	5.4	Azerbaijan
..	42	7.6	31	86	6.5	Bahamas, The
..	103	0.7	9	128	21.4	Bahrain
4.7	47	0.7	19	56	0.3	Bangladesh
..	49	16.3	..	127	5.0	Barbados
4.6	109	7.2	5	112	6.5	Belarus
..	172	18.0	4	117	9.8	Belgium
12.1	74	6.2	44	64	1.3	Belize
..	52	1.7	29	85	0.5	Benin
..	17	7.0	..	136	6.1	Bermuda
..	86	1.3	36	66	1.0	Bhutan
9.3	59	3.2	50	83	1.3	Bolivia
19.9	84	2.4	40	85	8.3	Bosnia and Herzegovina
1.5	69	1.8	61	143	2.5	Botswana
19.0	18	2.7	119	123	2.1	Brazil
..	98	4.0	101	109	27.5	Brunei Darussalam
14.2	97	3.4	18	141	6.6	Bulgaria
..	38	0.4	13	45	0.1	Burkina Faso
..	30	0.0	14	14	0.0	Burundi
..	111	7.0	85	70	0.3	Cambodia
3.6	39	0.0	15	52	0.3	Cameroon
..	50	2.4	5	75	16.3	Canada
5.3	47	6.7	11	79	0.6	Cape Verde
..	..	..	..	168	10.1	Cayman Islands
..	24	3.6	21	25	0.1	Central African Republic
..	71	9.1	66	32	0.0	Chad
..	..	..	..	..	..	Channel Islands
15.2	60	7.0	7	130	4.4	Chile
3.3	50	3.1	38	73	5.3	China
..	376	34.1	3	210	5.5	Hong Kong SAR, China
..	23	12.3	..	243	2.6	Macao SAR, China
21.0	28	4.0	14	98	1.5	Colombia
..	38	1.7	24	29	0.2	Comoros
3.8	75	22.4	65	23	0.0	Congo, Dem. Rep.
..	92	23.5	160	94	0.5	Congo, Rep.
7.7	63	5.1	60	92	1.8	Costa Rica
..	79	1.8	32	86	0.4	Côte d'Ivoire
..	52	2.3	7	116	5.3	Croatia
..	..	..	..	12	2.8	Cuba
..	..	..	..	..	..	Curaçao
..	43	1.0	8	98	7.9	Cyprus
..	131	2.5	20	122	11.2	Czech Republic
..	58	4.6	6	126	8.4	Denmark
7.5	..	..	37	21	0.6	Djibouti
9.8	58	5.2	14	164	1.9	Dominica
11.0	42	3.2	19	87	2.2	Dominican Republic
9.4	66	0.3	56	105	1.9	Ecuador
6.0	36	2.9	7	101	2.7	Egypt, Arab Rep.
19.0	61	1.5	17	126	1.0	El Salvador
..	112	4.8	137	59	7.3	Equatorial Guinea
..	33	2.6	84	4	0.1	Eritrea
..	127	0.8	7	139	13.6	Estonia
..	36	1.0	9	17	0.1	Ethiopia
..	..	..	..	122	14.6	Faeroe Islands
..	71	6.2	45	84	1.5	Fiji
..	58	0.0	14	166	10.6	Finland
..	44	1.5	7	105	5.9	France
..	..	..	..	81	3.4	French Polynesia
..	94	1.3	58	117	1.7	Gabon
7.2	28	3.2	27	89	0.3	Gambia, The
18.1	57	6.8	2	102	1.2	Georgia
..	72	1.1	15	132	9.6	Germany
3.4	58	7.9	12	85	0.4	Ghana
..	28	0.6	10	106	8.7	Greece

Economy	Total population millions 2011	Life expectancy at birth years 2010	Under-5 mortality rate per 1,000 live births 2011	Access to an improved water source % of population 2010	Gross national income (GNI)[a] $ billions 2011	per capita $ 2011
Greenland	0.06	..	..	100	1.5	26,020
Grenada	0.10	76	13	..	0.8	7,220
Guam	0.18	76	..	100	..	.. e
Guatemala	14.76	71	30	92	42.4	2,870
Guinea	10.22	54	126	74	4.5	440
Guinea-Bissau	1.55	48	161	64	0.9	600
Guyana	0.76	70	36	94	2.2	2,900
Haiti	10.12	62	70	69	7.1	700
Honduras	7.75	73	21	87	15.3	1,970
Hungary	9.97	74	6	100	126.9	12,730
Iceland	0.32	81	3	100	11.2	35,020
India	1,241.49	65	61	92	1,746.5	1,410
Indonesia	242.33	69	32	82	712.7	2,940
Iran, Islamic Rep.	74.80	73	25	96	330.4	4,520
Iraq	32.96	68	38	79	87.0	2,640
Ireland	4.49	80	4	100	173.1	38,580
Isle of Man	0.08	..	..	..	..	.. e
Israel	7.77	82	4	100	224.7	28,930
Italy	60.77	82	4	100	2,147.0	35,330
Jamaica	2.71	73	18	93	13.5	4,980
Japan	127.82	83	3	100	5,774.4	45,180
Jordan	6.18	73	21	97	27.1	4,380
Kazakhstan	16.56	68	28	95	136.1	8,220
Kenya	41.61	56	73	59	34.2	820
Kiribati	0.10	..	47	..	0.2	2,110
Korea, Dem. Rep.	24.45	69	33	98	..	.. h
Korea, Rep.	49.78	81	5	98	1,039.0	20,870
Kosovo	1.79	70	..	..	6.3	3,520
Kuwait	2.82	75	11	99	133.8	48,900
Kyrgyz Republic	5.51	69	31	90	5.1	920
Lao P.D.R.	6.29	67	42	67	7.1	1,130
Latvia	2.22	73	8	99	27.4	12,350
Lebanon	4.26	72	9	100	38.8	9,110
Lesotho	2.19	47	86	78	2.7	1,220
Liberia	4.13	56	78	73	1.0	240
Libya	6.42	75	16	..	77.1	12,320
Liechtenstein	0.04	..	2	..	4.9	137,070
Lithuania	3.20	73	6	..	39.3	12,280
Luxembourg	0.52	80	3	100	40.4	78,130
Macedonia, FYR	2.06	75	10	100	9.8	4,730
Madagascar	21.32	66	62	46	9.1	430
Malawi	15.38	53	83	83	5.2	340
Malaysia	28.86	74	7	100	243.1	8,420
Maldives	0.32	77	11	98	2.1	6,530
Mali	15.84	51	176	64	9.6	610
Malta	0.42	81	6	100	7.7	18,620
Marshall Islands	0.05	..	26	94	0.2	3,910
Mauritania	3.54	58	112	50	3.5	1,000
Mauritius	1.29	73	15	99	10.6	8,240
Mexico	114.79	77	16	96	1,060.2	9,240
Micronesia, Fed. Sts.	0.11	69	42	..	0.3	2,900
Moldova	3.56	69	16	96	7.1 i	1,980 i
Monaco	0.04	..	4	100	6.5	183,150
Mongolia	2.80	68	31	82	6.5	2,320
Montenegro	0.63	74	7	98	4.5	7,060
Morocco	32.27	72	33	83	97.6 j	2,970 j
Mozambique	23.93	50	103	47	11.2	470
Myanmar	48.34	65	62	83	..	.. h
Namibia	2.32	62	42	93	10.9	4,700
Nepal	30.49	68	48	89	16.6	540
Netherlands	16.70	81	4	100	830.2	49,730
New Caledonia	0.25	76	..	..	..	.. e
New Zealand	4.41	81	6	100	128.2	29,350
Nicaragua	5.87	74	26	85	6.8	1,170
Niger	16.07	54	125	49	5.8	360
Nigeria	162.47	51	124	58	195.3	1,200
Northern Mariana Islands	0.06	..	..	98	..	.. e
Norway	4.95	81	3	100	440.2	88,890
Oman	2.85	73	9	89	53.6	19,260
Pakistan	176.75	65	72	92	197.6	1,120
Palau	0.02	..	19	85	0.1	7,250
Panama	3.57	76	20	..	28.3	7,910
Papua New Guinea	7.01	62	58	40	10.4	1,480
Paraguay	6.57	72	22	86	19.5	2,970
Peru	29.40	74	18	85	161.7	5,500
Philippines	94.85	68	25	92	209.4	2,210
Poland	38.22	76	6	..	477.0	12,480
Portugal	10.64	79	3	99	226.0	21,250
Puerto Rico	3.71	79	..	..	61.6	16,560

Total debt service % of exports of goods, services and income[b] 2010	Merchandise trade % of GDP 2010	Foreign direct investment net inflows, % of GDP 2010	Starting a business time required in days June 2011	Mobile cellular subscriptions[c] per 100 people 2011	Carbon dioxide emissions per capita metric tons 2008	Economy
..	..	..	..	103	10.2	Greenland
14.3	40	7.7	15	117	2.4	Grenada
..	..	..	..	..	..	Guam
14.3	54	2.2	37	140	0.9	Guatemala
5.6	50	2.1	40	44	0.1	Guinea
..	41	1.1	9	26	0.2	Guinea-Bissau
..	101	11.9	26	69	2.0	Guyana
15.7	56	2.3	105	41	0.3	Haiti
7.6	93	5.9	14	104	1.2	Honduras
..	143	17.1	4	117	5.4	Hungary
..	68	7.2	5	106	7.0	Iceland
5.6	34	1.4	29	72	1.5	India
16.6	41	2.1	45	98	1.7	Indonesia
..	..	..	8	75	7.4	Iran, Islamic Rep.
..	117	1.8	77	78	3.4	Iraq
..	86	6.4	13	108	9.9	Ireland
..	..	..	..	..	..	Isle of Man
..	55	4.7	34	122	5.2	Israel
..	46	1.5	6	152	7.4	Italy
27.9	47	1.6	7	108	4.5	Jamaica
..	27	0.0	23	103	9.5	Japan
4.9	85	6.4	12	118	3.7	Jordan
71.4	60	6.9	19	143	15.1	Kazakhstan
4.4	54	0.6	33	65	0.3	Kenya
..	73	2.4	31	14	0.3	Kiribati
..	..	..	..	4	3.2	Korea, Dem. Rep.
..	88	0.4	7	109	10.4	Korea, Rep.
1.6	..	8.5	58	..	..	Kosovo
..	72	0.1	32	161	30.1	Kuwait
21.9	104	6.6	10	105	1.2	Kyrgyz Republic
..	47	3.9	93	87	0.3	Lao P.D.R.
76.4	88	5.5	16	103	3.3	Latvia
19.1	60	11.0	9	79	4.1	Lebanon
1.9	139	5.4	40	48	..	Lesotho
1.3	94	45.8	6	49	0.2	Liberia
..	..	..	..	156	9.5	Libya
..	..	..	..	102	..	Liechtenstein
34.3	122	2.9	22	151	4.5	Lithuania
..	82	542.9	19	148	21.5	Luxembourg
15.2	96	4.0	3	109	5.8	Macedonia, FYR
2.6	43	9.9	8	38	0.1	Madagascar
..	59	2.8	39	25	0.1	Malawi
5.2	153	3.9	6	127	7.6	Malaysia
21.3	62	7.9	9	166	3.0	Maldives
2.5	55	1.6	8	68	0.0	Mali
..	82	12.2	..	125	6.2	Malta
..	90	5.3	17	7	1.9	Marshall Islands
..	107	0.4	19	93	0.6	Mauritania
2.4	68	4.4	6	99	3.1	Mauritius
9.8	59	1.7	9	82	4.3	Mexico
..	61	3.4	16	25	0.6	Micronesia, Fed. Sts.
12.8	94	3.9	9	105	1.3	Moldova
..	..	..	..	86	..	Monaco
5.0	100	23.5	13	105	4.1	Mongolia
5.9	65	18.5	10	185	3.1	Montenegro
10.7	58	2.5	12	113	1.5	Morocco
2.9	84	8.6	13	33	0.1	Mozambique
..	..	..	..	3	0.3	Myanmar
..	85	7.1	66	105	1.8	Namibia
10.5	38	0.5	29	44	0.1	Nepal
..	141	1.9	8	115	10.6	Netherlands
..	..	..	..	89	12.9	New Caledonia
..	44	0.5	1	109	7.8	New Zealand
14.3	91	13.3	39	82	0.8	Nicaragua
..	57	17.5	17	27	0.1	Niger
0.4	64	3.1	34	59	0.6	Nigeria
..	..	..	..	..	..	Northern Mariana Islands
..	50	2.8	7	117	10.5	Norway
..	98	1.1	8	169	17.3	Oman
15.2	34	1.1	21	62	1.0	Pakistan
..	74	1.4	28	75	10.5	Palau
5.7	37	8.8	8	204	2.0	Panama
12.9	100	0.3	51	34	0.3	Papua New Guinea
4.6	80	2.1	35	99	0.7	Paraguay
16.7	43	4.8	26	110	1.4	Peru
18.4	55	0.6	35	92	0.9	Philippines
..	70	2.8	32	128	8.3	Poland
..	55	4.3	5	115	5.3	Portugal
..	..	..	6	83	..	Puerto Rico

Economy	Total population millions 2011	Life expectancy at birth years 2010	Under-5 mortality rate per 1,000 live births 2011	Access to an improved water source % of population 2010	Gross national income (GNI)[a] $ billions 2011	per capita $ 2011
Qatar	1.87	78	8	100	150.4	80,440
Romania	21.39	73	13	..	169.2	7,910
Russian Federation	141.93	69	12	97	1,476.1	10,400
Rwanda	10.94	55	54	65	6.2	570
Samoa	0.18	72	19	96	0.6	3,190
San Marino	0.03	83	2	..	..	.. e
São Tomé and Principe	0.17	64	89	89	0.2	1,360
Saudi Arabia	28.08	74	9	..	500.5	17,820
Senegal	12.77	59	65	72	13.7	1,070
Serbia	7.26	74	7	99	41.2	5,680
Seychelles	0.09	73	14	..	1.0	11,130
Sierra Leone	6.00	47	185	55	2.1	340
Singapore	5.18	82	3	100	222.6	42,930
Sint Maarten (Dutch part)	0.04	..	..	..	..	.. e
Slovak Republic	5.44	75	8	100	87.4	16,070
Slovenia	2.05	79	3	99	48.5	23,610
Solomon Islands	0.55	67	22	..	0.6	1,110
Somalia	9.56	51	180	29	..	.. h
South Africa	50.59	52	47	91	352.0	6,960
South Sudan	10.31	..	121	..	..	.. k
Spain	46.24	82	4	100	1,432.8	30,990
Sri Lanka	20.87	75	12	91	53.8	2,580
St. Kitts and Nevis	0.05	..	7	99	0.7	12,480
St. Lucia	0.18	74	16	96	1.2	6,680
St. Martin (French part)	0.03	..	..	..	..	.. e
St. Vincent and the Grenadines	0.11	72	21	..	0.7	6,100
Sudan	34.32	61	86	58	56.7 l	1,300 l
Suriname	0.53	70	30	92	4.0	7,640
Swaziland	1.07	48	104	71	3.5	3,300
Sweden	9.45	81	3	100	503.2	53,230
Switzerland	7.91	82	4	100	603.9	76,380
Syrian Arab Republic	20.82	76	15	90	56.3	2,750
Tajikistan	6.98	67	63	64	6.1	870
Tanzania	46.22	57	68	53	24.3 m	540 m
Thailand	69.52	74	12	96	307.1	4,420
Timor-Leste	1.18	62	54	69	3.1	2,730
Togo	6.15	57	110	61	3.4	560
Tonga	0.10	72	15	100	0.4	3,580
Trinidad and Tobago	1.35	70	28	94	20.2	15,040
Tunisia	10.67	75	16	..	43.4	4,070
Turkey	73.64	74	15	100	766.4	10,410
Turkmenistan	5.11	65	53	..	21.0	4,110
Turks and Caicos Islands	0.04	..	..	100	..	.. e
Tuvalu	0.01	..	30	98	0.0	5,010
Uganda	34.51	54	90	72	17.5	510
Ukraine	45.71	70	10	98	142.8	3,120
United Arab Emirates	7.89	77	7	100	321.7	40,760
United Kingdom	62.64	80	5	100	2,366.5	37,780
United States	311.59	78	8	99	15,097.1	48,450
Uruguay	3.37	76	10	100	40.0	11,860
Uzbekistan	29.34	68	49	87	44.2	1,510
Vanuatu	0.25	71	13	90	0.7	2,870
Venezuela, R.B.	29.28	74	15	..	349.1	11,920
Vietnam	87.84	75	22	95	110.9	1,260
Virgin Islands (U.S.)	0.11	79	..	..	..	.. e
West Bank and Gaza	4.02	73	22	85	..	.. k
Yemen, Rep.	24.80	65	77	55	26.4	1,070
Zambia	13.47	48	83	61	15.6	1,160
Zimbabwe	12.75	50	67	80	8.1	640
World	6,973.74 s	70 w	52 w	88 w	66,185.0 t	9,491 w
Low-income	816.81	59	95	65	463.0	567
Middle-income	5,021.92	69	47	90	20,717.3	4,125
Lower-middle-income	2,532.83	66	63	87	4,457.7	1,760
Upper-middle-income	2,489.10	73	20	93	16,253.0	6,530
Low- & middle- income	5,838.73	68	57	86	21,203.3	3,631
East Asia & Pacific	1,974.22	72	21	90	8,376.8	4,243
Europe & Central Asia	407.56	71	21	96	3,101.4	7,610
Latin America & Caribbean	589.02	74	19	94	5,032.8	8,544
Middle East & North Africa	336.63	72	32	89	1,280.6	3,869
South Asia	1,656.46	65	62	90	2,151.1	1,299
Sub-Saharan Africa	874.84	54	108	61	1,098.1	1,255
High-income	1,135.00	80	6	100	45,153.9	39,783
Euro area	332.99	81	4	100	12,844.3	38,573

See page 142 for explanation of symbols.
Note: Figures in *italics* are for years other than those specified.
a. Calculated using World Bank Atlas method.
b. Exports include workers' remittances.

c. Data are from the International Telecommunication Union's (ITU) World Telecommunication/ICT Indicators database. Please cite ITU for third-party use of these data.
d. Estimated to be upper-middle-income ($4,036 to $12,475).
e. Estimated to be high-income ($12,476 or more).

Total debt service % of exports of goods, services and income[b] 2010	Merchandise trade % of GDP 2010	Foreign direct investment net inflows, % of GDP 2010	Starting a business time required in days June 2011	Mobile cellular subscriptions[c] per 100 people 2011	Carbon dioxide emissions per capita metric tons 2008	Economy
..	67	4.3	12	123	49.1	Qatar
31.2	69	1.5	14	109	4.4	Romania
12.8	44	2.8	30	179	12.0	Russian Federation
2.3	31	0.8	3	41	0.1	Rwanda
5.2	62	0.1	9	91	0.9	Samoa
..	..	..	..	112	..	San Marino
6.5	61	12.3	10	68	0.8	São Tomé and Principe
..	77	2.8	5	191	16.6	Saudi Arabia
..	54	1.8	5	73	0.4	Senegal
30.9	69	6.0	13	125	6.8	Serbia
5.7	109	17.4	39	146	7.8	Seychelles
2.6	58	4.5	12	36	0.2	Sierra Leone
..	311	18.1	3	149	6.7	Singapore
..	..	..	..	..	..	Sint Maarten (Dutch part)
..	151	0.6	18	109	6.9	Slovak Republic
..	127	2.2	6	107	8.5	Slovenia
5.9	93	35.1	43	50	0.4	Solomon Islands
..	..	..	..	7	0.1	Somalia
4.9	48	1.4	19	127	8.9	South Africa
..	..	..	..	..	..	South Sudan
..	40	1.7	28	114	7.2	Spain
13.0	44	1.0	35	87	0.6	Sri Lanka
23.2	51	17.9	19	153	4.9	St. Kitts and Nevis
7.1	59	9.2	15	123	2.3	St. Lucia
..	..	..	..	..	..	St. Martin (French part)
16.4	62	15.3	10	121	1.8	St. Vincent and the Grenadines
4.2	32	3.1	36	56	0.3	Sudan
..	81	-5.9	694	179	4.7	Suriname
..	88	3.7	56	64	1.1	Swaziland
..	66	2.3	15	119	5.3	Sweden
..	70	0.4	18	130	5.3	Switzerland
..	51	2.5	13	63	3.6	Syrian Arab Republic
44.8	73	0.3	24	91	0.5	Tajikistan
3.0	50	1.9	29	56	0.2	Tanzania
4.8	118	3.0	29	113	4.2	Thailand
..	36	32.0	103	53	0.2	Timor-Leste
..	74	1.3	84	50	0.2	Togo
9.1	50	4.5	16	53	1.7	Tonga
..	82	2.6	43	136	37.4	Trinidad and Tobago
10.4	87	3.2	11	117	2.4	Tunisia
36.7	41	2.1	6	89	4.0	Turkey
..	60	10.4	..	69	9.7	Turkmenistan
..	..	..	..	..	4.4	Turks and Caicos Islands
..	52	4.8	..	22	..	Tuvalu
1.8	36	4.7	34	48	0.1	Uganda
40.7	82	4.4	24	123	7.0	Ukraine
..	128	1.3	13	149	25.0	United Arab Emirates
..	43	2.2	13	131	8.5	United Kingdom
..	22	1.5	6	106	18.0	United States
12.4	39	4.1	7	141	2.5	Uruguay
..	51	2.1	14	92	4.6	Uzbekistan
1.7	48	5.6	35	119	0.4	Vanuatu
8.8	27	1.7	141	98	6.1	Venezuela, R.B.
1.7	148	7.5	44	143	1.5	Vietnam
..	..	..	..	..	..	Virgin Islands (U.S.)
..	..	..	49	46	0.5	West Bank and Gaza
2.8	59	0.2	12	47	1.0	Yemen, Rep.
1.9	77	10.3	18	61	0.2	Zambia
..	84	1.4	90	72	0.7	Zimbabwe
.. w	48 w	2.6 w	31 u	86 w	4.8 w	World
4.8	52	3.1	33	41	0.3	Low-income
9.9	48	2.6	36	86	3.4	Middle-income
10.1	47	2.2	33	79	1.5	Lower-middle-income
9.9	48	2.7	40	92	5.3	Upper-middle-income
9.8	48	2.6	35	79	3.0	Low- & middle-income
4.8	57	3.1	39	80	4.3	East Asia & Pacific
24.2	52	3.1	16	132	7.8	Europe & Central Asia
13.8	35	2.4	58	107	2.8	Latin America & Caribbean
5.1	61	2.7	23	89	3.8	Middle East & North Africa
6.4	34	1.4	23	69	1.2	South Asia
3.3	58	2.3	34	53	0.8	Sub-Saharan Africa
..	48	2.6	17	117	11.9	High-income
..	66	4.7	12	126	8.0	Euro area

f. Data are for the area controlled by the government of the Republic of Cyprus.
g. Data excludes Abkhazia and South Ossetia.
h. Estimated to be low-income ($1,025 or less).
i. Data excludes Transnistria.

j. Data includes Former Spanish Sahara.
k. Estimated to be lower-middle-income ($1,026 to $4,035).
l. Data includes South Sudan.
m. Data refer to mainland Tanzania only.

Ranking of economies by GNI per capita

Rank	Economy	Atlas methodology $	Purchasing power parity international $	PPP rank
1	Monaco	183,150 a	..	..
2	Liechtenstein	137,070 a	..	..
3	Bermuda	.. a	..	..
4	Norway	88,890	62,970	6
5	Qatar	80,440	87,030	3
6	Luxembourg	78,130	64,410	5
7	Switzerland	76,380	52,320	12
8	Isle of Man	.. a	..	..
9	Denmark	60,390	42,300	22
10	Channel Islands	.. a	..	..
11	Sweden	53,230	42,200	23
12	Cayman Islands	.. a	..	..
13	Faeroe Islands	.. a	..	..
14	Netherlands	49,730	43,260	21
15	Kuwait	48,900 a	53,820 a	10
16	United States	48,450	48,890	16
17	Finland	48,420	38,500	32
18	Austria	48,300	42,080	24
19	Australia	46,200 a	36,410 a	33
20	Macao SAR, China	45,462 a	57,060 a	8
21	Belgium	46,160	39,270	31
22	Canada	45,560	39,730	30
23	Japan	45,180	35,530	36
25	Germany	43,980	39,970	27
27	Singapore	42,930	59,790	7
28	France	42,420	35,650	35
29	United Arab Emirates	40,760	48,220 b	17
32	Ireland	38,580	33,230	37
34	United Kingdom	37,780	35,940	34
35	Greenland	26,020 a	..	..
36	Italy	35,330	32,710	38
37	Hong Kong SAR, China	35,160	51,490	13
38	Iceland	35,020	30,760	43
39	Brunei Darussalam	31,800 a	49,790 a	14
40	Spain	30,990	31,660	39
41	Cyprus	29,450 a,c	30,910 a,c	42
42	New Zealand	29,350 a	28,970 a	46
43	Israel	28,930	27,120	51
46	Greece	25,030	26,090	54
47	Slovenia	23,610	26,960	52
48	Bahamas, The	21,970 a	29,850 a,b	45
51	Portugal	21,250	24,480	59
53	Korea, Rep.	20,870	30,340	44
55	Oman	19,260 a	25,770 a	53
56	Malta	18,620 a	24,170 a	58
57	Czech Republic .	18,520	24,280	60
58	Saudi Arabia	17,820	24,870	57
59	Puerto Rico	16,560 a	..	..
60	Bahrain	15,920 a	21,240 a	64
61	Slovak Republic	16,070	22,230	63
62	Estonia	15,200	20,830	65
63	Trinidad and Tobago	15,040	24,940 b	56
64	Equatorial Guinea	14,540	24,110	61
65	Croatia	13,850	19,330	71
66	Barbados	12,660 a	18,850 a,b	72
67	Hungary	12,730	20,260	67
69	Poland	12,480	20,480	66
69	St. Kitts and Nevis	12,480	14,490 b	87

Rank	Economy	Atlas methodology $	Purchasing power parity international $	PPP rank
71	Latvia	12,350	17,820	73
72	Chile	12,280	16,330	76
72	Lithuania	12,280	19,690	70
74	Antigua and Barbuda	12,060	15,670 b	77
75	Venezuela, RB	11,920	12,620	92
76	Uruguay	11,860	14,740	83
77	Seychelles	11,130	25,320 b	55
78	Brazil	10,720	11,500	98
80	Turkey	10,410	17,340	74
81	Russian Federation	10,400	19,940	69
82	Argentina	9,740	17,250	75
83	Mexico	9,240	15,060	81
84	Lebanon	9,110	14,000	88
85	Malaysia	8,420	15,190	78
86	Mauritius	8,240	14,760	82
87	Kazakhstan	8,220	11,310	100
88	Gabon	7,980	13,650	91
89	Panama	7,910	14,740 b	83
89	Romania	7,910	15,140	80
91	Suriname	7,640 a	7,710 a,b	120
92	Costa Rica	7,660	11,950 b	95
93	Botswana	7,480	14,560	85
94	Palau	7,250	12,330 b	94
95	Grenada	7,220	10,530 b	103
96	Dominica	7,090	12,460 b	93
97	Montenegro	7,060	13,720	90
98	Libya	12,320 a	16,750 a,b	107
99	South Africa	6,960	10,790	101
100	St. Lucia	6,680	9,080 b	111
101	Bulgaria	6,550	13,980	89
102	Maldives	6,530	8,540	114
103	Colombia	6,110	9,640	106
104	St. Vincent and the Grenadines	6,100	10,560 b	102
105	Belarus	5,830	14,560	85
107	Serbia	5,680	11,640	97
108	Peru	5,500	10,160	104
109	Azerbaijan	5,290	9,020	112
110	Dominican Republic	5,240	9,490 b	108
111	Iran, Islamic Rep.	4,520 a	11,400 a	96
112	Tuvalu	5,010	..	..
113	Jamaica	4,980	7,770 b	121
114	China	4,940	8,450	115
115	Bosnia and Herzegovina	4,780	9,200	109
116	Macedonia, FYR	4,730	11,490	99
117	Namibia	4,700	6,600	125
118	Algeria	4,470	8,370 b	117
119	Thailand	4,420	8,390	116
120	Jordan	4,380	5,970	131
121	Ecuador	4,140	8,310	119
122	Turkmenistan	4,110	8,350 b	118
123	Tunisia	4,070	9,090	110
124	Angola	4,060	5,290	137
125	Albania	3,980	8,900	113
126	Marshall Islands	3,910	..	..
127	Belize	3,690	6,070 b	129
128	Fiji	3,680	4,590	144
129	Tonga	3,580	4,690 b	143
130	Cape Verde	3,540	4,000	150
131	Kosovo	3,520	..	..
132	El Salvador	3,480	6,690 b	124
133	Armenia	3,360	6,140	127
134	Swaziland	3,300	5,970	131
135	Samoa	3,190	4,430 b	147
136	Ukraine	3,120	7,080	123

Rank	Economy	Atlas methodology $	Purchasing power parity international $	PPP rank
137	Morocco	2,970 d	4,910 d	141
137	Paraguay	2,970	5,310	136
139	Guyana	2,900 a	3,460 a,b	157
140	Indonesia	2,940	4,530	145
141	Micronesia, Fed. Sts.	2,900	3,610 b	156
142	Guatemala	2,870	4,800 b	142
142	Vanuatu	2,870	4,500 b	146
144	Georgia	2,860 e	5,390 e	135
145	Syrian Arab Republic	2,750 a	5,090 a	139
146	Timor-Leste	2,730 a	5,210 a,b	137
147	Iraq	2,640	3,770	153
148	Egypt, Arab Rep.	2,600	6,160	126
149	Sri Lanka	2,580	5,560	133
150	Mongolia	2,320	4,360	148
151	Congo, Rep.	2,270	3,280	160
152	Philippines	2,210	4,160	149
153	Kiribati	2,110	3,480 b	158
154	Bhutan	2,070	5,480	134
156	Bolivia	2,040	4,920	140
157	Moldova	1,980 f	3,670 f	154
158	Honduras	1,970	3,840 b	151
159	Uzbekistan	1,510	3,440 b	159
160	Papua New Guinea	1,480	2,590 b	165
161	Ghana	1,410	1,820	181
161	India	1,410	3,620	155
163	Djibouti	1,270 a	2,450 a	166
164	São Tomé and Principe	1,360	2,080	175
165	Sudan	1,300 a,g	2,020 a,g	178
166	Vietnam	1,260	3,260	161
167	Lesotho	1,220	2,070	176
168	Cameroon	1,210	2,360	168
170	Nigeria	1,200	2,300	171
171	Nicaragua	1,170	2,840 b	163
172	Zambia	1,160	1,490	188
173	Lao P.D.R.	1,130	2,600	164
174	Pakistan	1,120	2,880	162
175	Solomon Islands	1,110	2,360 b	168
176	Côte d'Ivoire	1,100	1,730	183
177	Senegal	1,070	1,960	179
177	Yemen, Rep.	1,070	2,180	174
179	Mauritania	1,000	2,410	167
180	Kyrgyz Republic	920	2,290	172
181	Tajikistan	870	2,310	170
182	Cambodia	830	2,260	173
183	Kenya	820	1,720	184
184	Benin	780	1,630	186
185	Bangladesh	770	1,940	180
185	Comoros	770	1,120	198
188	Haiti	700	1,190	196
189	Chad	690	1,370	189
190	Zimbabwe	640	..	..
191	Gambia, The	610	2,060	177
191	Mali	610	1,050	201
193	Guinea-Bissau	600	1,250	194
194	Burkina Faso	570	1,310	192
194	Rwanda	570	1,240	195
196	Togo	560	1,030	203
197	Tanzania	540 h	1,510 h	187
199	Uganda	510	1,320	191
200	Nepal	540	1,260	193
201	Central African Republic	470	810	208
201	Mozambique	470	980	204
203	Guinea	440	1,050	201
204	Eritrea	430	580 b	211

Rank	Economy	Atlas methodology $	Purchasing power parity international $	PPP rank
204	Madagascar	430	950	205
206	Afghanistan	410 a	1,060 a,b	200
207	Ethiopia	400	1,110	199
208	Niger	360	720	209
209	Malawi	340	870	206
209	Sierra Leone	340	850	207
211	Burundi	250	610	210
212	Liberia	240	520	212
213	Congo, Dem. Rep.	190	350	214

Note: Rankings include all 214 World Bank Atlas economies presented in the key indicators table, but only those with confirmed GNI per capita estimates or those that rank among the top twenty for the Atlas method are shown in rank order.

Estimated ranges for economies that do not have confirmed World Bank Atlas GNI per capita figures are :

High-income ($12,476 or more):
    Andorra
    Aruba
    Curaçao
    French Polynesia
    Guam
    New Caledonia
    Northern Mariana Islands
    San Marino
    Sint Maarten (Dutch part)
    St. Martin (French part)
    Turks and Caicos Islands
    Virgin Islands (U.S.)

Upper-middle-income ($4,036 to $12,475)
    American Samoa
    Cuba

Lower-middle-income ($1,026 to $4,035)
    South Sudan
    West Bank and Gaza

Low-income ($1,025 or less)
    Korea, Dem. Rep.
    Myanmar
    Somalia

.. Not available. Figures in *italics* are for 2010 or 2009.
a. 2011 data not available; ranking is approximate.
b. Estimate is based on regression; other PPP figures are extrapolated from the 2005 International Comparison Program benchmark estimates.
c. Data are for the area controlled by the government of the Republic of Cyprus.
d. Data include Former Spanish Sahara.
e. Data exclude Abkhazia and South Ossetia.
f. Data exclude Transnistria.
g. Data include South Sudan.
h. Data refer to mainland Tanzania only.

Definitions, sources, notes, and abbreviations

Adjusted net saving Net national saving plus education expenditure minus energy depletion, mineral depletion, net forest depletion, and carbon dioxide and particle emissions damage. (World Bank)

Adolescent fertility rate The number of births per 1,000 women ages 15–19. (UN Population Division)

Agricultural land Permanent pastures, arable land, and land under permanent crops. Permanent pasture is land used for five or more years for forage, including natural and cultivated crops. Arable land includes land defined by the FAO as land under temporary crops (double-cropped areas are counted once), temporary meadows for mowing or for pasture, land under market or kitchen gardens, and land that is temporarily fallow. Land abandoned as a result of shifting cultivation is excluded. Land under permanent crops is land cultivated with crops that occupy the land for long periods and need not be replanted after each harvest, such as cocoa, coffee, and rubber. Land under flowering shrubs, fruit trees, nut trees, and vines is included, but land under trees grown for wood or timber is not. (FAO)

Agricultural products Commodities classified in SITC revision 2 sections 0,1, 2, excluding 27 and 28, and 4.

Agricultural support, total The value of gross transfers from taxpayers and consumers arising from policy measures, net of associated budgetary receipts, regardless of their objectives and impacts on farm production and income or production of farm products. (OECD)

Aid, net Aid flows classified as official development assistance, net of repayments. (OECD DAC)

Aid, untied Bilateral official development assistance commitment not subject to restrictions by donors on procurement sources. (OECD)

Antiretroviral therapy coverage The percentage of adults and children with advanced HIV infection currently receiving antiretroviral therapy according to nationally approved treatment protocols (or WHO/UNAIDS standards) among the estimated number of people with advanced HIV infection. (WHO)

Bilateral ODA commitments Firm obligations, expressed in writing and backed by the necessary funds, undertaken by official bilateral donors to provide specified assistance to a recipient country or a multilateral organization. Bilateral commitments are recorded in the full amount of expected transfer, irrespective of the time required for completing disbursements. (OECD DAC)

Birth at health facility Percentage of live births in the years preceding the survey that took place at a health facility. (Household Surveys)

Births attended by skilled health staff The proportion of deliveries attended by personnel trained to give the necessary supervision, care, and advice to women during pregnancy, labor, and the postpartum period, to conduct deliveries on their own and to care for newborns. (Household Surveys)

Bonds Securities issued with a fixed rate of interest for a period of more than one year. They include net flows through cross-border public and publicly guaranteed and private nonguaranteed bond issues. (World Bank)

Business, time to start up The time, in calendar days, needed to complete all the procedures required to legally operate a business. If a procedure can be speeded up at additional cost, the fastest procedure, regardless of cost, is chosen. Time spent gathering information about the registration process is excluded. (World Bank)

Carbon dioxide emissions Emissions from the burning of fossil fuels (including the consumption of solid, liquid, and gas fuels and gas flaring) and the manufacture of cement. (CDIAC)

Cereal production Cereals generally of the gramineous family harvested for dry grain only. (FAO)

Cereal yield The production of wheat, rice, maize, barley, oats, rye, millet, sorghum, buckwheat, and mixed grains, measured in kilograms per hectare of harvested land. Refers to crops harvested for dry grain only. Cereal crops harvested for hay or harvested green for food, feed, or silage, and those used for grazing are excluded. The FAO allocates production data to the calendar year in which the bulk of the harvest took place. Most of a crop harvested near the end of the year will be used in the following year. (FAO)

Child labor Children ages 7–14 who are involved in economic activity for at least one hour in the reference week of the survey. (UCW)

Child labor, Agriculture Children ages 7–14 who are involved in economic activity in the agricultural sector. Agriculture corresponds to division 1 (ISIC revision 2), categories A and B (ISIC revision 3), or category A (ISIC revision 4) and includes agriculture and hunting, forestry and logging, and fishing. (UCW)

Child labor, Manufacturing Children ages 7–14 who are involved in economic activity in the manufacturing sector. Manufacturing corresponds to division 3 (ISIC revision 2), category D (ISIC revision 3), or category C (ISIC revision 4). (UCW)

Child labor, Service Children ages 7–14 who are involved in economic activity in the service sector. Services correspond to divisions 6–9 (ISIC revision 2), categories G–P (ISIC revision 3) or categories Q–U (ISIC revision 4) and include wholesale and retail trade, hotels and restaurants, transport, financial intermediation, real estate, public administration, education, health and social work, other community services, and private household activity. (UCW)

Child labor, paid workers Children ages 7–14 who are involved in economic activity and hold the type of jobs defined as "paid employment jobs." (UCW)

Child labor, self-employed workers Children ages 7–14 who are involved in economic activity and hold the type of jobs defined as a "self-employment jobs," working on their own account or with one or a few partners. (UCW)

Child labor, unpaid family workers Children ages 7–14 who are involved in economic activity and work without pay in a market-oriented establishment or activity operated by a related person living in the same household. (UCW)

Children out of school, primary school-age children The number of children of primary school age who are not enrolled in primary or secondary school. (UNESCO Institute for Statistics)

Commercial bank and other lending Net flows of commercial bank lending (public and publicly guaranteed and private nonguaranteed) and other private credits. (World Bank)

Contraceptive prevalence rate The percentage of women married or in-union ages 15–49 who are practicing, or whose sexual partners are practicing, any form of contraception. (Household Surveys)

Corruption is the abuse of public office for private gain and is an outcome of poor governance, reflecting the breakdown of accountability. (World Bank)

Debt, private nonguaranteed The long-term external obligations of private debtors that are not guaranteed for repayment by a public entity. (World Bank)

Debt, public and publicly guaranteed The long-term external obligations of public debtors, including the national governments and political subdivisions (or an agency of either) and autonomous public bodies, and the external obligations of private debtors that are guaranteed for repayment by a public entity. (World Bank)

Debt, short term All debt having an original maturity of one year or less and interest in arrears on long-term debt. (World Bank)

Debt, total external Debt owed to nonresidents repayable in foreign currency, goods, or services. It is the sum of public, publicly guaranteed, and private nonguaranteed long-term debt, use of International Monetary Fund credit, and short-term debt. (World Bank)

Debt service, public The sum of principal repayments and interest actually paid in foreign currency, goods, or services for long-term public and publicly guaranteed debt and repayments (repurchases and charges) to the International Monetary Fund. (World Bank)

Debt service, total The sum of principal repayments and interest actually paid in foreign currency, goods, or services on long-term debt, interest paid on short-term debt, and repayments (repurchases and charges) to the International Monetary Fund. (World Bank)

Deforestation The permanent conversion of natural forest area to other uses, including shifting cultivation, permanent agriculture, ranching, settlements, and infrastructure development. Deforested areas do not include areas logged but intended for regeneration or areas degraded by fuelwood gathering, acid precipitation, or forest fires. Negative numbers indicate an increase in forest area. (FAO)

Education, primary The level of education that provides children with basic reading, writing, and mathematics skills along with an elementary understanding of such subjects as history, geography, natural science, social science, art, and music. (UNESCO Institute for Statistics)

Education, secondary The level of education that completes the provision of basic education aimed at laying the foundations for lifelong learning and human development by offering more subject- or skill-oriented instruction using more specialized teachers. (UNESCO Institute for Statistics)

Education, tertiary The level of education leading to an advanced research qualification that normally requires, as a minimum condition of admission, the successful completion of education at the secondary level. (UNESCO Institute for Statistics)

Energy and minerals rents The product of unit resource rents and the physical quantities extracted. Energy covers coal, crude oil, and natural gas; minerals include bauxite, copper, gold, iron, lead, nickel, phosphate, silver, tin, and zinc. (World Bank)

Energy use The use of primary energy before transformation to other end-use fuels, which equals indigenous production plus imports and stock changes, minus exports and fuels supplied to ships and aircraft engaged in international transport. (IEA)

Enrollment rate, gross The ratio of children who are enrolled in an education level, regardless of age, to the population of the corresponding official school age, as defined by the International Standard Classification of Education 1997 (ISCED97). (UNESCO Institute for Statistics)

Enrollment rate, net The ratio of children of official school age who are enrolled in school, to the population of the corresponding official school age, as defined by the International Standard Classification of Education 1997 (ISCED97). (UNESCO Institute for Statistics)

Exchange rate, official The exchange rate (local currency units relative to the U.S. dollar) determined by national authorities or the rate determined in the legally sanctioned exchange market. It is calculated as an annual average based on monthly averages. (IMF)

Exports of goods, services, and income International transactions involving a change in ownership of general merchandise, goods sent for processing and repairs, nonmonetary gold, services, receipts of employee compensation for nonresident workers, and investment income. (IMF)

Exports to developing economies outside region
The sum of merchandise exports from the reporting
economy to other developing economies in other
World Bank regions as a percentage of total
merchandise exports by the economy. (World Bank)

Exports to developing economies within region
The sum of merchandise exports from the reporting
economy to other developing economies in the
same World Bank region as a percentage of total
merchandise exports by the economy. (World Bank)

Exports to high-income economies The sum of
merchandise exports from the reporting economy
to high-income economies as a percentage of total
merchandise exports by the economy. (World Bank)

Female-to-male enrollments in secondary schools
The ratio of female-to-male gross enrollment rates
in secondary schools. (UNESCO Institute for Statistics)

Fertility rate, total The number of children that would
be born to a woman if she were to live to the end of
her childbearing years and bear children in accordance
with the age-specific fertility rates of the specific year.
(World Bank)

**Financing from abroad (obtained from nonresidents)
and domestic financing (obtained from residents)**
The means by which a government provides financial
resources to cover a budget deficit or allocates financial
resources arising from a budget surplus. Includes all
government liabilities—other than those for currency
issues or demand, time, or savings deposits with
government—or claims on others held by government,
and changes in government holdings of cash and
deposits. Excludes government guarantees of the
debt of others. (IMF)

Food price index Includes the average of six commodity
group price indexes of meat, dairy, cereals, oil and
fats, and sugar. These commodities are weighted with
the average export shares of each of the groups for
2002–2004. (FAO)

Food production index Covers food crops that are
considered edible and that contain nutrients. (FAO)

Foreign direct investment, net inflows Net inflows
of investment to acquire a lasting interest in or a
management control over (10 percent or more of
voting stock) in an enterprise operating in an economy
other than that of the investor. It is the sum of equity
capital, reinvestment of earnings, other long-term
capital, and short-term capital as shown in the
balance of payments. (IMF)

Forest area Land under natural or planted stands of trees
of at least 5 meters in height in situ, whether productive
or not, excluding trees stands in agriculture production
systems (for example, in fruit plantations and agroforestry
systems) and trees in urban parks and gardens. (FAO)

Freshwater resources, internal renewable resources
Average annual flows of river and groundwater from
rainfall. (FAO)

Freshwater withdrawals, annual Total water withdrawals,
not counting evaporation losses from storage basins but
including water from desalination plants in countries
where they are a significant source. Withdrawals also
include water from desalination sources. Withdrawals
for agriculture and industry are total withdrawals
for irrigation and livestock production and for direct
industrial use (including for cooling thermoelectric
plants). Withdrawals for domestic uses include drinking
water, municipal use or supply, and use for public
services, commercial establishments, and homes. (FAO)

Gross capital formation (commonly called *investment*)
Outlays on additions to the fixed assets of the economy,
net of changes in the level of inventories, and net
acquisitions of valuables. Fixed assets include land
improvements (such as fences, ditches, and drains);
plant, machinery, and equipment purchases; and
the construction of roads, railways, and dwellings.
(World Bank, OECD, UN)

Gross domestic product (GDP) The sum of gross value
added by all resident producers in the economy plus
any product taxes (less subsidies) not included in the
value of the products. It is calculated using purchaser
prices and without deductions for the depreciation of
fabricated assets or for the depletion and degradation
of natural resources. (World Bank)

Gross domestic product (GDP) per capita Gross domestic
product divided by midyear population. (World Bank)

Gross national income (GNI) Gross domestic product
plus net receipts of primary income (compensation of
employees and property income) from abroad. Data are
converted to dollars using the World Bank *Atlas* method.
(World Bank)

Gross national income (GNI) per capita Gross national
income divided by midyear population. (World Bank)

Gross national income (GNI), PPP Gross national income
converted to international dollars using purchasing
power parity rates. An international dollar has the same
purchasing power over GNI as a U.S. dollar has in the
United States. (World Bank)

Heavily Indebted Poor Countries (HIPC) Initiative
A program of official creditors designed to relieve
the poorest, most heavily indebted countries of their
debt to certain multilateral creditors, including the
World Bank and the International Monetary Fund.
(World Bank)

High-income economies Those with a gross national
income (GNI) per capita of $12,476 or more in 2011.
(World Bank)

HIV, adult prevalence of The proportion of people ages
15–49 who are infected with HIV. (UNAIDS)

**Households reporting adult women and men as
the usual person collecting water** Proportion of
households reporting adult women and men as
the usual person collecting water. (Nistha Sinha, 2010,
"Infrastructure, Gender Differences, and Impacts: The Evidence")

Immunization rate, measles, child Percentage of children ages 12–23 months who received a vaccination for measles before 12 months of age or at any time before the survey. A child is considered adequately immunized against measles after receiving one dose of the vaccine. (WHO and UNICEF)

Individuals using the Internet Refers to the percentage of individuals who have used the Internet (from any location) in the past 12 months. The Internet can be used via a computer, mobile phone, personal digital assistant, games machine, digital TV, etc. (ITU)

Industry The output of the industrial sector corresponding to International Standard Industrial Classification (ISIC) divisions 2–5 (ISIC revision 2) or tabulation categories C–F (ISIC revision 3). (ILO)

Interest payments Payments of interest on debt—including long-term bonds, long-term loans, and other debt instruments—to both domestic and foreign residents. (World Bank)

International migrant, stock The number of people born in a country other than that in which they live; this includes refugees. (UN Population Division)

Irrigated land Areas purposely provided with water, including land irrigated by controlled flooding. (FAO)

Labor force participation rate The proportion of the population ages 15 and older that is economically active: all people who supply labor for the production of goods and services during a specified period. (ILO)

Land area A country's total area, excluding area under inland water bodies and national claims to the continental shelf and to exclusive economic zones. In most cases, definitions of inland water bodies includes major rivers and lakes. (FAO)

Land under cereal production Refers to harvested areas, although some countries report only sown or cultivated areas. (FAO)

Life expectancy at birth The number of years a newborn infant would live if prevailing patterns of mortality at the time of its birth were to stay the same throughout its life. (World Bank)

Lifetime risk of maternal death The probability that a 15-year-old female will die eventually from a maternal cause, if throughout her lifetime she experiences the maternal death risk and overall fertility and mortality rates of the specified year for a given population. (WHO, UNICEF, UNFPA, and World Bank)

Low-income economies Those with a gross national income (GNI) per capita of $1,025 or less in 2011. (World Bank)

Malnutrition, underweight children, prevalence of The percentage of children under 5 whose weight for age is more than two standard deviations below the median for the international reference population ages 0–59 months. The data are based on the international child growth standards for infants and young children, *Child Growth Standards*, released in 2006 by the World Health Organization. (WHO)

Manufactured products Commodities classified in SITC revision 2 sections 5–8 excluding division 68.

Manufacturing The output of industries corresponding to International Standard Industrial Classification (ISIC) divisions 15–37.

Merchandise trade The sum of merchandise exports and imports measured in current U.S. dollars. Also referred to as *trade in goods*. (WTO)

Middle-income economies Those with a gross national income (GNI) per capita of $1,026 or more but less than $12,476 in 2011. (World Bank)

Mobile cellular telephone subscriptions Subscriptions to a public mobile telephone service using cellular technology, which provides access to the public switched telephone network. Post-paid and pre-paid subscriptions are included. (ITU)

Mortality rate, infant The number of infants dying before reaching one year of age, per 1,000 live births in a given year. (UN Inter-agency Group for Child Mortality Estimation)

Mortality rate, under-5 The probability that a newborn baby will die before reaching age 5, if subject to the age-specific mortality rates of the specified year. The probability is expressed as a rate per 1,000. (UN Inter-agency Group for Child Mortality Estimation)

Mortality ratio, maternal The number of women who die from pregnancy-related causes while pregnant or within 42 days of pregnancy termination, per 100,000 live births. The data shown are modeled estimates based on an exercise by the World Health Organization, the United Nations Children's Fund, the United Nations Population Fund, and the World Bank. (WHO, UNICEF, UNFPA, and World Bank)

Multilateral Debt Relief Initiative (MDRI) An initiative that further reduces the debt of heavily indebted poor countries and provides resources for meeting the Millennium Development Goals. Under the MDRI, the International Development Association, the International Monetary Fund, the African Development Fund, and the Inter-American Development Bank provide 100 percent debt relief on eligible debts due to them from countries that completed the HIPC Initiative process. (World Bank)

Nationally protected terrestrial and marine areas Totally or partially protected areas of at least 1,000 hectares that are designated as national parks, natural monuments, nature reserves or wildlife sanctuaries, protected landscapes or seascapes, or scientific reserves with limited public access. The terrestrial protected areas exclude marine areas, unclassified areas, littoral (intertidal) areas, and sites protected under local or provincial law. Marine protected areas (territorial waters up to 12 nautical miles) are areas of intertidal or subtidal terrain (and overlying water and associated flora and fauna and historical and cultural features) that have been reserved to protect part of or the entire enclosed environment. (UNEP/WCMC)

Net migration The total number of immigrants less the total number of emigrants, including both citizens and noncitizens. Data are five-year estimates. (UN Population Division)

Number of people receiving antiretroviral therapy The number of adults and children with advanced HIV infection currently receiving antiretroviral therapy according to nationally approved treatment protocols (or WHO/UNAIDS standards). (WHO)

Official development assistance (ODA) Disbursement of loans made on concessional terms (net of repayments) and grants by official agencies of the members of the Development Assistance Committee (DAC), by multilateral institutions, and by non-DAC countries to promote economic development and welfare in countries and territories in the DAC list of ODA recipients. (OECD DAC)

Overqualification rate The share of people working in jobs or occupations for which their skills are too high. Education and job qualification levels are grouped into three categories: low, intermediate, and high. An overqualified individual is one who holds a job that requires lesser qualifications than one that would theoretically be available at his or her education level. Overqualification rates are calculated for individuals with an intermediate or higher education. (OECD)

Particulate matter concentration Fine suspended particulates less than 10 microns in diameter (PM10) that are capable of penetrating deep into the respiratory tract and causing significant health damage. Data are urban-population-weighted PM10 levels in residential areas of cities with more than 100,000 residents. The estimates represent the average annual exposure level of the average urban resident to outdoor particulate matter. (World Bank)

Percent of repeaters, primary The number of students enrolled in the same grade as in the previous year as a percentage of all students enrolled in primary school. (UNESCO Institute for Statistics)

Population, average annual growth rate The exponential rate of change in population for the period indicated. (World Bank)

Population, rural Calculated as the difference between the total population and the urban population. (UN Population Division, World Bank)

Population, total Midyear population that includes all residents regardless of legal status or citizenship—except for refugees not permanently settled in the country of asylum, who are generally considered part of the population of their country of origin. (World Bank)

Population, urban The midyear population of areas defined as urban in each country and reported to the United Nations. (UN Population Division, World Bank)

Population ages 0–14 The percentage of total population whose ages are between 0 and 14. (UN Population Division)

Population ages 15–64 The percentage of total population whose ages are between 15 and 64. (UN Population Division)

Population ages 65+ The percentage of total population whose ages are 65 and older. (UN Population Division)

Population below $1 a day The proportion of the population living on less than $1.08 a day at 1993 purchasing power parity prices. (World Bank)

Population below $2 a day The proportion of the population living on less than $2.15 a day at 1993 purchasing power parity prices. (World Bank)

Population density Midyear population divided by land area in square kilometers. (World Bank)

Portfolio equity flow Net inflows from equity securities other than those recorded as direct investment, including shares, stocks, depository receipts, and direct purchases of shares in local stock markets by foreign investors. (World Bank)

Pregnant women receiving prenatal care The proportion of women attended to at least once during pregnancy by skilled health personnel for reasons related to pregnancy. (Household Surveys)

Primary completion rate The proportion of students completing the last year of primary school, calculated by taking the total number of students in the last grade of primary school, minus the number of repeaters in that grade, divided by the total number of children of official graduation age. (UNESCO Institute for Statistics)

Private participation in infrastructure Investment commitments in infrastructure projects in telecommunications, energy, transport, and water and sanitation with private participation that have reached financial closure and directly or indirectly serve the public. All investment (public and private) in projects in which a private company assumes the operating risk is included. (World Bank)

Programme for International Student Assessment (PISA) Internationally comparable assessment, coordinated by the Organisation for Economic Co-operation and Development (OECD), that measures the knowledge and skills of 15-year-olds. The assessment tests reading, mathematical, and scientific literacy in terms of general competencies. (OECD)

Public sector management and institutions A proxy measure of governance that includes assessments of property rights and rule-based governance; quality of budgetary and financial management; efficiency of revenue mobilization; quality of public administration; and transparency, accountability, and corruption in the public sector. (World Bank)

Purchasing power parity (PPP) conversion factor The number of units of a country's currency required to buy the same amount of goods and services in the domestic market as a U.S. dollar would buy in the United States. (World Bank)

Ratio of female-to-male hourly wage The ratio of the female hourly wage to male hourly wage. (Household Surveys)

Refugees People recognized as refugees under the 1951 Convention Relating to the Status of Refugees or its 1967 Protocol; the 1969 Organization of African Unity Convention Governing the Specific Aspects of Refugee Problems in Africa; people recognized as refugees in accordance with the UNHCR statute; people granted a refugee-like humanitarian status; and people provided with temporary protection. Palestinian refugees are people (and their descendants) whose residence was Palestine between June 1946 and May 1948 and who lost their homes and means of livelihood as a result of the 1948 Arab-Israeli conflict. (UNHCR and UNRWA)

Renewable internal freshwater resources Average annual flows of rivers and groundwater from rainfall in the country. Natural incoming flows originating outside a country's borders are excluded. Overlapping water resources between surface runoff and groundwater recharge are also deducted. (FAO's AQUASTAT)

Sanitation, access to an improved facility The share of the urban population with access to at least adequate excreta disposal facilities (private or shared but not public) that can effectively prevent human, animal, and insect contact with excreta. Improved facilities range from simple but protected pit latrines to flush toilets with a sewage connection. (WHO/UNICEF)

Services Corresponds to International Standard Industrial Classification (ISIC) divisions 6–9 (ISIC revision 2) or tabulation categories G–P (ISIC revision 3). (ILO)

Southern and Eastern Africa Consortium for Monitoring Educational Quality (SACMEQ) A regional network consisting of 15 Ministries of Education in Southern and Eastern Africa. It measures student performance on reading and mathematics. (SACMEQ)

Tariff, simple mean The unweighted average of the effectively applied rates for all products subject to tariffs. (World Bank, UNCTAD, WTO)

Textiles Commodities classified in SITC revision 2 divisions 26, 65 and 84.

Time spent fetching water Minutes per day that people spent fetching water (Nistha Sinha, 2010, "Infrastructure, Gender Differences, and Impacts: The Evidence")

Trade The two-way flow of exports and imports of goods (merchandise trade) and services (service trade). (IMF)

Trade in services The sum of services exports and imports. (IMF)

Treated bednets, use of The proportion of children ages 0–59 months who slept under an insecticide-impregnated bednet the night before the survey. (UNICEF)

Tuberculosis, incidence of The number of new and relapse cases of tuberculosis (all types) including patients with HIV per 100,000 people. (WHO)

Unofficial payments to public officials The percentage of firms expected to make unofficial or informal payments to public officials to "get things done" with regard to customs, taxes, licenses, regulations, and services. (World Bank)

Value added The net output of an industry after adding up all outputs and subtracting intermediate inputs. The industrial origin of value added is determined by the International Standard Industrial Classification (ISIC) revision 3.

Water source, access to an improved The share of the population with reasonable access to an adequate amount of water from an improved source, such as a household connection, public standpipe, borehole, protected well or spring, or rainwater collection. Unimproved sources include vendors, tanker trucks, and unprotected wells and springs. Reasonable access is defined as the availability of at least 20 liters a person per day from a source within one kilometer of the dwelling. (WHO and UNICEF)

Women in parliament The percentage of parliamentary seats in a single or lower chamber occupied by women. (IPU)

Workers' remittances and compensation of employees, received and paid Current transfers by migrant workers and wages and salaries earned by nonresident workers. (World Bank and IMF)

World Bank Atlas method A conversion factor to convert national currency units to U.S. dollars at prevailing exchange rates, adjusted for inflation and averaged over three years. The purpose is to reduce the effect of exchange rate fluctuations in the cross-country comparison of national incomes. (World Bank)

Data sources

The indicators presented in this *Atlas* are compiled by international agencies and by public and private organizations, usually on the basis of survey data or administrative statistics obtained from national governments. The principal source of each indicator is given in parentheses following the definition.

The World Bank publishes these and many other statistical series in the *World Development Indicators*, available in print, CD-ROM, and online. Excerpts from this *Atlas*, additional information about sources, definitions, and statistical methods, and suggestions for further reading are available at data.worldbank.org.

Data notes and symbols

The data in this book are for the most recent year, unless otherwise noted.
- Growth rates are proportional changes from the previous year.
- Regional aggregates include data for low- and middle-income economies only.
- Figures in *italics* indicate data for years or periods other than those specified.

Data are shown for economies with populations greater than 30,000, or less if they are members of the World Bank. The term *country* (used interchangeably with *economy*) does not imply political independence or official recognition by the World Bank, but refers to any economy for which the authorities report separate social or economic statistics.

The regional groupings of countries include only low- and middle-income economies. For the income groups, every economy is classified as low-income, middle-income, or high-income.
- *Low-income economies* are those with a gross national income (GNI) per capita of $1,025 or less in 2011.
- *Middle-income economies* are those with a GNI per capita of $1,026 or more but less than $12,476.
- *Lower-middle-income economies* and *upper-middle-income economies* are separated at a GNI per capita of $4,035.
- *High-income economies* are those with a GNI per capita of $12,476 or more.

Symbols used in the data table

.. means that data are not available or that aggregates cannot be calculated because of missing data.
0 or **0.0** means zero or less than half the unit shown.
$ means current U.S. dollars.
The methods used to calculate regional and income group aggregates are denoted by:
m (median), **s** (simple total), **t** (total including estimates for missing data), **u** (unweighted average), and **w** (weighted average).

Abbreviations

CDIAC	Carbon Dioxide Information Analysis Center	PPI	Private Participation in Infrastructure
CPIA	Country Policy and Institutional Assessment	PPP	Purchasing Power Parity
DAC	Development Assistance Committee of the Organisation for Economic Co-operation and Development	UCW	Understanding Children's Work
		UN	United Nations
		UNAIDS	Joint United Nations Programme on HIV/AIDS
DHS	Demographic and Health Surveys	UNDP	United Nations Development Programme
FAO	Food and Agriculture Organization of the United Nations	UNEP	United Nations Environment Programme
		UNESCO	United Nations Educational, Scientific and Cultural Organization
FDI	Foreign Direct Investment		
GDP	Gross Domestic Product	UNFPA	United Nations Population Fund
GNI	Gross National Income	UNHCR	The Office of the United Nations High Commissioner for Refugees
HIPC	Heavily Indebted Poor Countries		
ICT	Information and Communications Technology	UNICEF	United Nations Children's Fund
IDA	International Development Association	UNIFEM	United Nations Development Fund for Women
IEA	International Energy Agency	UNPD	United Nations Population Division
ILO	International Labour Organization	UNSD	United Nations Statistics Division
IMF	International Monetary Fund	UNRWA	United Nations Relief and Works Agency for Palestine Refugees in the Near East
IPU	Inter-Parliamentary Union		
ITU	International Telecommunication Union	WCMC	World Conservation Monitoring Centre
MDGs	Millennium Development Goals	WDI	World Development Indicators
MDRI	Multilateral Debt Relief Initiative	WHO	World Health Organization
ODA	Official Development Assistance	WRI	World Resources Institute
OECD	Organisation for Economic Co-operation and Development	WTO	World Trade Organization

For more information

- *World Development Indicators (WDI)* is the World Bank's premier compilation of data about development. This *Atlas* complements the *World Development Indicators* by providing a geographical view of pertinent data. The *World Development Indicators* is available at data.worldbank.org/data-catalog/world-development-indicators
- *International Debt Statistics (IDS)* (formerly *Global Development Finance*) is the World Bank's comprehensive compilation of data on external debt and financial flows. It is available at data.worldbank.org/data-catalog/international-debt-statistics
- *African Development Indicators*, the World Bank's most detailed collection of data on Africa, is available in one volume at www.worldbank.org/adi
- The **Millennium Development Goals (MDG)** and the data and indicators required to track progress toward them are available at www.developmentgoals.org
- The **MDG database** is available at mdgs.un.org
- The **PARIS21 Consortium** and information about how it promotes evidence-based policy making and monitoring are available at www.paris21.org
- The **Statistical Capacity Building Program**, which offers tools and advice for statistical capacity building in developing countries, can be accessed at www.worldbank.org/data/bbsc
- The **International Comparison Program (ICP)** and information about the ICP and the final results from the 2005 round can be found at www.worldbank.org/data/icp
- **United Nations data** can be accessed at unstats.un.org/unsd/databases.htm

Index

Note: Page numbers in **bold** refer to maps; page numbers in *italics* refer to information presented in graphs and tables.